Kings for a Day: Aintree's Bravest Sons

MAINSTREAM SPORT

KINGS FOR A DAY

AINTREE'S BRAVEST SONS

REG GREEN

MAINSTREAM
PUBLISHING

EDINBURGH AND LONDON

First published in Great Britain in 2002 by
MAINSTREAM PUBLISHING COMPANY
(EDINBURGH) LTD
7 Albany Street
Edinburgh EH1 3UG

ISBN 1 84018 679 8

This edition, 2002

A catalogue record for this book is available
from the British Library

Typeset in Perpetua and Cheltenham
Printed and bound in Great Britain by
Cox & Wyman Ltd

CONTENTS

INTRODUCTION

In every walk of life and sphere of activity, there lies the hope that one's efforts will some day, somehow, be recognised in a meaningful and memorable manner. There are few better examples of this desire invoking such commitment and dedication to a purpose than that of the most exacting of all equestrian contests, the Grand National Steeplechase at Aintree.

Above all else, for over 160 years, through the reigns of six British monarchs, this totally unique sporting event has captivated the imagination of successive generations from every corner of the world. Between those who risk so much competing in the race as riders, there exists intense yet friendly rivalry, a camaraderie rare within high-profile endeavours and a superb level of sportsmanship which is an example to us all.

My love affair with this incredible steeplechase began one bright spring Friday in 1946 when, just eight years old, I sat on my father's shoulders in the 'well' of Becher's Brook and marvelled at the amazing panoply of emotions played out before me. The exciting atmosphere engendered amongst the vast crowds of spectators; the athletic grace and beauty of the horses jumping such daunting obstacles and admiration for the bravery of their riders combined to leave an indelible impression which has been enriched with every subsequent visit to this unique sporting event.

I consider myself highly fortunate in that I live so close to Aintree's historic racecourse, a fact which makes it much easier to make that unmissable annual pilgrimage to the greatest steeplechase on earth, and since that long-past day when the meaning of courage unfolded before that impressionable kid with his dad, I have been privileged to witness some of the greatest horsemen in racing become 'kings for a day'.

The deeds of every Grand National-winning jockey, from Bobby Petre in 1946 to Richard Guest in 2001, are recorded within the following pages, as a humble tribute to their invaluable contributions to the history of steeplechasing in general – and in particular to the most severe test for a horse and rider ever devised.

ONE

Captain Robert Charles Petre

With the benefit of hindsight, nothing could appear more appropriate than the fact that the first Grand National to be staged after six years of war should be won by a man who had only recently returned from the struggle to restore peace and freedom to a troubled world.

As was the case for many of his generation and background, riding horses was as normal an activity for Bobby Petre as attending school, or the choice of military service as a career, also an important part of family tradition.

It was at his first preparatory school in St Neots, Eversley in Hampshire, that young Bobby made friends with Frank Furlong, a boy with a similar passion for horses as himself, and when becoming an officer cadet at Sandhurst in his late teens, was delighted to discover that Cadet Furlong was already there. Another would-be soldier at the academy, Fulke Walwyn, soon shared their friendship when it became known that their common interests involved riding horses over obstacles. When all three competed at the Garth Hunt in 1930 they won a race each and their enthusiasm for steeplechasing increased greatly when Walwyn became champion amateur rider in both 1933 and 1934.

It was also in that 1934 season that Bobby Petre first became licensed to compete under rules as a member of the unpaid ranks and if any further inspiration was needed it came within 12 months, when the other member of that formidable Sandhurst trio, Frank Furlong, rode his father's horse Reynoldstown to victory in the Grand National. Increasing weight prevented Frank from partnering the horse for a second attempt at the National but a more than capable substitute was at hand in the form of his friend and brother officer in the 9th Lancers, Fulke Walwyn.

The 1936 Aintree showpiece is remembered by many as the occasion in which the front-running outsider Davy Jones ran-out as a result of a damaged bridle at the final fence with the race at his mercy, although there could be no denying that

Reynoldstown and Fulke Walwyn were eventually very worthy winners.

It was Bobby Petre's turn to gain the spotlight in 1938 when riding a perfectly judged contest to win a very close finish on St George II in Cheltenham's National Hunt 'Chase and then rounding off an excellent season by finishing as the leading amateur for that year.

With the storm clouds of war gathering over Europe the following year, all men on Britain's military reserve waited anxiously to be recalled to the colours, among them, of course, Walwyn, Furlong and Petre. On Friday, 24 March 1939, Aintree staged what many considered was likely to be the final Grand National before another major European conflict began and among the 37 riders taking part was Bobby Petre, aboard his famous Cheltenham winner St George II.

After completing a clear first circuit of the race, St George II was still in the race on the run back into the country, but at the fence before Becher's Brook was baulked badly by another horse and refused the obstacle. It was an abrupt and disappointing end to Bobby's first appearance in the race and, although unaware of it at the time, it was to be a long, weary and danger-fraught seven years before another opportunity of Aintree glory presented itself to him again. Less than six months after Workman triumphed in that 1939 National, Britain declared war on Germany when Hitler refused to remove his troops from Poland after invading and occupying it.

A wartime Grand National did take place at Aintree, however, in March 1940, and of the huge crowd in attendance that day, the vast majority wore uniforms of various branches of the armed forces, both domestic and colonial. The race was won by Bogskar, ridden by Flight Sergeant Mervyn Jones, who arrived at, and left, the racecourse in the uniform of the Royal Air Force. Although not competing on that memorable, though very sad day, present as spectators were Lieutenant Commander Francis Furlong, RNVR, of the Fleet Air Arm, Captain Fulke Walwyn of the 9th Lancers and Captain Robert Charles Petre of the Scots Guards.

Throughout the period cynically referred to as 'the phoney war', horse racing continued in Britain on a greatly reduced scale, allowing jockeys awaiting overseas postings the chance to continue their profession, albeit on a part-time basis. However, after the evacuation of the British expeditionary force from the Dunkirk beaches and the subsequent fall of France to the invading German army, everything changed dramatically with England and the British Empire standing alone against Hitler's tyranny.

At the height of these sombre reversals of fortune, one action on the high seas did increase the belief that the British lion still had teeth, though. As the enemy pocket battleship *Bismarck* was returning from a raid on shipping in the

North Atlantic, three squadrons of rather antiquated Fairy Swordfish aircraft from HMS *Ark Royal* attacked and disabled the pride of the German navy. The *Bismarck* eventually sank the following day and one of the brave pilots who returned safely from this daring mission was none other Frank Furlong of the Fleet Air Arm.

While home on leave in early November 1940, Captain Bobby Petre took a brief reminder of what his life was intended for when riding Mixed Foursome in the Southam Handicap 'Chase at Cheltenham. He displayed all his old exuberance and won by a head from one of the leading jockeys in the country, Frenchie Nicholson. What made this success all the sweeter was the fact that the horse was owned by Bobby's father, Captain C.B. Petre. Although he was to encounter much action and danger in the many months ahead, it was to be more than five years before the young officer proudly rode into a winner's enclosure again.

After almost six years of brutal conflict, Nazi troops in north-west Germany finally surrendered and on 8 May 1945 the Second World War against Germany was officially declared to be at an end. Allied soldiers everywhere began counting the days when they would eventually become civilians again, yet even after victory over Japan in the Far East was achieved in September, the long frustrating wait for demobilisation continued.

On the last day of January 1946, one of those desirous of being relieved of the regimentation which had governed his existence for so long was Captain Bobby Petre, returning to the racecourse for the first time in too many years. Teaming up with a nine-year-old gelding named Lovely Cottage as a contender in the Warminster Handicap Steeplechase at Wincanton, the long-awaited return to racing activity proved something of a disappointment, for they fell. A very frustrating period followed for the soldier home from the war, with offered rides few and far between. The only consolation from his next six attempts was getting Lovely Cottage safely round in the Henry VII 'Chase at Windsor, even if it was a long way behind the winner, Silver Fame.

In retrospect, it appears highly appropriate that Bobby Petre's return to the winner's enclosure after an enforced interval for wartime duties should be provided by the Tommy Rayson-trained Lovely Cottage and the convincing six-length victory came in the Exmoor Handicap 'Chase at Taunton on 8 March 1946. With but one wind-up race at the Cheltenham Festival remaining for the horse before the first Grand National since Bogskar's wartime victory, Bobby Petre was more than pleased to accept the engagement for Aintree.

In the region of 300,000 people crowded onto the racecourse for the big race, the majority of them so convinced the recent Irish winner of the Cheltenham Gold Cup, Prince Regent, would triumph that Tim Hyde's mount was sent off the 3–1 favourite of the 34 runners. Although far from foot-perfect in the early part of the race, the favourite was well to the fore approaching the Water Jump at the halfway stage and, having mastered the peculiarities of the obstacles, a roar of approval came from the crowd as Prince Regent took up the running after jumping Becher's Brook. Surrounded by an ever-increasing pack of loose horses from the Canal Turn back over the remaining fences, Tim Hyde tried again and again to gallop his mount clear of them and, coming to the final fence, Prince Regent was still clear of just five others left in the contest.

Within seconds of landing safely, however, it was apparent that the Irish champion was beginning to flag, as both Lovely Cottage and Jack Finlay rapidly made ground on him and, striking the front at the elbow, Bobby Petre rode out his Hampshire-trained mount to win by four lengths from the 100–1 outsider Jack Finlay, with the gallant top-weight Prince Regent three lengths further back in third place.

Still surprised at the relative ease of his victory, Captain Petre was sympathetic in his description of the plight of the defeated market leader when saying,

> Tim Hyde was so hampered by those loose horses, he had to ride about three finishes in the last half-mile. Between the last two fences I was four lengths behind him. Lovely Cottage was gaining slowly, but I thought Tim was only giving his horse a breather. Then I saw Prince Regent was no longer on the bit. In a flash I realised that the favourite was beaten. I set my horse alight, he responded gamely, jumped the last fence just behind Prince Regent and stayed on, as I knew he would.

By the beginning of the following season Petre had turned professional, his first ride as such being aboard Carrick Castle when finishing third in a Selling 'Chase at Wye. The very severe winter of 1947 curtailed a large portion of the jumping season, causing an interruption to the preparations of many of the 57 hopefuls taking part in the Grand National at the end of March.

With Prince Regent again favourite, though this time at the more realistic price of 8–1, Bobby partnered Silver Fame, a promising chestnut owned by Lord Bicester, which was to develop into a future Cheltenham Gold Cup winner. On that foggy, damp day at Aintree, however, the pair were never in contention and eventually fell three fences from home.

This was Captain Petre's final appearance in the race and as offers of rides became fewer he acquired a trainer's licence, enjoying some small success in this capacity before tragedy struck in the cruellest possible way. One day, during a cold spell he took his horses to exercise on the beach, supervising their work from a low breakwater. When stepping down he fell, breaking his leg so severely that it had to be amputated.

Always cheerful and energetic, Bobby refused to allow this freak accident to subdue his activities and in a remarkably short time he was riding out again with his string. Sadly, and to many within racing unjustly, he was subsequently held responsible by the Jockey Club when, at a meeting, one of his runners was found to have been doped. The fact that the trainer was many miles from the scene of this incident at the time held no sway in his defence. For the rules of racing at that time insisted that wherever the animal was, its welfare was always the responsibility of the trainer. In an outrageous turn of events, Bobby Petre, who had served racing and his country so well, was deprived of his livelihood by the loss of his licence, and a racing career which held so much promise was brought to a regrettable and premature end.

With the modification of the ruling concerning the administration of illegal substances within racing, Bobby was welcomed back onto the racecourses of Britain at least as a spectator, but by then possibly his most productive years had passed. Lord John Oaksey fondly remembers when, going out to ride in the 1963 National, the last person to wish him well was the man who 18 years earlier had ridden Lovely Cottage to victory in the race.

Captain Robert Charles Petre passed away peacefully in August 1996 at the age of 84.

Edward Dempsey

It can reasonably be said that the career of Irish jockey Eddie Dempsey is as shrouded in mystery today as it was 55 years ago, when he shocked the world of racing to its very foundations by winning the Grand National on a horse as unheard of as himself.

From the scant information available it would certainly appear that, although he was certainly riding for many years in Ireland, the County Meath-born jockey's main source of income was earned away from the racecourse, in riding work for trainers on the gallops. It is a sad fact within horse racing that many so-called unfashionable riders spend more of their lives preparing thoroughbreds at exercise than in competition on the track.

The earliest records to hand indicate that Eddie Dempsey was first seen in action in 1933, when he took part in six races. He was successful twice: on Brave Edna at Punchestown and Poor Chance at Mullingar. As is so often the case, rides came few and far between for Eddie and it was not until 1941 that he gained his first real claim to fame.

Trainer Tom Dreaper selected him to partner a promising six year old named Prince Regent in the gelding's first race over fences, the St Patrick's Steeplechase at Baldoyle. Giving his mount a confident though sympathetic ride, Eddie finished fifth behind the Dan Moore ridden winner Red Wind. Some seven weeks later, on 7 May 1941, they teamed up again at Phoenix Park, Dublin, in the Enniskerry Hurdle over two miles and from a highly competitive field Dempsey rode a brilliant finish to win by a neck from the 6–4 favourite Antrim.

Tried over three miles for the first time the following November, Eddie Dempsey was again in the saddle when Prince Regent finished a good second in the Avonmore Steeplechase at Leopardstown and again the following week, when winning the Webster Champion Cup 'Chase at the same venue.

Mr James V. Rank's gelding was very obviously a champion in the making, yet sadly the services of the jockey who had assisted so well in his progress were dispensed with, as a more ambitious campaign was arranged for the animal. Two of Ireland's leading riders, Jimmy Brogan and Tim Hyde, took over for the remainder of the season, by the end of which Prince Regent had added another four victories to his tally including the Irish Grand National at Fairyhouse.

Although understandably disappointed, Dempsey went back to the chore so many jockeys experience, that of searching for rides in a highly competitive market. Thanks to such loyal owners as Mr T.F. Baker and Mr J. Sutherland, Eddie continued to ride competitively, albeit infrequently. It was when riding Never No More at Baldoyle's Whitsuntide meeting in May 1944 that he first caught sight of the horse which was destined to bring him such undreamt-of fame and recognition. A narrowly beaten second that day in the Clonard Hurdle, the horse four lengths behind in third place was a wiry-looking five year old called Caughoo, owned by jeweller John McDowell from Dublin and trained on the nearby Sutton Strand beach by his brother Herbert. It was to be many months before Dempsey got the chance of a closer look at the Wexford-bred gelding and on that occasion it was as the jockey of the then six year old in Leopardstown's Bray Steeplechase over three miles on 27 December 1945. Although unplaced behind the older and more experienced Lough Conn, all connected with the horse were nevertheless pleased with the performance, for his main target of the season was an attempt to win the Ulster National at Downpatrick for a second successive time. With Eddie now his regular partner, Caughoo made steady progress with every run and in his final race before the April engagement at Downpatrick was a 'most promising runner-up' in the Baldoyle Handicap 'Chase.

Unfortunately, the perils of his profession caught up with Eddie Dempsey in the three weeks leading up to the big race, when he suffered an injury in a race fall which put him out of action for a few months. In his absence, the brilliant Irish champion Aubrey Brabazon took the mount on Caughoo, who jumped brilliantly throughout to win his second Ulster National in a most convincing manner.

Reunited with the gelding, Eddie began the 1946–47 campaign at Leopardstown in a humble hurdle race over two miles and, although they completed the course, they finished a long way behind the placed horses. It was a situation which became frustratingly familiar through the remainder of 1946 and some way into the following year. The pair were beaten out of sight in October, again at Leopardstown in the Laragh Steeplechase, with this particular defeat all the more painful for Dempsey with the winner being the horse he had helped to 'make', Prince Regent.

In the early weeks of 1947, racing in mainland Britain began to suffer from what developed into an extended period of harsh winter weather, with meeting after meeting abandoned due to frost. Even the National Hunt meeting at Cheltenham fell victim to what was generally accepted as the most severe cold spell in living memory.

Apart from the problems in England, the McDowell brothers in Dublin were facing their own uncertainties and these of course involved the recent lacklustre displays of Caughoo. Originally the intention for the remainder of the season was to direct all efforts towards a third Ulster National success, yet they had serious doubts and had begun to question the viability of such a plan. Late into many long nights, any decision became more difficult. The brothers eventually involved their mother and sister in attempting to find a solution to the quandary and fortuitously one of the family quartet suggested an alternative engagement for their only racehorse in the Grand National some four days before the Downpatrick event. Finally Aintree was decided upon and Edward Dempsey was able to look forward to making his first visit to England and, incredibly enough, to take part in the greatest steeplechasing contest in the world.

Forty-two days after finishing down the course in the Leopardstown 'Chase, Caughoo lined up with 56 others in the fog and rain – which can often blight the most exciting day in the jumping calendar. For this rider and the entire McDowell family, though, it was the one place to be however slim their chances may have appeared. With fellow-countryman Prince Regent again favourite at 8–1, betting was, as always, heavy on what is always the biggest gamble of the racing year. The fact that his mount carried the derisory market price of 100–1 in no way daunted Eddie's delight. For the first time in their lives the jockey and Caughoo arrived in England – unheralded, unheard of, but fully prepared for the greatest test they had yet encountered.

So dreadful were the conditions that very little could be seen of the proceedings from the stands and enclosures, but straight from 'the off' it was another of the Irish challengers, Lough Conn, who struck the front and led the way down to Becher's. Falls came in regular succession in the heavy going. Still at the head of affairs over the Brook, Lough Conn was followed by Kilnaglory, Bricett, Domino, Tulyra, Gormanstown, Prince Regent and Silver Fame. Among those already out of the contest, though, was the well-fancied Revelry, together with Day Dreams, Bullington, Wicklow Wolf and Michael's Pearl. Another of the better-backed horses, Luan Casca, failed to negotiate the tricky drop at the Brook.

Jumping the Water Jump at the halfway stage, Lough Conn still held the advantage from Musical Lad. The pair were surrounded by a host of riderless horses and the remaining survivors of the large field were strung out a long way in the rear. Over Becher's Brook for the final time, Lough Conn had increased his lead to ten lengths, with the improving Caughoo now in second place, followed by Bricett, Musical Lad, Kilnaglory and, some way off the pace, Prince Regent. With five fences left, Caughoo overtook the tiring Lough Conn and, increasing his lead with every stride, came back onto the racecourse for the final two fences well clear of his rivals. At the last fence Caughoo got in too close and made his only mistake. Although pitching badly on landing, his jockey sat tight to recover and gallop on to a 20-length victory from Lough Conn, Kami and the top-weighted favourite Prince Regent.

The shock result was hardly welcomed by the general public but for the McDowell family and Eddie Dempsey it was the greatest racing moment of their lives.

Regrettably, some little time after the most meritorious day of Eddie Dempsey's career, a most unjust accusation was levelled against him by Daniel McCann, the rider who came second in the race on Lough Conn. After a casual meeting of the two, it was suggested that during the course of the race, taking advantage of the foggy conditions, Dempsey had taken an illegal short-cut across the racecourse on the first circuit and waited for the runners to come round again before rejoining the contest. During the ensuing altercation, blows were exchanged between the two and upon appearing before a magistrate the claim was repeated. That there was absolutely no substance to the allegation is very evident from the newsreel film of the race, which clearly shows Caughoo in continuous action throughout the course of the entire Grand National.

The build-up to a second tilt at the Aintree marathon in 1948 followed the same pattern as before, but all concerned with the horse feared that a certain sparkle was missing from his performances and, despite a promising run into second place in Baldoyle's Bray 'Chase, an uncharacteristic fall at Navan was followed in the National by Dempsey having to pull Caughoo up at the Canal second time round.

Sadly, by the end of the 1948–49 season Caughoo was dead and for the man who had shared his greatest moment of turf glory, Eddie Dempsey, the loss was doubly painful, with the knowledge that the man who replaced him as jockey in the gelding's final Grand National in 1949 was none other than Daniel McCann.

There was one final visit to Aintree left for the previously unknown, unfashionable and sparsely employed Dempsey, and that came in 1950 when he considered himself lucky to pick up the mount on 66–1 shot Cadamstown. They only got as far as the fence after Becher's the first time round and at the end of that season, Eddie relinquished his jockey's licence. He retired to Donaghmore House in County Meath, hopefully with some comforting memories of one day in the fog at Liverpool, when the gods smiled his way and Caughoo provided that unbelievable taste of glory. Eddie died in February 1989, aged 77.

Arthur Patrick Thompson

As an Irishman without any racing background in his pedigree, Arthur Thompson was a rarity among his compatriots, who became renowned for their talent riding horses over obstacles. Born in County Carlow, Arthur was the son of a watchmaker. His family knew little or nothing about the sport and had it not been for the tragic death of his mother when he was still only a small boy it may well have been that chasing would have been deprived of one its greatest contributors.

Sent to live with an aunt in the country, the youngster quickly became friends with her son, Paddy Claxton, and it was thanks to his influence that Arthur became involved with horses. An accomplished rider himself, Paddy detected in young Arthur an enthusiasm worthy of encouraging and he persuaded trainer John Kirwan to take the boy on as an apprentice at his yard near Gowran in Kilkenny.

Weighing just four stone, he made his first public ride a winning one when partnering a mare named Good Thing in a one-and-a-half-mile hurdle race on 26 August 1931 at Mallow, beating the odds-on favourite Calendio comfortably by two lengths. In no time at all, his services were much in demand and, despite becoming Champion Apprentice at all codes of racing for a number of seasons, Arthur was becoming concerned about the increase in his weight.

It was because of this that he decided to try his luck in England, where the range of weights in handicaps was higher and in 1936 he settled in Yorkshire, proceeding to ride 16 winners for trainer John Harper. A brief spell riding for Matt Peacock at Middleham was followed by employment at the nearby yard of Colonel Wilfred Lyde but upon the outbreak of war both the Colonel and his jockey joined the armed forces.

Posted to the Middle East with his regiment, the Northumberland Fusiliers, he was continuously in action during the to and fro of the desert conflict with Rommel's Afrika Korps. Surviving the entire siege of Tobruk, Arthur Thompson and his comrades found a brief period of relative security when sent back to Cairo, but within weeks were back at the sharp end of desert warfare and were eventually overpowered by German tanks to become prisoners of war. Shipped to Italy, he was one of some 15,000 captured troops who shared the humiliation and inhumanity of various prison camps before being transferred to Germany, where their German guards at least showed some concern for their welfare. A prisoner for three years, until the spring of 1945 when the Russians advanced through Germany, Arthur and an Australian colleague at last broke free and decided the best plan would be to attempt to reach the American divisions on the far side of the river. With the aid of a couple of requisitioned bikes, they finally cycled their way to freedom.

Upon being demobilised, Arthur made his way back to Middleham, concerned again about his weight of 11st 7lb, but determined to pick up his career from where it had been interrupted. He was back in the saddle for the first time in over four years at Wetherby on 3 November 1945.

Another man who endured the rigours of military combat during the recent conflict was trainer Neville Crump. Re-starting his livelihood with but a handful of horses for the 1946–47 jumping season, he formed what was to become one of the most successful partnerships in racing by employing Arthur Thompson as his stable jockey.

Another recent addition to the trainer's team was a headstrong, vicious seven-year-old bay mare with the inappropriately endearing name of Sheila's Cottage, who was owned by the adjutant of nearby Catterick Camp, Sir Hervey Bruce. It quickly became obvious to everyone in the yard that the only person who could handle her was Arthur Thompson and, despite hitting every fence in their first race together at Carlisle in October 1946, they finished third in the three-mile novice 'chase. A greatly improved performance followed at Haydock Park just over a month later when she won the Makerfield 'Chase over three miles by a distance and after finishing second at Doncaster the following week, she returned to Haydock in early January to make all the running in the three-and-a-half-mile Gerard Handicap 'Chase.

While Britain was suffering an extremely cold winter, the bold decision to run Sheila's Cottage in the 1947 Grand National was taken, but a spell of work on Redcar sands saw the mare arrive at Aintree as one of the few fully fit contestants among the 57 runners. On very heavy ground, Sheila's Cottage was travelling well until she was brought down at the 12th fence. Her final outing of that, her first season, was in the Scottish Grand National at Bogside, but when well in contention at the third-last, she met it wrong and fell.

A well-planned campaign for a second tilt at the National was put into gear at once, with a gradual build-up of five races carefully chosen for the mare before crossing the Pennines to Aintree again. After finishing down the course in a pipe-opener hurdle race at Doncaster in mid-November, the bad-tempered daughter of Cottage jumped brilliantly to win at Haydock a fortnight later. Having already caught the attention of the handicapper, Sheila's Cottage was steadily rising in the weights, which suited the tall Arthur Thompson, and after finishing third over four miles at Cheltenham's December meeting, was allocated 11st 13lb at the Haydock Park New Year meeting eight days later. Carrying the colours of her new owner, Mr John Procter (a Grimsby trawler owner), she gave another splendid display of jumping to finish third, again in the Gerard Handicap 'Chase. Owner Procter, trainer Crump and jockey Arthur Thompson were more than happy with her progress and began thinking seriously about that Aintree engagement. Her final race before that appointment came in Doncaster's Great Yorkshire 'Chase at the end of February on ground much too fast for her. Even so, Sheila's Cottage ran a fine race to finish fifth behind the winner, Cool Customer, with two future champions, Russian Hero and Freebooter some way behind her.

In complete contrast to the previous year's weather, Aintree was seen at its best on National day, spring sunshine swelling the crowds to near record proportions on 20 March 1948. Favourite of the 43 runners was Lord Bicester's promising Silver Fame at 9–1, with Loyal Antrim, Rowland Roy, Cloncarrig, Roimond and the previous year's runner-up, Lough Conn, also well backed. Sheila's Cottage was at the somewhat generous price of 50–1 and from a good start was well up with the leaders jumping the first. Lough Conn led over Becher's, closely followed by Cloncarrig, First of the Dandies and Rowland Roy but Silver Fame was brought down by a falling horse at the Brook. Just off the pace, Arthur Thompson kept his mount well in touch, very pleased with the mare's jumping while always aware of the danger from loose horses. First of the Dandies was left in front when Cloncarrig pecked badly at the Chair and the new leader led the way back onto the final circuit, closely followed by Rowland Roy, Parthenon, Maltese Wanderer and Happy Home. With the field thinning out rapidly approaching the second Becher's, Zahia,

Sheila's Cottage and Cromwell moved closer to the leaders and on the run back from Valentine's these were among just a handful left with a realistic chance of winning. First of the Dandies was still in front jumping the penultimate fence but was now being strongly pressed by Zahia and with Arthur Thompson beginning to make a run on his mare. An error of judgement on the part of Zahia's jockey caused her to take the wrong course when approaching the final jump and from there on, First of the Dandies looked all over the winner. On the run to the post, however, Arthur suspected the leader was beginning to tire and, driving his mount through on the inside, produced one final effort from her. Sheila's Cottage got up to win close home by one length from First of the Dandies, with Cromwell six lengths back in third place and Happy Home fourth of the fourteen finishers.

It was a wonderful victory for trainer Neville Crump so early in his career, which understandably received a tremendous boost, and in no time at all it brought many new owners and horses to his Warwick House stables. It was the last time Sheila's Cottage appeared on a racecourse but, before leaving the yard to begin stud duties, the 'ornery, vicious old cow', as her trainer affectionately referred to her, left her jockey with one final gesture to remember her by. A few days after winning the National, Arthur Thompson was tacking her up in preparation for a photo shoot when the horse only he could handle savagely bit the top off one of his fingers. Refusing to go to the hospital, Arthur simply mounted his attacker and gently persuaded her to be a good girl and pose for their picture. Years later, when Sheila's Cottage died, her final resting place was a grave at the bottom of Arthur Thompson's garden at Kamolin in County Wexford.

Such was the rush of people now wanting Neville Crump to train their horses, the stabling facility at Warwick House had to be extended and the meagre half dozen equine athletes he began with soon numbered over 30. Winners came thick and fast for the northern yard now making such an impact on the jumping scene and for the 1949 National they had two representatives, Wot No Sun and the Thompson ridden Astra. Both showed prominently during the course of the race, the former bowing out at the second Becher's and Arthur keeping Astra up with the leaders until they were brought down three from home. A fortnight later Wot No Sun made amends for his lapse by making all the running to win the Scottish Grand National, this time with Thompson aboard.

At the end of that season the trainer finished in the top seven of leading prize-winners, while Arthur Thompson took third place in the jockey's championship with 46 wins to his credit, just 14 behind champion Tim Molony.

Now fully established as one of the leading National Hunt teams in the country, the Middleham establishment went from strength to strength through the next season, with Arthur again finishing third in the jockey's table with 60 winners and also riding Wot No Sun into second place in the Grand National behind that superb Aintree horse Freebooter. He was still beset with weight problems, however, and in the disastrous National of 1951 put up three pounds overweight to partner Major Straker's Partpoint, who, unsettled by the disturbance at the start, came down at the first Canal Turn. Another good term for the Middleham yard ended with him again finishing third of the most successful riders, with his guvnor in second place in the trainers' list.

It was in April 1951, while watching an amateur riders' Hunter Chase from the stands at Hexham, that Arthur first set eyes on a nine-year-old bay gelding named Teal and was impressed with the manner in which the horse rallied after being remounted to finish third. In conversation afterwards with the heavy-betting owner Harry Lane, he remarked that if he wanted to win a National he should buy the animal. Within a fortnight Teal had become the property of the burly construction magnate from South Shields for three thousand pounds, a massive estimated value in the days when the gelding's breeder was unable to sell him for five pounds.

Although the horse had won a couple of point-to-points, he was really still just a novice, with only two events under rules behind him; but placed in the skilful hands of Neville Crump, Teal soon showed his outstanding ability. Both trainer and jockey were convinced they had a very good horse, and after finishing second at Kelso in his first race for his new connections, he made most of the running to win at Cheltenham in mid-November. Just ten days later, with a superb display of jumping, Teal literally hacked-up in the Boston Spa Handicap 'Chase at Wetherby to win by 20 lengths and the betting pundits already began wondering about Aintree.

A slight hiccup at Newbury followed, when he fell at the open-ditch after catching his foot in a hole, but at Birmingham in his final race before the National, Teal spread-eagled a good field of staying jumpers to romp home four lengths to the good. His price for the big Aintree event was immediately cut by the bookies from 50–1 to 100–8.

On 5 April 1952, 47 runners gathered in Aintree's paddock before going out to contest the Grand National. Four of them were saddled by Captain Neville Crump, and stable jockey Arthur Thompson had no hesitation in making Teal his chosen mount. The other three, Wot No Sun, Skyreholme and Traveller's Pride were ridden by Dave Dick, Dick Francis and Larry Stephens respectively, and with previous winner Freebooter the 10–1 favourite, Teal was the next best backed at 100–7.

With constant rain reducing visibility, the patience of the vast crowd became stretched when the start was delayed for eleven minutes by three runners breaking the tape. When a nearby spectator expressed his annoyance to the waiting jockeys, Arthur Thompson confidently replied, 'I know what you mean, mate, I should be back in the winner's enclosure by now.'

When they were finally despatched, Freebooter went straight to the front, even though he was carrying top weight, with Teal hard on his heels. Adroitly avoiding another pile-up at the first fence, both continued to comfortably dictate the pace while the casualties increased behind them. Approaching the Chair Jump near the end of the first circuit, Teal was in danger of being hampered by the riderless Caesar's Wife and, aware of the danger, Arthur took one hand off his reins to reach across and steer the offender away. Now clear, Teal took the mighty ditch in splendid style and the Water beyond to lead just 17 still in the race back out for the final round. Closely pressed on the way to Becher's by Freebooter, Royal Tan, Legal Joy and his stablemate Wot No Sun, it was only the brilliant horsemanship of his jockey which again kept Teal in the race. Striking the top of the fence, the gelding landed over the famous Brook almost on his belly but, sticking like glue to his mount, Arthur Thompson kept his seat as they skidded along the ground. Recovering superbly, Teal was back in contention alongside Freebooter as they jumped the Canal Turn in front. The mistake here, however, involved the favourite, with Freebooter stumbling on landing and falling. Left in front, Teal now started to make the best of his way home, jumping fence after fence beautifully. It was only when coming to the second-last fence that Michael Scudamore drew level on Legal Joy. Touching down together after the last, Teal produced the better finishing speed to pass the winning post five lengths clear of Legal Joy, with the brave Wot No Sun a bad third and Uncle Barney fourth.

The jubilant owner Harry Lane had every reason to kick his hat around the winner's enclosure, having won a small fortune in bets at long odds. The victory guaranteed Neville Crump his first trainer's championship and Arthur Thompson joined the select band of men to ride more than one Grand National winner.

Tragedy struck during the build-up to achieve that elusive double National victory for Teal in 1953, when an injury in that year's Cheltenham Gold Cup led to his premature death. It was a particularly devastating blow for the man who discovered the obscure former point-to-pointer, for Arthur Thompson always maintained that Teal was the best horse he had ever ridden.

Without his old favourite, Arthur settled for the stable's Larry Finn on the big day at Aintree in 1953, but the pair were brought down at the eleventh fence. Twelve months later he finished eighth in the race on Southern Coup and, nearing the end of his distinguished career, he made his final appearance in the 1956 race, the event most remembered for the dramatic collapse of Devon Loch, with the race at his mercy. His conveyance that year was High Guard and, although they only got as far as the first fence, Arthur left the racecourse content in the knowledge that he'd tasted not once but twice the joy denied to so many.

By the end of that year he retired at the age of 40, fully aware that he was suffering some heart trouble – but also, more importantly to a man so dedicated to his demanding profession, that his reflexes were becoming blunted.

Arthur Thompson passed away peacefully at his home in Kamolin, County Wexford, in June 1988 and is fondly remembered for his kindness and concern for everyone he knew.

Michael Leo Aloysius McMorrow

Leo McMorrow was probably one of the least known of that intrepid band of Irishmen who, after developing their riding skills in their native land, crossed the Irish Sea to further their career. For many years his only claim to fame was having the longest name in horse racing. At a time when there was an abundance of superlative talent competing on Irish racecourses, Leo shared the fate of many who were overshadowed by such contemporaries as Tim Hyde, Aubrey Brabazon, Dan Moore, Bryan Marshall and the brothers Tim and Martin Molony.

After a promising beginning as an amateur when he came third with Queen of War at Navan in March 1937, it was to be a long time before he could experience the thrill of winning his first race. Undaunted, Leo persevered with commendable stoicism, taking rides whenever and wherever he could find them, but still that longed-for first victory eluded him. Some three years later, on 28 March 1940 at Rathkeale, a little bay mare named Lucid Eyes rewarded the young amateur's determination, and after 40 failed attempts Leo discovered the thrill of unsaddling his mount in the winner's enclosure. A little over six weeks later he repeated the process at the little Tramore racetrack, bringing his mount Glendine to win the Seaside Plate by two and a half lengths with a good late challenge. An unexpected reward as he returned to the weighing room were the congratulations of the man he had beaten into second place, the former Grand National-winning jockey Tim Hyde.

His strike rate improved during the 1940–41 season, with four wins and seven placings from only fifteen rides, and in October 1942 he was entrusted with introducing to racing a three-year-old brown gelding by the name of Caughoo. In a driving finish for Limerick's Greenpark Plate, Leo held on to win by a short head and on the same track four months later he scored again with Caughoo, who four years later carried Eddie Dempsey to a memorable Aintree victory.

Another spell in the doldrums followed as McMorrow found it increasingly difficult to obtain engagements to ride and after turning professional early in 1944 the situation worsened. With just two winners to his credit that year (Mark Twain at Leopardstown in April and Gussie Goose at Limerick six months later), he began to consider leaving the sport and seeking another profession. Having no doubt suffered many hours of painful deliberation, Leo finally decided to try his luck in England. After arriving, he was soon riding work for Northants trainer Cliff Beechener.

His first racecourse appointment for his new stable was memorable for all the wrong reasons. For after finishing a close second on Ethie Agnes in the Southam Novices Chase at Cheltenham, an objection was lodged on the grounds that he had carried the wrong weight. His mount was disqualified, placed last, and the trainer fined five sovereigns. He came second again six days later with Ethie Agnes at Southwell, this time without incurring the wrath of the stewards, and his subsequent win on Final Folly for the same yard at Wetherby quickly brought the delicious taste of the turf back to him. With three other successes before the end of the season – two aboard Shillaly and the other at Wetherby again with Fear the Worst – his confidence took a much needed upward surge.

Such are the vagaries of the jumping game, however, that another lean spell followed and, apart from winning on Cottage Welcome at Wolverhampton, the only other high spot of the 1946–47 season for Leo was taking part in a race over Aintree's notorious fences. Although falling with Sydney Smith's Steel Flame at the fence after Valentine's in the Becher Steeplechase, the occasion reinforced his reason for continuing. Further encouragement came 24 hours later, with Caughoo, the horse he taught to jump, winning the Grand National.

An insignificant chance ride on Lovely Job at Haydock Park in November 1947 led to a fall at the halfway stage of the contest but his presence at the Lancashire course that day provided him with an opportunity to witness the outstanding amateur Dick Francis win the County Handicap 'Chase on Russian Hero. Little could he have known what this brief encounter would lead to.

The following March, Leo McMorrow returned to Liverpool for the real thing – the greatest steeplechase on earth. Partnering the oldest runner of the 43 contestants, he piloted the 14-year-old Schubert into 13th place, one place in front of former winner Lovely Cottage.

In a surprising twist of fate, it was around this time that the good fortune of another steeplechase rider opened up the biggest opportunity yet to come Leo McMorrow's way. Dick Francis turned professional and was quickly snapped up by that leading owner of jumpers, Lord Bicester. Consequently, an opening presented itself at the stables of George Owen at Cholmondley Castle in Cheshire, and as the new National Hunt season of 1948–49 got under way, Leo began riding for his new employer on a regular basis. His first success for Mr Owen's yard came in late October at the picturesque Worcester racecourse, when riding the 20–1 shot Russian Hero to a head victory in the Severn Handicap 'Chase over two miles. The partnership was successful again in December, this time over three miles at Birmingham.

After a third victory with Mr Williamson's gelding early in 1949, the owner's thoughts began turning towards the National but after three dismal displays later that spring, which included two falls, such a plan appeared grossly over-optimistic. When the big day arrived, however, Russian Hero and Leo McMorrow were among the 43 contestants at Aintree, listed among the 66–1 others in the betting.

Away to a good start, the big field surged across Melling Road led by Monaveen, Acthon Major and the favourite Cromwell. With little change in the order, they jumped Becher's Brook safely, except for Magnetic Fin and Perfect Night. The list of fallers mounted rapidly on the run back to the racecourse and, jumping the Water at the end of the first circuit, the Dick Francis-ridden top-weight Roimond held the foremost position. Royal Mount, Cromwell, Wot No Sun and the improving Russian Hero were next in line and back at Becher's for the final time there were still a dozen in close contention. Royal Mount was now showing the way to Roimond, Southborough, Astra, Russian Hero, Cromwell and Wot No Sun. With the race now on in earnest, Royal Mount surrendered the lead to Roimond when blundering at the fence after Valentine's and, to everyone's surprise, Russian Hero emerged quickly from the remainder to join issue. Staying on the better over the final fences, Russian Hero won by eight lengths from Roimond, with Royal Mount third and Cromwell fourth of the 11 which completed the course.

A hurried late celebration was organised for the winner's connections at the Blossoms Hotel in Chester that evening and a most considerate gesture by the hosts was the inclusion as a guest of Dick Francis who, besides coming second in the race, had played a large part in preparing Russian Hero for his day of glory.

One week after that incredible day at Aintree, Leo McMorrow won a humble hurdle race on the novice Onekin at Bangor-on-Dee and by the end of the season had taken his total for the campaign to 12 wins. He rode Russian Hero a further three times in the National but sadly without completing the course. They came down at the first fence in 1950, suffered like so many others from the bad start the following year when they failed to get beyond the Chair, and in 1952 they again fell victims to the first obstacle.

Returning to the role of a freelance jockey, Leo based himself back in Yorkshire. He was without a mount in the big race in 1953 but finished seventh in 1954 aboard the Harrogate-trained Uncle Barney and 13th on the same horse 12 months later. Partnering Merry Windsor in the 1956 race, they fell three from home and when making his last appearance in the Grand National of 1957 he represented his old guv'nor George Owen when riding Morrcator. The pair fell at the Canal Turn on the first circuit when up with the leaders.

Finding it more difficult to continue his career in this country, Leo McMorrow was persuaded to travel to the United States, where he rode for some time for both Paddy and Mick Smithwick, the cousins of Dan Moore. He later became assistant trainer to Jack Fisher but in the autumn of 1973 he was tragically killed in a car crash in Pennsylvania.

James Joseph Power

Already a professional at the age of 19, Jimmy Power had his last ride in his native Ireland at Bellewstown on 2 July 1947 before following the example of both Arthur Thompson and Leo McMorrow to seek his fortune in mainland Britain.

Born in 1924 at Waterford, he also headed for the north of England, hoping to attract the attention of some of the many smaller stables which were scattered in some profusion within that area. The first to offer him the occasional ride was John Stewart Wight of Grantshouse, Berwickshire, whose owners included Colonel Lord Joicey and his wife Lady Joicey. It was in his Lordship's pink and olive-green colours that Jimmy made his first appearance on an English racecourse, finishing second at Catterick Bridge on the novice hurdler Paintbox in early November 1947.

By the end of that first season in this country, the young Waterford jockey had rewarded trainer Wight's trust with three winners, which included Paintbox at Hexham and the 20–1 shot Scotch Muffler at Haydock. Jack Ormston, an amateur rider turned trainer, of Richmond in Yorkshire, was also rewarded for his allegiance when Jimmy partnered his Shareholder to a three-length victory at Wetherby at the end of the season.

Quickly aware of the newcomer's ability, trainers Marshall, Dodd and Kitching joined John Wight in acquiring Power's services and their judgement proved well founded when they shared between them seven successes with Jimmy by the beginning of March 1949. An indication of John Wight's appreciation for his new-found jockey came with his choice of Jimmy Power as the pilot for the ageing gelding Clyduffe, the second of his two entries in that year's Grand National. To actually be selected to ride a competitor in the most challenging steeplechase in the world so early in his career was a dream come true for the young Irishman and the fact that the more experienced Dick Curran was to ride the yard's better fancied Ulster Monarch in no way lessened Jimmy's delight.

Always well to the rear, Clyduffe made an unholy mess at the first Becher's Brook, taking off too early and coming down so steeply on the landing side that all four legs went from under him. Jockey Power, however, stuck like glue to his mount and, in what many described as a perfect rodeo act, recovered brilliantly to bring the horse to its feet and continue in the race. They eventually finished in tenth place, a long way behind the winner Russian Hero. Rounding off the remainder of the season with another four winners in the north, Jimmy now looked forward to hopefully improving his record in the forthcoming campaign, little realising just how rewarding it was to be.

A sparkling double early on, with Curransport and Orinoco at Perth in September, was immediately followed by a chance ride on Mrs Lurline Brotherton's Blancador and, although finishing unplaced, it was encouraging to have been selected by such a distinguished owner. In charge of her horses was the highly successful Yorkshire trainer Bobby Renton, a man who regularly turned out numerous jump winners and who was also respected for his fine judgement of both horses and men. That he was impressed by Power's talent was quickly evidenced when, a few weeks after first engaging him at Perth, he gave the jockey the leg-up on another of Mrs Brotherton's horses, Chimay, at Wetherby. It was the gelding's first outing of the current term, and although neglected in the betting, Jimmy rode a clever and considerate race to bring him home the three-length winner at 100–8.

While still competing for the men in the north who gave him his first chances, Jimmy began riding Renton's horses more often and at the Nottingham October meeting made his first racecourse appearance on the stable's champion Freebooter. A winner earlier in the year over Liverpool's big fences in the Champion 'Chase when ridden by the leading jockey Tim Molony, the gelding's new partner felt a certain affinity with the horse, for by a curious coincidence both Power and Freebooter were born in Waterford. Always prominent and jumping beautifully throughout, Freebooter finished third in that Nottingham event, behind Knight of the Deep and the most recent National winner, Russian Hero.

For a delighted jockey the next step was Aintree for the Grand Sefton

Steeplechase over two miles, seven furlongs of the most notorious fences in the world. Once again Freebooter gave Jimmy an 'armchair ride'. Lying third crossing the Melling Road back onto the racecourse, they took over approaching the last fence and, jumping that as perfectly as all the others, ran out a convincing eight-lengths winner from Her Majesty the Queen and HRH Princess Elizabeth's Monaveen. It was clear to all who witnessed that terrific performance that this was very possibly a future Grand National winner. Certainly, with a little over four months left before that appointment, Bobby Renton's Ripon yard were already making plans.

The long journey south to Hurst Park was made for the New Year's eve fixture and the valuable Queen Elizabeth 'Chase, in which Freebooter was to take on some of the best three-mile jumpers in the country. A right-handed track, this racecourse, situated near Hampton Court, was completely unsuited to the Yorkshire animal's action, yet despite this Freebooter ran on strongly towards the finish to get within six lengths of the winner, Monaveen. Both first and second were to meet again on their most important day at Aintree, together with seven of those who finished behind them.

Now performing at his peak, Jimmy Power was totting up the wins on a regular basis and after piloting Freebooter to an impressive victory in Doncaster's Great Yorkshire 'Chase he rewarded both the owner and trainer for their confidence in him by winning for them the prestigious County Hurdle at the Cheltenham National Hunt Meeting on the 25–1 chance Blue Raleigh. From there on, at least until 25 March, it was merely a matter of avoiding injuries, staying fit and making sure that the same applied to his partner in the build up to their greatest test.

Grand National day was for once blessed with perfect spring weather, the sun blazing down on Aintree, as if aware that the entire British Royal Family were to be present for the occasion. Of the 49 runners, Freebooter and the previous year's runner-up Roimond headed the market as 10–1 joint favourites, with Wot No Sun, Cromwell and the Royal representative Monaveen also well supported in the betting. The race itself certainly lived up to all expectations, containing drama at its most dynamic, determination at its most deadly and pride at its most profound.

With Monaveen at the head of affairs from the very start, patriotism was rife among throngs of spectators and as he took off in front over Becher's for the first time hopes rose that the Royal victory of 50 years before was to be repeated. Freebooter was well to the fore, though, and for a brief moment headed the leader, but with Valentine's and the fences alongside the Canal causing many problems, the race was wide open when they came back onto the racecourse for the end of the first round. Cloncarrig held a slight advantage over a group including Monaveen, Rowland Roy, Wot No Sun, Acthon Major and Freebooter coming to the 14th, but it was here that the Royal horse made a horrendous mistake. Hitting the plain fence hard, Monaveen shot his rider Tony Grantham forward, leaving the jockey clinging on for dear life and it was only the quick thinking of Arthur Thompson aboard Wot No Sun who kept them in the race. Reaching out with one hand, he pulled Grantham back into the saddle to keep the Windsors' hopes alive. At the very next obstacle, the Chair, it was Freebooter's turn to make a near-fatal error. Misjudging his take-off, the gelding struck the fence with his chest full-on, catapulting his jockey forwards and over his mount's head, leaving him clinging literally to the favourite's ears. Employing the identical expertise demonstrated in last year's race with Clyduffe, Jimmy Power made what was probably the most remarkable and decisive recovery ever achieved in horse racing. Back out on the second circuit he allowed his mount plenty of time to settle and, responding to the considerate handling, Freebooter was back within striking distance of the leaders jumping Becher's for the final time. At the head of the field after the Brook, Angel Hill took command but after unseating her rider Tom Shone at the Canal Turn, Cloncarrig took over and, closely pressed by the ever-improving Freebooter, made his way back towards the home stretch. Well clear of the remainder, the pair came to the second-last fence where Cloncarrig made his only mistake, striking the top of the obstacle. Completely unbalanced, he crumbled to the ground. Just a quick glance behind assured Jimmy Power that the race was at his mercy and, leaping the last fence in superb style, he rode out Freebooter to a 15-length victory over Wot No Sun, Acthon Major, Rowland Roy and the first Royal representative for 42 years, Monaveen.

For the gentle, unassuming jockey, the aftermath of this victory became a greater ordeal than the race itself, yet there could just about be seen a flicker of recognition at the importance of the occasion as he hurried to weigh-in.

With five other successes to his credit before the end of that season of seasons, Jimmy Power finished 12th in the top jockey's table, but perhaps his finest satisfaction was the knowledge that his efforts had assisted in Bobby Renton, the man who had believed in him, coming second in the top 12 trainers of the year.

Having succeeded in the supreme test of any jockey's career, Jimmy Power went on to become a particular favourite of the Aintree crowds, scoring victories in a second Grand Sefton with Freebooter and the Topham Trophy 'Chase with John Jacques in 1956.

Caught up in the shambles of the 1951 National start, he was brought down with Freebooter early in that race, repeated it with Cardinal Error at the first in the 1952, and refused close to home when aboard the favourite Little Yid in 1953. Royal Stuart in 1954, Sun Clasp the following year and Pippykin in 1956 all failed to carry Power to the end of the National journey and, although he managed to finish fifth in the race with The Crofter in 1957, it was obvious to all that this rider's racing days were coming to an end. Unseated aboard The Crofter in the 1958 Aintree spectacular, his final ride in the race came the following year when he was brought down with 100–1 shot Sundawn III at the first Becher's.

A wonderful credit to the profession of National Hunt jockeys, towards the end of his riding career Jimmy gave a superb example of horsemanship when winning the Cheltenham Gold Cup on Limber Hill in 1956, the year in which he finished sixth in the jockeys' table.

Always with a genuine smile on his face, Jimmy Power in retirement provides the same care and attention to his sheep on the small farm he runs on the outskirts of York as he did to Freebooter and the rest when he was in the saddle.

TWO

John Arthur Bullock

Born in Walsall in 1917, Johnny Bullock first rode under rules as a professional in 1937, one of his earliest winners being Keshar in a Plumpton hurdle race in December of that year. With the outbreak of war interrupting his and countless others' careers, he became a paratrooper and in September 1944 took part in Operation Market Garden, the allied attempt to seize the bridges across the Rhine in enemy-occupied Holland.

Surviving the bitter house-to-house fighting in and around Arnhem, John Bullock was taken prisoner when the mission failed to capture that one 'bridge too far' and spent the remainder of the war in a German POW camp.

It was not until November 1945 that John Bullock returned to the more familiar and far happier surroundings of a racecourse, finishing unplaced with Iambic in the Abberley Handicap Hurdle at Worcester. After securing just one more ride that season, he realised that the future looked far from rosy. There was little sign of any improvement the following season either, although he did partner three winners for two small stables, those of Tom Yates and Charles Birch.

Slowly but surely his success increased, with seven victories coming his way in the 1947–48 campaign, but it was in the following year that his fortunes really took a turn for the better. When former four-times champion jockey Fred Rimell suffered a serious injury in 1947, he set up as a trainer in Kinnersley, Worcestershire, and in April 1949 he offered Johnny Bullock the mount on a young hurdler named Croupier. The pair duly won the Chepstow Novices Hurdle and as Rimell began to increase the number of horses in his care, the ex-paratrooper became regularly employed as the stable jockey. As success followed success, Bullock's patience and determination through the years of struggling were at last rewarded. Within the first six months of the 1949–50 season he had repaid Fred Rimell's trust with ten winners, including a storming victory at Cheltenham's National Hunt Meeting with High Level in the Cotswold Steeplechase.

Liverpool's spring meeting at Aintree found Johnny Bullock at the venue with four mounts for the Kinnersley yard, and although they did not complete their respective contests, it gave the jockey a tremendous sense of recognition after the years in racing's wilderness. Falling with Camas Bridge in the Topham Trophy 'Chase on the opening day, both High Level and Middle Arch also failed to oblige later in the week. Although his partner in the Grand National, Cavaliero, was among the outsiders at 66–1, nothing could disguise the sense of pride he felt at the prospect of his first encounter with the legendary event. Even though Cavaliero carried him no further than Becher's Brook on the first circuit, it was a never-to-be-forgotten experience for Johnny and, although naturally disappointed, he knew when leaving the course that day that he just had to try again.

Before the season closed in late May he had provided another seven victories for himself and the Rimell yard, among them a hurdle race at Ludlow on a chestnut gelding named Arnhem, a reminder for the jockey of far less happy times.

Riding Bosco at Newton Abbot early in the new campaign, the Rimell–Bullock partnership began where it had left off, winning the Ideford Hurdle very comfortably and setting the pattern for another successful period. By the end of December 1950 they had notched up a tally of 19 victories, the last of these being with Mighty Fine in the Stayers Handicap Steeplechase over four miles at Cheltenham. Among the also-rans behind him that day was the bay mare Nickel Coin with jockey Dick Francis aboard. A daughter of the 1936 2,000-guineas winner Pay Up, this was a 'lady' Johnny Bullock was soon to become associated with.

A rising star of the Kinnersley stable at this time was the young gelding Land Fort, who, after first having Bullock as his partner, subsequently became the regular mount of champion jockey Tim Molony. After a brilliant sequence of four successive victories, it was obvious that he was to be aimed at the forthcoming Grand National and, very probably at the insistence of the gelding's owner, one of the leading jockeys was requested to partner him. With Tim Molony required for Arctic Gold, the second in the jockeys' table, Bryan Marshall, was engaged by Fred Rimell to team up with Mr Oliver's Land Fort. As this was the Worcestershire trainer's sole representative in the National, John Bullock gladly accepted the ride on the mare he not only had previously beaten but which he had since ridden to victory in the Manifesto 'Chase at Lingfield and finished second with at Sandown Park – Mr Jeffrey Royle's Nickel Coin.

On an overcast afternoon at Aintree on the first Saturday in April, 36 runners milled around at the start of the National, their riders still undecided where to place their mounts in the line-up. To the amazement of everyone present, the starter released the gate while at least a third of the competitors where facing the wrong way. The shambles which ensued forced those left to attempt to make up lost ground and in the resultant mad dash they met the first fence far too fast. Twelve came down at this point; a third of the entire field eliminated from the contest they had been preparing for since the beginning of the season. Among those making a premature exit was Fred Rimell's Land Fort. Approaching the Canal Turn, the favourite Arctic Gold was in front but he too became a victim, totally misjudging the obstacle and depositing Tim Molony on the ground. When stablemates Russian Hero and Dog Watch fell at the Chair, only five were left to clear the Water Jump and commence the final circuit. Gay Heather came down at Becher's, bringing down Derrinstown in the process, and when Broomfield went at the next only Nickel Coin and the Irish challenger Royal Tan were left to make their exhausted way home. Slightly in front at the last obstacle, the latter made a bad mistake and with a perfect leap John Bullock raced ahead with Nickel Coin to win by six lengths. Having remounted, another Irish-trained horse, Derrinstown, finished a long way behind in third place, the only other survivor in a most calamitous contest.

In the post-race interview, Bullock described how he settled the mare early on, always going smoothly close to the leaders, and continued:

> I led Royal Tan by several lengths but he jumped to the front two fences out because he took the obstacle slightly better. I felt, though, that I was always going the better and when Royal Tan blundered badly at the last fence, I again went into the lead.

It was the last race that Nickel Coin took part in, for she was retired to stud duty, where she bred three foals, the best being King's Nickel by Kingsmead, who in due course won four races.

That thrilling, unexpected National victory was a perfect complement to a fabulous season for John Bullock, which culminated in him finishing seventh in the leading jockeys' table with 32 winners and contributed in no small measure to Fred Rimell heading the list of trainers.

It was five full years before he again weighed out for the Grand National and although during that period a reasonable number of winners had come his way each year, a younger, more dynamic generation of jockeys had emerged. In that waterlogged Aintree marathon of 1955, Bullock partnered Steel Lock for the Chelmsford trainer Ken Bailey and when still in touch with the leaders was knocked over at the last open ditch.

That most dramatic National of 1956, with Devon Loch getting within 50 yards of victory before inexplicably tumbling to the ground, saw Johnny finish eighth behind probably the luckiest winner of all, ESB, the representative of Fred Rimell's Kinnersley establishment. An early exit at the fourth fence with Armorial III the following year was repeated in 1958 when he fell with Rendezvous III at the fifth, and in his final Aintree appearance in 1959 his mount Eagle Lodge refused three from home.

His last big success was when riding Stenquill to victory in Manchester's Emblem Steeplechase in October 1962, for the Whitchurch stable of trainer Laidler. Shortly afterwards, John Arthur Bullock hung up his boots and returned to Walsall, where he died peacefully in 1988.

Bryan Andrew Marshall

If ever it can be truly stated that a man was born to the saddle, then that distinction must surely apply to Bryan Marshall, one of the greatest jockeys ever to grace a racecourse with an incredible talent that is so rare. His mother was the legendary international horsewoman Mrs Binty Marshall, who won all the major showjumping events in both England and Ireland, more often than not riding side saddle. After Bryan was born at Cloughjordan, North Tipperary, in February 1916, it was the most natural thing on earth that he would quickly be introduced to the magical and tough world of the horse.

In the saddle at the age of three, he was hunting on a lead-rein by the time he was five and before long was galloping over the walls, ditches and banks in the hunting field. Soon demonstrating a standard of horsemanship way beyond his tender years, at the age of 11 he spent his summer holidays in England at the racing stables of Atty Persse. The following year he returned to begin his apprenticeship with the famous Stockbridge-based trainer.

Soon riding work regularly with such famous jockeys as Freddie Fox and Harry Beasley, Bryan quickly adapted to the harsh regime essential in the preparation of thoroughbred racehorses. So impressed with the youngster's talent was the famous trainer that he gave him his first public ride on a racecourse within the year, at Lingfield Park. Soon after his 13th birthday the following year, Bryan enjoyed his first taste of turf success. At Kempton Park on 10 May 1929, he rode Cheviotdale to a memorable victory.

With increasing weight came the realisation that young Marshall would be unable to pursue a career on the flat but with his love and expertise of hunting his alternative choice within racing was most welcome. A spell in America with trainer Gerald Balding led to his first really serious accident, when Bryan broke his leg while schooling. Upon recovering, he did succeed in riding one 'Chase winner before returning to Ireland. He was recruited as assistant trainer to Hubert Hartigan in 1933 and this position at the Penrith stables included riding their horses in competition, but even with spare rides from other sources, further on-course success eluded him.

Towards the end of 1937 he took up an appointment as jockey to the newly licensed Noel Murless at Hambledon and at Manchester the following February guided his charge Carlore to victory, his long-awaited first jumping success in England. His season's-end winning tally was extended to seven, followed the subsequent term by 11, but by then the clouds of war were gathering over Europe. Joining the army at the outbreak of hostilities, Bryan Marshall became a trooper with the 3rd Cavalry Training Regiment based in Edinburgh. While awaiting embarkation to an unknown destination, Bryan made an impromptu appeal to his Commanding Officer. His request for leave to ride at Aintree's final fixture until peace was restored was met with approval and Trooper Marshall duly weighed-out for his first appearance over the notorious Liverpool fences. Although falling with Shining Blade in the Stanley Steeplechase, the day after Flight Sergeant Mervyn Jones steered Bogskar to victory in the National, the young soldier experienced the flavour of the magnetism of Aintree.

Commissioned in the 5th Inniskilling Dragoon Guards, Bryan Marshall saw action with his regiment in a number of theatres of combat and on the first day of the Normandy landings he received a sniper's bullet through his neck. Within a month, Captain Marshall was back with the regiment, now part of the 7th Armoured Division which fought through France, Belgium and Germany. Demobilised early in 1946, he rode freelance for some time, scoring a total of 22 winners before the season's end.

During the summer of 1946, Bryan became first jockey to the powerful Lambourn stable of Fulke Walwyn, creating a partnership which set the world of steeplechasing alight. Walwyn finished up leading trainer that year with Bryan taking second place among the top riders – but more significantly for the latter, he finished eighth in his first Grand National attempt on Miss Dorothy Paget's Kilnaglory. Although still plagued by increasing weight, Marshall was in full flow and at the peak of his form by now and in winning the jockeys' championship the next term he displayed all the skill, tenacity and judgement of pace gained from so many years in the saddle. In addition to the 66 winners which took him to the top of his profession, Bryan enjoyed another fine ride in that year's Aintree spectacular, when coming home sixth on his stable's Rowland Roy.

He filled the same position in the 1949 National aboard another of Miss Paget's brilliant team of jumpers, Happy Home. He missed the next year's race through injury, then made an early exit from the contest in 1951 when coming down at the first with Land Fort. By now the battle with the scales had become so futile that he was severely restricted in the number of mounts he was able to accept and, as a result, his position as Walwyn's first jockey was coming to an end. Taking the mount on top-weight Freebooter in the 1952 National looked like providing Bryan with his first winner in the race until, after being among the leading group from the start, the gelding made an uncharacteristic blunder at the second Canal Turn and exited from the contest.

The emergence of the Ballydoyle genius Vincent O'Brien was at this time the major talking point of the racing media and, being an ardent admirer of his fellow-countryman's exceptional talent, the trainer engaged Bryan Marshall to partner his runners when available. Concerned about the occasional erratic jumping of his eight-year-old Early Mist, O'Brien selected Bryan Marshall as the perfect pilot for the gelding in the 1953 Grand National. Of the 31 runners, Yorkshire-trained Little Yid was a well-supported favourite, ahead of Whispering Steel, Glen Fire and O'Brien's more fancied contender Lucky Dome, but one of the most exciting prospects among the contestants was Fulke Walwyn's former Cheltenham Gold Cup winner Mont Tremblant.

A fast pace was set straight from the start by the latest recruit to the professional ranks, Michael Scudamore, with Fred Rimell's Ordnance. Although they held a clear lead over the Water Jump, both Mont Tremblant and Early Mist were well in touch. With the front-runner falling at the 20th, Early Mist was left in front somewhat earlier than his connections would have wished – but undeterred, Marshall held his mount together well, closely followed by Mont Tremblant, Armoured Knight, Cloncarrig and Irish Lizard. Holding a clear lead from three out, Early Mist justified his trainer's wisdom in choosing Marshall as jockey by responding well to the immaculate assistance from the saddle to romp home 20 lengths clear of Mont Tremblant, with Irish Lizard third and the grey Overshadow a distant fourth.

For owner Joe Griffin, trainer Vincent O'Brien and the ecstatic jockey Bryan Marshall, it was a first-time victory they would, or could, never want to forget and yet, unbelievably, 12 months later the same combination again entered Aintree's winner's enclosure. This time the horse involved was that gallant Aintree stalwart of O'Brien's, Royal Tan. The triumph that day was a resounding tribute to the outstanding skill and jockeyship of Bryan Marshall. After giving his mount a copybook ride through the entire trip, Royal Tan landed clear over the last fence from a seemingly tired Tudor Line. The latter, however, rallied in the most courageous manner and from the elbow the gap between the two narrowed at an alarming rate. In one of the closest finishes ever witnessed at Aintree, Marshall summoned up every last ounce of energy and determination to hold on and win by the narrow margin of a neck. In a manner typical of the men who risk their lives on a daily basis in this most demanding of all endeavours, beaten jockey George Slack made the simple yet sincere announcement that, 'It was a privilege to be beaten by such a brilliant jockey as Bryan Marshall, in such a wonderful race.'

In a determined attempt to make it three Grand National victories in a row, Vincent O'Brien saddled four of his team at Aintree in 1955: Oriental Way, Royal Tan, Early Mist and the newcomer Quare Times. Despite the unjust reputation Early Mist had acquired, Bryan Marshall chose the now ten year old as his conveyance. Finishing in ninth place in hock-deep going, Bryan was nonetheless overjoyed at the winner ahead of him, Quare Times, who provided Vincent with an unprecedented third successive win in the toughest race of all.

By now beset by a number of injuries, in addition to his ongoing weight struggle, Bryan Marshall prepared for his imminent retirement from the saddle by taking out a licence to train. Nothing could have been more appropriate, therefore, than his final appearance in the annual test of equine greatness – he chose a horse now prepared by himself which had already supplied the sweetest moment of his riding life. Early Mist, now with top weight at the age of 11 and owned by John Dunlop, regrettably came down with Bryan at the very first fence in that 1956 Grand National which was to end in such outrageous drama.

Having ridden 508 winners in a career shortened by the war, Bryan Marshall eventually retired from race riding in 1957, setting up his training establishment at Berkeley House in Lambourn. Although sending out a number of winners, Bryan achieved less success in this role. A greatly respected teacher of jockeys, he moved to Newbury later, where he set up a prosperous horse transport business.

Included among his many other famous winners were Rowland Roy in the 1947 King George VI 'Chase; the County Hurdle of 1952 with Ballymacan; the Mildmay Memorial 'Chase in the same year, and the 1954 Liverpool Hurdle on Galatian. Apart from his National victories with Early Mist and Royal Tan, however, possibly his proudest moment was being led into the winner's enclosure at Kempton Park after winning on Manicou in the King George VI Steeplechase. That success provided her Majesty Queen Elizabeth with her first major success in National Hunt racing.

Patrick Taaffe

Another superb horseman from across the Irish Sea, Pat Taaffe was a man also blessed with a quiet unassuming manner and an inbred love of horses. Born in Rathcoole, County Dublin, on 12 March 1930, it really can be said that he was bred for racing. His father was steeplechase trainer Tom Taaffe and his mother Kitty was the sister of another distinguished trainer, Barney Nugent. Almost from the time he took his first steps, he found himself astride a pony and was introduced to the hunting field at the age of eight. He progressed rapidly to showjumping and the following year was awarded the recognition of Best Boy Rider Under 11 Years of Age at the Dublin Horse Show.

Soon competing in hunt races, Pat's first winner came at the Bray Harriers point-to-point on Merry Coon. When just 16 years old, at Phoenix Park in 1947, he steered home Ballincarona for his first success under rules. Riding many of his father's horses as an amateur, he ran up such a string of victories that within 12 months he lost the right to claim any weight allowance. As so often happens in competitive sport, it was the misfortune of another which provided the opportunity that changed his life: Eddie Newman broke his leg in a fall in December 1949. Left without a jockey through this mishap, Greenogue trainer Tom Dreaper engaged Pat Taaffe to ride Mr J.V. Rank's Stormhead in the Glasthule Handicap 'Chase at Leopardstown later in the month and was duly impressed when the amateur brought the gelding home eight lengths clear of his rivals. A little over a week later, Pat provided the same owner-trainer combination with the perfect festive gift when bringing home Shagreen as the winner at the same track's Boxing Day meeting.

Early in January 1950 he relinquished his amateur status after his final ride as such, when finishing fourth on Phone Castletown in a novices' 'chase at Naas. His first outing as a professional came exactly one week later when finishing down the course on Bright Cherry at Leopardstown. Most appropriately, he recorded his opening victory among the paid ranks aboard Osbertstown's Sister in a hurdle race at Thurles in mid-February for his father, the trainer Tom Taaffe. Now first jockey to the powerful Tom Dreaper yard, Pat scored their initial victory at Mullingar the following week with Ballymacarney in a novices' 'chase. Thus began a partnership which was to last a full 21 years and would become one of the most successful in turf history. Always generous in his praise, Pat Taaffe always declared, 'I owe everything to Mr Dreaper'.

Although they were fierce rivals when racing, Pat struck up a lasting friendship with Martin Molony, a man considered by experts as one of the finest jockeys to be seen over jumps in the twentieth century. Refusing to live in England, Martin Molony (whose elder brother Tim became champion jockey five times) had no qualms, though, in making regular raids on the mainland to capture many important steeplechasing trophies. Enjoying the valuable retainer to partner Lord Bicester's strong team of jumpers, Martin and Pat competed against each other often, particularly after Pat joined Tom Dreaper. Sadly, Martin's career was cut short by a serious accident on the racecourse and from that point on it was the elder brother Tim who figured prominently as a rival.

Shortly after his 21st birthday, in the Festival of Britain year, 1951, Pat prepared to make his first trip to Aintree, with two rides over the famous fences booked. Partnering False Scent for trainer Dan Moore in the Topham Trophy 'Chase on the opening day of the Spring Meeting, he finished a good second behind the favourite Culworth.

Weighing-out three days later to partner Lord Sefton's gelding Irish Lizard in the Grand National, Pat welcomed the advice of senior jockeys, including Tim Molony who was making his fifth attempt to win the race aboard the 8–1 favourite, Arctic Gold.

For the majority of those competing, the race was over almost as soon as it began when, from a very poor start, 12 of the 36 came down at the first fence. Pat Taaffe was among them. The favourite got as far as the eighth and only two completed the course without falling. A similar pile-up at that same obstacle again put paid to Taaffe's chances the following year when his mount Early Mist was knocked over by another horse and in 1953, 24 hours after recording his first Aintree success on Teapot II in the Liverpool Hurdle, he finished fourth in the Grand National on Overshadow. It was a cruel coincidence, however, that the winner in front of him in that race was none other than Early Mist.

Riding winners with increasing regularity, Pat was in much demand by now, not only by Tom Dreaper's yard but by other discerning trainers, clamouring for his services whenever he was available. In November 1953 he partnered the giant Coneyburrow to victory in the Grand Sefton Steeplechase over one circuit of the National course for trainer Joe Osborne, a man he had ridden against as an amateur. The following March, the pair teamed up again at Aintree for the toughest test of all and, with Coneyburrow joint second-favourite with Royal Tan, Pat was confident they would give a good account of themselves. And that they truly did, for apart from an error when leading at the Water Jump, they were still in contention until Coneyburrow struck the top of the third-last jump and crumpled, fatally injured, to the ground. It was one of the saddest moments of the young man's life, as he returned to the stables with just his late mount's saddle.

In action again within days, however, Pat won the Conyngham Cup on Mr O'Meara's Boro's Pet and then, to his intense delight, the Irish Grand National at Fairyhouse for Lord Bicester and Tom Dreaper with Royal Approach.

The man of the moment so far as jump racing was concerned at that time was Vincent O'Brien, the Master of Ballydoyle. This was a man who had captured every major prize on both sides of the Irish Sea, including successive Grand Nationals in 1953 and 1954. As the new season approached, O'Brien was determined to make an all-out effort to achieve the impossible: a third victory in Aintree's uniquely demanding event. Of the 30 runners competing in the 1955 National, no fewer than four came from his abode of champions, Ballydoyle. Topping the handicap were his two former Aintree heroes Royal Tan and Early Mist, with the improving seven-year-old winner of the Munster National Oriental Way the outsider of the four, even with the assistance of jockey Fred Winter. Chosen as a conveyance for Pat Taaffe was former winner of Cheltenham's National Hunt 'Chase over four miles Quare Times, a bay gelding Pat had already won with at Naas and more recently finished a respectable two-length second with, behind the Tim Molony-ridden Limber Hill, at the Cheltenham Festival.

For the first time in 54 years Aintree's showpiece jumping event was threatened by atrocious weather. Inspection after inspection took place amid torrential rain before the decision to continue was taken; then only on the condition that the Water Jump be omitted. Rising well to the occasion, the beautifully turned-out Quare Times relieved all fears concerning his ability to cope with the daunting obstacles, jumping brilliantly to be among the leaders at the halfway stage. Taking up the running from a greatly thinned-out field at the second Becher's, Pat Taaffe still had plenty in hand when he was overtaken three from home. Sending his mount again to the front approaching the last fence, he came home a decisive 12-length winner. Second for a successive second time was Yorkshire-trained Tudor Line. Particularly satisfying to the winning jockey, third place was secured by his younger brother Tos Taaffe, on his father's representative Carey's Cottage.

That dream ride at Aintree was quickly added to by another success in the Irish equivalent at Fairyhouse, this time with the brown gelding Umm, who went on to crown a wonderful season for Pat Taffe by winning the Galway Plate. In a gesture typical of the man, Vincent O'Brien provided his fellow countrymen with an opportunity to see his third Grand National hero in action at Leopardstown, in a humble two-mile hurdle race worth a mere £133. In what became little more than an exercise gallop, Pat Taaffe brought home Quare Times as the six-length winner from 14 opponents.

The jockey's outstanding achievements on the racecourse went from strength to strength, through association with such equine wonders as Zonda, Fortria and Ben Stack. His record at Aintree, with Icelough in 1957, Sentina

40

in '58, Slippery Serpent in '59 and Jonjo the next year, though, all ended with that long walk back to the jockeys' room. His fame reached new heights when the offspring of his first professional ride, the consistent mare Bright Cherry, entered Tom Dreaper's establishment. Certainly an enigma, her son Arkle, in conformation alone, was hardly what one would envisage as a future prospect for the highest honours. His sire, Archive, although bred to be an Epsom Derby possible, proved so disappointing that his stud fee was a meagre 48 guineas. Yet the brilliant Tom Dreaper recognised something beyond the animal's gawkiness, lack of interest and general apathy; that essential ingredient he always sought in any horse, the ability to jump. History tells its own story, and the path of Arkle and his constant partner Pat Taaffe became their own heritage, with three Cheltenham Gold Cups, a King George VI Steeplechase, the Irish Grand National, the Whitbread Gold Cup and two Hennessy Gold Cups won for the charming owner, Anne, Duchess of Westminster.

All through this incredibly stimulating experience with Arkle, Pat continued to make his annual pilgrimage to Aintree for that single event which was like a magnet to him, the Grand National. Seventh on Jonjo in 1961, failing to complete with Kerforo, seventh again with Hollywood actor Gregory Peck's entry Owen's Sedge in 1963, tenth on Pappageno's Cottage the following year, and less than perfect displays with Quintin Bay, Flying Wild and Rosinver Bay, gave rise to the perception that, so far as Aintree glory was concerned, Pat Taaffe was yesterday's man. Now approaching his 40th year, the man himself might well have been merely counting out the days to his imminent retirement. But then, for the second time in his thrill-packed life as a jockey, fate dealt that unexpected and decisive card.

Champion English jockey Terry Biddlecombe suffered an injury which ruled out his prospects of riding trainer Fred Rimell's Gay Trip in the 1970 Aintree epic. To his eternal credit, the perceptive Biddlecombe suggested the ageing Pat Taffe as a more than appropriate substitute. Nearing the end of a career in the saddle which could not fail to be an inspiration to all, Pat Taaffe lined up with the stout-hearted Gay Trip at Aintree on 4 April 1970 and, with one of the immortal displays of sheer jockeyship, proceeded to ride the race of his life in bringing home Fred Rimell's third Grand National winner by 20 lengths.

Hanging up his boots almost immediately, Pat applied for and received a licence to train. His most difficult task was encountered and overcome with the erratic Captain Christy, which he prepared for victory in the 1972 Irish Sweeps Hurdle, the Scottish Champion Hurdle 12 months later, the Cheltenham Gold Cup in 1974 and Kempton's King George VI Steeplechase in both 1974 and 1975.

A gentleman in every sense of the word, Pat Taaffe was the epitome of all that is good and meaningful in life, a credit to humanity and an everlasting inspiration to all who wish to improve themselves. His premature death in 1992 was an irreplaceable loss to the world of steeplechasing and to mankind in general.

David Victor Dick

Regarded, somewhat unfairly by many, as the luckiest person ever to succeed in the world's supreme test of horse and man, Dave Dick was a big man in every sense of the word. A swashbuckler with a sense of humour not out of place in a music hall, he added a vibrant and often controversial element to the sometimes austere world of the 'Sport of Kings'.

Born in March 1924, the son of an Epsom trainer, he grew up in the rather dubious company of another rebel, Fred Winter, with whom he attended, somewhat irregularly, Ewell Castle School. Lifelong friends from an early age, they shared the same youthful adventures, committed the same adolescent indiscretions and, like all young men before and since, believed the world was their oyster. Apprenticed in 1936 to his father, he rode his first winner at Brighton in September two years later on Carton, a three year old owned and trained by his best friend's father, Frederick Neville Winter. His first major success came in 1941 when riding Gloaming to victory in the Lincolnshire Handicap for that most knowledgeable racehorse trainer George Lambton.

From that encouraging first important victory, Dave suffered, as many others did, from the problem of increasing height and weight, which severely restricted any plans he had for continuing a livelihood on the flat. As things eventually turned out, flat racing's loss became the winter sport's gain and although too heavy to ever be in a position to challenge for the jockeys' championship, from the early 1950s Dave Dick gained a reputation as a big race specialist.

Taking the mount on Fulke Walwyn's Rowland Roy in the Grand Sefton 'Chase at Aintree provided him with a golden opportunity from one of the leading trainers and, without ever troubling his principal rivals, Shagreen, Freebooter and, Finnure, the jockey gave a competent display. Five months later they teamed up again for the 1951 Grand National, a race in which Rowland Roy had finished fourth last time. By a pleasant coincidence, also making a first appearance in the event was his closest friend, Fred Winter on Syd Mercer's Glen Fire. Although both avoided the calamitous chaos at the first fence, Dave exited six jumps later at the one after Becher's and Fred was unseated at the very next obstacle, the Canal Turn.

Now riding with much success for Fulke Walwyn and his principal owner

Miss Dorothy Paget, Dave Dick reached his highest level of winners the next season. His proudest moment of those 50 victories was when he brought home the six-year-old chestnut Mont Tremblant to a ten-length victory in the 1952 Cheltenham Gold Cup. With his stable's sights now firmly set on the approaching Liverpool meeting, there was all-round disappointment when Dave was unable to make the weight for their leading National fancy Legal Joy. He did, however, welcome the chance provided by Neville Crump to ride Wot No Sun in the big race and, as a prelude to the daunting task ahead, gave Mr Walwyn's Telegram II a superb ride to win Aintree's Coronation Hurdle the day before the feature event.

Amid a constant downpour, the first fence in the Grand National again claimed a heavy toll but with Wot No Sun jumping well and avoiding trouble his jockey was enjoying himself and was pleased with his position of third place at the Water Jump. Though tiring from three out, his mount gamely battled on to settle for third position behind Teal and Legal Joy. In what turned out to be his best season in terms of winners ridden, Dave Dick finished the season fourth in the jockeys' list behind Tim Molony, Fred Winter and Bryan Marshall.

The bold decision was taken in 1953 to attempt to win the National with Mont Tremblant, still only a seven year old, unaccustomed to the peculiarities of Aintree and more importantly burdened by the handicapper with top weight of 12st 5lb. Winning twice from four outings on the run-up to another crack at the Gold Cup, each time in the hands of Dick Francis, the gelding was back in the care of Dave Dick for Cheltenham's Blue Riband. Always well up with the pace during the race, Mont Tremblant ran courageously to finish fourth, a little over eight lengths behind the Irish-trained winner Knock Hard.

Another heroic performance followed at Aintree, with Mont Tremblant giving a perfect display of jumping for most of the way over those uniquely treacherous fences. Always to the forefront, he jumped Becher's Brook the first time like a stag, with a leap which had those nearby gasping in admiration. A close third over the Water Jump behind Ordnance and Little Yid, Dave kept his horse well in touch going back into the country and it was here that Bryan Marshall ranged alongside with Early Mist. The latter took over when Ordnance fell at the twentieth and two fences later Mont Tremblant made his only mistake when blundering badly at Becher's. Staying on, the stronger in the closing stages and with the benefit of a weight concession of 17lb, Early Mist won comfortably from Mont Tremblant and Irish Lizard, with only two others getting round.

Fourth again with Mont Tremblant in the Gold Cup of 1954, Dave was successful at that year's Cheltenham Festival with Miss Paget's Glenbeigh in the Broadway Novices 'Chase and was pleased to accept the mount on the same owner's Legal Joy in the National. Parting company when challenging for the lead at the 13th in that 1954 contest won by Royal Tan, it was Legal Joy which carried Dave into 12th place the following year.

It will remain forever a shame that David Dick's greatest triumph was shrouded in so much sadness and uncertainty, through the manner of its conclusion. His and ESB's victory is always referred to as 'Devon Loch's National', yet coldly but realistically every yard of Aintree's punishing four and a half miles has to be strenuously fought for and held to the victorious – or, too often, bitter – end. As an international sporting event of the highest calibre, the 1956 Grand National had everything. The customary heroism; outrageously unbelievable uncertainty; the prospect of a worthy triumph for the best-loved owner in steeplechasing; and the pathos which only such an event of total commitment can produce. A gentleman supreme, Dick Francis, carried Her Majesty the Queen Mother's colours with dignity and pride above her outstanding brown gelding Devon Loch, specially prepared to lay his trainer Peter Cazalet's long running Aintree jinx to rest.

Given a copybook ride by his immaculate jockey, Devon Loch jumped beautifully the whole way, lying a handy seventh at the halfway stage, moving smoothly into second place behind Armorial III at the second Canal Turn and taking command at the third from home. Always well in attendance, ESB was fifth at the Water Jump, recovered nicely from an error at the Canal Turn to maintain his fifth position, and was within a length of the leader Devon Loch over the final fence. Once on the flat, however, the royal representative stormed clear, running on strongly without his jockey moving a muscle and he appeared certain to win. In his own words, Dave Dick dropped his hands, content to settle for second place, when suddenly, without the merest warning, Devon Loch collapsed to the ground barely 50 yards from the winning post. Anyone could have been excused for losing concentration with such a grotesquely freak incident unfolding before them but, always the consummate professional, Dave Dick gathered his mount with renewed vigour and rode out a finish not even the wildest imagination could have envisaged. With Gentle Moya ten lengths behind in second place and Royal Tan, Eagle Lodge and Key Royal his other nearest rivals, ESB became the winner of the Grand National, few of those present even aware of the outcome until some ten minutes after his incredible victory.

With typical graciousness, Dave's immediate response when interviewed was: 'I was beaten stone cold and must be the luckiest winner of all time', a sentiment equalled by Her Majesty the Queen Mother's reply when questioned about the tragic demise of Devon Loch – 'Well of course, that's horse racing, isn't it?'

Having provided Fred Rimell with his first great Aintree winner, Dave finished eighth with ESB in the race 12 months later and in 1958 again gained a clear round to be sixth. With former winner Mr What under him, in 1961 they completed in 11th place and another National hero, Merryman II, was ridden into 13th position by David a year later. In 1963, Frenchman's Cove carried the veteran Dave Dick into 20th place and on his final appearance in the race in 1964, Pas Seul, with which he had won the 1961 Whitbread Gold Cup, fell with him at the 12th fence.

In his last season this incredible, loveable and quite often indiscreet jockey, won on two horses which may have been (but then again perhaps they weren't) apologies for his supreme Aintree moment. Riding in the Queen Mother's colours, Dave won the Spa Hurdle on Antiar and the Coventry Handicap Steeplechase with The Rip. Then after riding Utopia to victory at Stratford in October 1965, he left the jockeys' room for the final time. Having suffered a serious accident shortly afterwards while schooling a horse, Dave Dick, a throwback to those noble knights of old and flamboyant cavaliers, never rode in a race again.

One of the all-time greats of post-war National Hunt racing and still the only man to ride the winner of both the Lincolnshire Handicap and the Grand National, many of David Dick's exploits off the racecourse were as daring as those on it and he could always be relied upon to bring a smile to anyone's face.

It was a great loss to the racing world when David Dick passed away on 15 February 2001 at the age of 76, but the exceptional example he left will live on in all who appreciate outstanding skill, natural bravery and a ready wit capable of softening the hardest heart.

Frederick Thomas Winter CBE

Fred Winter, and the man who was to become his lifetime friend, Dave Dick, shared many similarities from their earliest year, not least their backgrounds.

Fred was the son of Frederick Neville Winter, a successful flat-race jockey who won, among other important events, The Oaks on Cherimoya in 1911; the Stewards Cup with Braxted in the same year; The Doncaster Cup in 1928 aboard Pons Asinorum; and the Irish Derby the following year riding Kopi. It was in a bungalow at Andover (appropriately named Cherimoya) that Mr and Mrs Winter added a son to the two daughters they already had. Frederick Thomas was born in September 1926. In 1930, Fred senior took out his first trainer's licence.

Moving to his new establishment at Bredenbury near the station at Epsom Downs, before the age of five Fred junior could often be seen on Epsom High

Street at the head of his father's 'string', sitting regally above a towering racehorse. The youngster also cantered on the Downs alongside his father on his pony while weighing no more than three stone.

It was at Epsom that young Fred first encountered Dave Dick, a boy also endowed with a better than average understanding of the ways of the turf. Like all boys since 'Adam was a lad', the inseparable friends laid the ground rules for their future friendship and escapades, sampling all that was forbidden, tempting providence and generally making bloody nuisances of themselves. Yet behind everything lay their determination that the world of horses should always be theirs, no matter what. The pranks, the dares, the constant attempt to outdo each other in sheer naughtiness, were all preparations for what lay ahead in their future life.

In terms of horsemanship, Fred Winter matured at an alarming rate, winning prizes here there and everywhere in shows and gymkhanas well before the age of ten. When he was only 13 he shared the honours in a jumping class at the Richmond Horse Show. One of his co-winners was a young lady by the name of Pat Smythe and among those behind them were such future famous showjumping champions as Peter Robeson and Douglas Bunn.

Riding out every morning with his father's horses was the perfect grounding for the future champion, particularly with his favourite involvement, taking the jumpers over practice hurdles.

Receiving permission for a day off from school while still in his first teenage year, Fred made his first public appearance on a racecourse at Newbury, riding his father's horse Tam O'Shanter in a six-furlong nursery and finished ninth of 21. After just a couple of more rides the youngster gained his initial victory on the same horse at Newbury in May 1940, beating the veteran flat-race jockey Tommy Lowrey by a length.

Fred was soon acknowledged by racing pundits as an exciting new riding prospect. His father decided Fred would find better chances of good rides if indentured to larger stables and so it was that the rising star of flat-race jockeys found himself under the directorship of Henri Jellis at Newmarket. Although he appeared more frequently on the racecourse, this period failed to bring Fred the success he hoped for, with Winter junior gaining only two wins from about 80 rides during 1941. Equally depressing was the fact that his weight was increasing alarmingly for a profession dependant on the diminutive extent of one's body size.

Another problem he encountered was a growing disenchantment with the sport, due largely to the reduction of racing because of the war and with so many of his friends already in uniform, Fred began considering what role he could play in serving his country.

A brief period in a factory at Feltham repairing damaged planes was followed by nine months as a stable lad for Epsom trainer Walter Nightingall until, in a flurry of patriotism, he joined the Army. The temptation of half a crown a day extra pay convinced Frederick Thomas Winter to volunteer for the Parachute Regiment and, discovering that jumping from aeroplanes provided a tremendous thrill, he qualified for the role with flying colours. After receiving a commission from the West Kent Regiment, Fred was posted to Palestine, but by this time the war was almost at an end and he began considering what awaited him in civvy street. Fully aware that his weight now ruled out any chance of resuming a career riding on the flat, and that his training in the Army was hardly conducive to gaining employment, his options were limited. Reluctantly, he accepted the fact that there was little else he was able to do except ride horses and decided to enquire from his father if he would let him ride one of his jumpers in a race.

While on demobilisation leave in December 1947, he was given the leg-up by his father on Bambino II in a hurdle race at Kempton Park's Boxing Day meeting. Completely misjudging the pace for this kind of race, Fred attempted to make too much of the running and his mount had little left towards the end of the race. It was a chastening afternoon for the young jockey, yet undeterred, he went out the following afternoon aboard another horse trained by his father, the ageing 'chaser Carton, in the two-mile Kenton Handicap Steeplechase. Following his father's instructions to the letter, they came home comfortable winners by six lengths at the attractive odds of 100–8. By the weirdest of coincidences, Carton was the animal which ten years earlier had given his friend Dave Dick his first victory on the flat at Brighton and had now provided Fred with his initial taste of victory over obstacles.

After his immediate exuberance, Fred Winter quickly sized up the differences between the two codes of racing and in that first season 'over the sticks', he scored two wins from nine rides, despite a month on the sidelines through injury. Rapidly adapting to the peculiarities of the jumping game, Fred began the new campaign in the best possible manner, winning again on that gallant old stager Carton, this time at Folkestone. With his natural ability, coupled with his intense enthusiasm, he had the racing press enthusing over this newcomer's obvious potential.

In only the second week of that new season, however, the fickle hand of fate, so notorious for wreaking havoc on even the best, struck in the most cruel and painful way. Fred partnered a bay mare with the ludicrous name of Tugboat Minnie in a novice hurdle race at Wye on 13 September 1948. She made not the slightest attempt to rise at the first flight and, crashing to the ground, she rolled over her jockey. Obviously in agonising pain, it was seven

47

days before Fred was diagnosed as having two fractured vertebrae in his spine. This was to be the most soul-searching period Fred ever encountered; every pain-wracked day questioning his resolve, commitment and dedication to a life on the turf.

Yet despite the daily hammering doubt generated by the continuous painful agony, Fred Winter remembered the exultation, sense of achievement and gut-tingling thrill of battling out a tight finish on a horse bravely responding to your every request. Only a person with immense inner strength and inscrutable determination could even contemplate returning to the unpredictable and highly dangerous world of riding horses at speed over obstacles. Fred himself would be the first to admit that he received tremendous support during this period from a very considerate source. As he regained his fitness, Fred's sister Patricia's husband, flat-race champion Doug Smith, encouraged him to do some schooling for Newmarket trainer and former leading jockey, George Archibald.

With his confidence and fitness gradually returning, Fred Winter at last arrived back on a racecourse at Folkestone in September 1949 to partner his old mate Carton. Although favourites, in the view of many observers they gave a dismal display to finish last of five. Fred did, though, make his first race ride for George Archibald a winning one when, benefiting from the last-fence fall of the favourite in a Plumpton hurdle race in November, he raced home with Dick the Gee to win by six lengths.

Coming at the time it did, this victory renewed his flagging confidence, but more importantly it was witnessed by a man who was to change the jockey's whole future. Captain Ryan Price, a small trainer based at Findon in Sussex, had already employed Winter's services earlier that month and without the jockey being aware, he was pleased with performance, which gained them victory by only a neck. Fred's success with Dick The Gee increased Captain Price's belief that the rider possessed real talent and by the end of that season of such pain and uncertainty, Fred became stable jockey to the Findon handler. A little-known jockey and a struggling trainer amalgamating their energies in an attempt to find success on the turf was hardly earth-shattering news within the media at the time, but over the next 16 years theirs was a story of ongoing success which took the racing world by storm.

In a complete reversal of fortune, Fred Winter rode 38 winners during the 1950–51 season, many of them trained by Ryan Price. He also finished fifth behind the champion Tim Molony in the jockeys' table. It was also during this period that he first became smitten with the allure of the Grand National.

Partnering Glen Fire in that notorious 1951 race, his journey ended at the first Canal Turn and, although it was to be four years before his second bid for Aintree glory, the experience obviously left a deep impression. Second in the championship (again behind Tim Molony) the next season, this time with 85 victories, Fred rode a record 121 winners during the 1952–53 season to take the crown and enable Ryan Price to finish second in the trainers' list. On the opening day of the new campaign, however, Fred was brought well and truly down to earth in the worst and most painful manner.

In his first ride that day at Newton Abbot, Fred fell at the first fence with Cent Francs, suffering a compound fracture of his left leg, which kept him out of action for a full 12 months. In what was to be one of the most testing periods of his life, Fred Winter was sustained by the thought of once more continuing his association with the brilliant former hunter Halloween, a partnership that for many years was to thrill racing enthusiasts everywhere. A second victory with him in Kempton's King George VI 'Chase set the pattern for another memorable season.

At the Cheltenham Festival the following March, Fred repaid Ryan Price's loyalty by winning him the Champion Hurdle on Clair Soleil, and the next day rode Halloween into second place in the Cheltenham Gold Cup behind Gay Donald.

Booked by Vincent O'Brien to partner one of his four entries in the 1955 National, he was well in attendance with Oriental Way until falling at the 11th fence. His nerve unimpaired and his will to win as great as ever, Fred partnered 65 winners in his first season back after that injury, to finish only two behind Tim Molony's total. The following year, Winter became champion again with 74 winners and appeared to have his best chance yet of winning the Grand National.

Less than 24 hours before the great race, he won an all-the-way victory with Ryan Price's Amoureux II in Liverpool's Coronation Hurdle, giving rise to the expectancy that his mount in the National, Sundew, would provide a great double.

Lying handily in second place, the huge chestnut tracked the front-running leader Armorial III back onto the final circuit, jumping with an impressive exuberance. Still ahead of the eventual principals, Devon Loch and ESB at Becher's Brook, Sundew misjudged his leap, giving Fred Winter no chance of staying in the saddle. His only consolation that dramatic National day was his dearest friend Dave Dick's sensational win with ESB.

Having studied that great Aintree jockey Pat Taaffe's technique over those enormous Liverpool obstacles, Fred was convinced that the Irishman's was the correct manner in which to plan a route to success across the most potentially dangerous land on earth. Determined to overcome the Aintree hoodoo which had dashed so many dreams for so long, Fred also sought the advice of that brilliant horseman of yesteryear, Dudley Williams. Having achieved his moment of glory with Kellsboro' Jack in 1933, Welshman Dudley made a regular habit of showing his rivals the best way home over those mighty fences by winning several less prestigious events across Aintree. Having twice failed to even get round the National course, Sundew's abysmal performance in Aintree's Grand Sefton 'Chase was hardly encouraging, but still the animal's Warwickshire trainer, Frank Hudson, felt convinced that the only 'chaser in his small yard could still achieve the ultimate accolade in the jumping world.

Learning well from all the advice he had sought, Fred Winter allowed Sundew free passage from the very beginning of the 1957 National and after the early demise of the leader Armorial III, was never again headed. Derek Ancil on Athenian threatened momentarily on the final circuit and after surviving a mistake at the second Becher's Sundew was still at the head of affairs. By the time his old friend Dave Dick loomed alongside on last year's winner ESB with just two jumps left, Fred already knew that his mount was nearing the end of his tether and was relieved to discover that the challenge was of no substance. Holding his mount together with authority and sympathy, Fred held on tenaciously to withstand the late challenge of Scottish-trained Wyndburgh and win somewhat easily by eight lengths.

Another championship season ended with Fred Winter at the head of the winning jockeys' table with 80 winners to his credit – the most important by anyones' standards being the one gained at Aintree on Sundew.

Another top title followed the next year, this time with 82 successes to his credit but with Springsilver in that year's Aintree spectacular, they exited at the 19th.

By now universally recognised as the supreme artist of all jump jockeys, Fred brought off an incredible Cheltenham double in 1961 by winning the Champion Hurdle with Eborneezer and the Gold Cup on Saffron Tartan, after already carrying off Sandown's Triumph Hurdle aboard that brilliant hurdler Cantab. In the interim period, sadness had loomed large with the death of Sundew at Haydock in November 1957, and failure to complete the National trip in the following three years with Springsilver, Done Up and Dandy Scot left many feeling that, in terms of Aintree, Fred Winter's days were complete.

Those who did had second thoughts when the Ryan Price-trained Kilmore finished a very respectable fifth behind Nicolaus Silver in that strongly contested Aintree spectacular of 1961. From that day on, Fred Winter sought to present the man who brought his genius to the fore when his life was at its lowest ebb, Captain Ryan Price, with a victory no one could question or ever dispute. That most severe, treacherous and demanding victory of all – the Grand National.

Under the worst possible conditions, the 1962 Aintree epic was run in such very heavy ground that all were prompted to fantasise about the outcome. In a race which eventually was dubbed the 'success of the veterans', Fred Winter gave a superlative exhibition of horsemanship which will last forever in the memories of those privileged to see it. The brave 12-year-old Kilmore answered every request of his jockey in the most exacting conditions one could ever imagine, to restrain the determined late challenges of two same-aged heroes, Wyndburgh and Mr What.

That long euphoric walk back to the winner's enclosure told its own story that day. Two men, so often consigned to the scrapheap, joining as one in a celebration of mutual confidence, commitment and loyalty, to provide each other with a demonstration of total appreciation.

Having earlier that year won the Cheltenham Gold on Mandarin, surely little more could have been expected from the pint-sized jockey with the heart of a lion, but within weeks Fred Winter completely re-wrote the record books across the English Channel. Partnering once again the French-bred Mandarin at Auteuil in France, Fred rode the race of his life, while suffering a debilitating weight-loss illness, to snatch victory from certain defeat in the Grande Steeplechase de Paris. Despite a broken bit, early in the contest the genius of Fred Winter came into play with a superlative display of horsemanship in guiding home to victory his mount, effectively without the aid of steering or brakes.

In 1963 Kilmore finished sixth in the National, and with his final run 12 months later he came down approaching Becher's second time round. Few could have guessed that this was the last time such a racing phenomena as Fred Winter would be seen working his mastery over Aintree's unique fences.

After retiring from the saddle in 1964, Fred was justifiably honoured with the recognition of the CBE. He became a trainer and unbelievably took over from where he left off when a 'mere' jockey. Establishing his base at Uplands in Lambourn, Wiltshire, he began the second chapter of re-writing the record books, this time by preparing jumpers to win every major contest in the National Hunt calendar. Respected by all in racing and admired by racegoers everywhere, Fred Winter was only 61 when, after a fall on the stairs of his home, he suffered his second stroke. Cruelly, the man who for over 30 years faced every danger and setback which are basic ingredients of steeplechasing with a natural equanimity, was so stricken that his speech was severely impaired and mobility seriously affected.

That racing genius affectionately referred to as 'Mr Grand National' left the sport he loved and lived for with a legacy of excellence, dedication and honest endeavour which will never be forgotten.

THREE

Arthur Robert Freeman

Arthur Freeman was born on 7 January 1926, a nephew of the famous Pytchley huntsman Frank Freeman. He became apprenticed to the illustrious classic flat-race trainer the Honourable George Lambton at Newmarket. After 30 rides in public for the yard and still without a winner to his credit, Arthur was beginning to feel disconsolate when along came the war and, as a private in the Green Howards and the Somerset Light Infrantry, he spent his 18th birthday on the border of Holland and Germany. Still abroad after the war, he rode a few winners in army events at Hanover but upon demobilisation found it difficult at home to get back into flat racing. It was only when an older rider suggested he tried the jumping game that he even considered the prospect of competing 'over the sticks'.

After acquiring his first National Hunt jockey's licence in 1950, Arthur went through a lean spell, riding just four winners in his first two seasons, but then slowly but surely he began to find his way. One of the first trainers to use his services on a regular basis was John Morant, who as an owner led in the 1946 Grand National winner Lovely Cottage. It was with this man's gelding, Game Gambler, that Arthur won one of his earliest races, the Heavitree Novices Hurdle at Devon and Exeter in September 1951. Later that season, he finished unplaced with him in the Prospect Hurdle at Aintree.

After hearing a whisper that Newmarket trainer George Archibald may possibly need a jockey, he boldly applied. Arthur was initially taken on as an ordinary lad but Archibald quickly recognised his potential and winners suddenly began coming Arthur's way. One of these was a good novice hurdler, Ronald, with whom he won three races early in 1953 before finishing a good third in Liverpool's Coronation Hurdle the day before the National. Taking the ride on Archibald's entry Wait and See in the big race the next day gave Arthur Freeman his first taste of Aintree's jockeys' room during the final countdown to the National. As it happened, the race itself was over far too soon for his liking, he and his mount being brought down at the first open ditch. Something about Aintree's atmosphere, though, had captured his imagination and the hope persisted that he would have another opportunity to sample it more fully.

It was to take rather longer than he would have wished, however, and although by now he was favourably noticed by the racing press, who began referring to him as 'a very promising jockey' and even more encouragingly 'the find of the season', Arthur failed to secure a ride in the 1954 Grand National. Later in the year, with the new season underway, he did receive a pleasant surprise when asked by the royal trainer Peter Cazalet to ride a novice hurdler named Gipsy Love in a race at Fontwell. Although finishing unplaced, Major Cazalet was sufficiently impressed that a couple of weeks later Arthur Freeman was again engaged to carry Her Majesty the Queen Mother's colours on the improving M'as-tu-Vu. The event was the Walton Green Handicap 'Chase at Sandown Park and after coming fourth behind the winner Gay Donald, he was offered the job of second jockey to Dick Francis at the powerful Fairlawne establishment of Major Peter Cazalet.

With that distinguished owner Lord Bicester having first claims on Dick Francis, Arthur now came in for plenty of rides and the fact that Dick was required to ride His Lordship's Mariner's Log in the 1955 Grand National left the way clear for Freeman to partner M'as-tu-Vu at Aintree.

Having won with the gelding at Lingfield ten days earlier, Arthur was confident the horse would provide him with a lengthier experience of the National than his first attempt – and so it proved.

Always well up with the pace, they figured prominently throughout the first circuit, M'as-tu-Vu lying second over the Water behind Sundew and taking up the running after the 18th. A bad mistake at the second Becher's cost them a lot of ground and eventually the royal competitor fell four from home.

The following year the process was repeated, with M'as-tu-Vu winning with Arthur in the saddle at Lingfield before going on to Aintree, where they were accompanied by Devon Loch, the better fancied of the royal pair. The latter almost pulled it off in a climax which saw Her Majesty's horse fall on the flat barely 30 yards from victory. Arthur Freeman again showed prominently with his charge until coming down at the 19th fence.

For the first time Arthur finished among the leading riders the next season, finishing in fifth place with 35 wins, but still success in the greatest challenge of all remained elusive. His mount in that year's Grand National, Rendezvous III, was brought down at the very first fence.

With the retirement of Dick Francis, Arthur became first jockey to Major

Cazalet and during the 1957–58 campaign he won six races for the Queen Mother; three with the very promising Double Star and one each aboard King of the Isle, Wild West and King's Point. It was to be another highly successful term for the man from Newmarket, but with Derek Ancil already booked by his owner Colonel W.H. Whitbread to ride the only Cazalet entry in the National, Arthur looked like missing the 1958 race.

Scottish-trained Wyndburgh, runner-up in 1957, was a hot favourite from the moment ante-post betting began on the event and as the moment of truth drew closer, his odds reduced even more. Of the five Irish challengers, the eight-year-old Mr What was considered by most to be little more than a novice, but he had won five 'chases in his own country and was prepared for the race by Thomas Taaffe, father of that outstanding jockey Pat. With both Pat and his younger brother, Tos, already committed to other owners, a somewhat late decision was taken to offer Arthur Freeman the ride. At the opening of the Aintree meeting Mr What was readily available at 33–1 among most bookmakers, yet those odds were to reduce rapidly over the next two days, despite Arthur having to put up six pounds overweight.

In the Mildmay 'Chase over Aintree's Mildmay course on the Friday, Arthur Freeman had the first of his only two booked rides at the meeting, taking the leg-up from Peter Cazalet on Just Awake in the colours of Colonel W.H. Whitbread. Riding a perfectly judged race, Arthur produced a great response from his mount in the closing stages to hold on and win by a neck. It was the ideal fillip for his next appointment exactly 24 hours later: the Grand National.

Avoiding the usual trouble in the early part of the race, Arthur made a forward move with Mr What, coming back onto the racecourse towards the 13th fence. Three fences later he leapt the Water Jump in sixth place. Tracking Goosander, Athenian and The Crofter back out into the country, Mr What was jumping splendidly the whole time, making a nonsense of his alleged novice status. Taking up the running after landing over the second Becher's, the little Irish horse jumped from fence to fence, appearing stronger the further he went. Crossing the Melling Road for the final time, only a fall could prevent Mr What from winning, as he drew ever further away from his pursuers. Well clear at the final fence, the gelding made his only mistake in what had been a trouble-free round. Hitting the fence hard, it was simply pure horsemanship on the part of his jockey which kept the partnership intact. Allowing his mount ample time to recover, Arthur Freeman brought home Mr What an incredible 30-length winner from Tiberetta, Green Drill and the favourite, Wyndburgh.

At the season's end he finished in third place among the top jump jockeys with 53 winners and in July he crowned a memorable year when marrying his delightful fiancée Joanna.

In 1959, when Arthur again took third position in the jockeys' list with 49 winners, he was sidelined from riding Mr What when Tos was available to represent his father, and they finished third behind OXO and Wyndburgh. Arthur did, however, excel at the Cheltenham Festival, winning on Sword Flash and Mac Joy, and finishing third in the Gold Cup on Lochroe. His tally of victories for the Queen Mother also increased that season, producing nine winners in the royal colours, which included four with Double Star, two on Out of Town and three aboard Sparkling Knight.

Reunited once more with Mr What in the 1960 Aintree showpiece, they came down at Becher's second time round when well in touch with the leading group. It was his last ride in the race and, having endured increasing weight and a serious skull fracture, Arthur finally retired at the end of that season, though not before riding another three winners for his royal patron.

In total he rode 22 winners for Her Majesty the Queen Mother and when granted his trainer's licence in July 1960, he set up operations at Bury Lodge, Bury Road, Newmarket. Among the big races he won as a trainer were the Mildmay of Flete Challenge Cup and the National Hunt Centenary 'Chase at Cheltenham, and by far the best horse he ever saddled was Tibidabo.

Suffering from poor health for a number of years, Arthur Freeman sadly passed away in 1988.

Michael John Scudamore

The son of a farmer, Michael Scudamore was born in 1932 and, thanks to his father John Geoffrey, he immediately inherited the strongest possible affection for horses. From his earliest days it seems he had only one idea of the perfect way of life; to be able to ride horses for a living.

When just 14 years old he rode in a point-to-point and soon afterwards, at the suggestion of some of his dad's racing friends, he found himself taking part in a hunter 'chase at Hereford. Growing up quickly brought him increasing weight and with barely a dozen flat races under his belt Michael was forced to switch to the National Hunt side of the sport. As an amateur he took the mount on a five year old trained by his father called Wild Honey in a hurdle race at Wolverhampton. Putting in a strong late challenge, he was only beaten by three-quarters of a length by Jimmy Power on Aghavannagh. Less than three weeks later, Michael scored his first victory riding the same horse in a Selling Hurdle at Chepstow on 15 February 1950.

Early in the new season, while still an amateur, Michael became associated with a gelding called East A' Calling, owned and trained by Mr Knipe, and it was soon apparent that they worked well together. After winning two of their first three races, the young rider had his first encounter with Aintree, when they formed part of the line-up for the Becher 'Chase over two and a half miles of the world-famous obstacles. After jumping the third, the mighty Chair, East A'Calling went to the front and, leaping well from there on, proceeded to lead until being caught close home by the Liverpool veteran Cloncarrig. Beaten by only a head after issuing a renewed challenge, young Scudamore was well pleased with his mount's performance. After winning the Tetbury 'Chase at Cheltenham in January on the horse, preparations began for a crack at the Grand National three months later.

Of the 36 riders competing in that 1951 National, seven others besides Scudamore were amateurs, and as they paraded in front of the stands nobody could have known this traditional procession was one which Michael would be involved with each spring for the next 15 years. On this occasion, though, many hopes were dashed with the dreadful start which caused so much trouble, and Michael was among the 12 riders prematurely put out of the contest at the first fence.

At Stratford-upon-Avon on the last day of the season, Michael Scudamore had his last ride as an amateur when finishing down the course on Simonagh in the final Hunters' 'Chase. His first professional engagement came at Worcester on 8 September 1951 with Buxton's First carrying him into second place in a two-mile hurdle race. It was not until the following February, however, that he broke his duck among the paid ranks, with Double D at Ludlow, and this was quickly followed when Michael partnered Fred Rimell's Signal Prince to a well-judged victory in the National Hunt Juvenile 'Chase at the Cheltenham Festival.

Through this somewhat frustrating period, his good judgement and determination had been noticed and he was hired by top trainer Fulke Walwyn to accompany Miss Dorothy Paget's exciting new prospect, Legal Joy, in the Grand National. Third favourite in the race at 100–7, behind Freebooter and Teal, Legal Joy's usual rider, Dave Dick, was unable to make the weight and chose to partner Yorkshire-trained Wot No Sun.

This time surviving the first fence despite another heavy toll there, Michael gave his mount a perfect ride all the way, being fourth at the halfway stage behind Freebooter, Teal and Wot No Sun. When the leader fell at the second Canal Turn, Legal Joy moved alongside Teal then took up the running at the third-last. Touching down together over the final fence, it was, however, Arthur Thompson's mount which found the better turn of foot and Teal raced clear in the home straight to win by six lengths from Legal Joy, Wot No Sun and Uncle Barney.

It was a tremendous effort by the young jockey in only his second appearance in the race and already the racing press began predicting a great future for the 19 year old.

In 1953 it was Kinnersley trainer Fred Rimell who sought Michael's services in the big Liverpool feature, as partner of his improving youngster Ordnance, a horse the young jockey had already won with at Chepstow. Blazing a trail from the first fence, they set a hot pace for the remainder of the first circuit, only to tire and come down two before the second Becher's. The year was not without its rewards, though, with Michael finishing the season in tenth place among the top riders with an impressive 34 victories.

Another good year came with the new term and he finished the campaign this time with 20 winners and once more proved he knew his way around Aintree when piloting Lord Sefton's Irish Lizard into third place in the National. Twelve months later the same pair finished 11th in the race but in the next three Nationals he failed to complete the course, twice with Neville Crump's Much Obliged and in 1958 when teaming up with racing journalist Oliver Gilbey's Valiant Spark.

Even so, this interim period was not without its thrills and rewards. Among the 39 wins which gained him fourth position in the jockeys' table of 1956 were triumphs on Rose Park in the King George VI 'Chase and with Square Dance in the Triumph Hurdle at Hurst Park. The Cheltenham Gold Cup also fell to him in 1957 when giving Linwell a copybook ride at Prestbury and another fine performance on Creeola II won him the Welsh Grand National at Chepstow the same year. His tally of victories for that term numbered 58, making him the second most successful jockey next to Fred Winter.

With the 1959 Grand National the target of Royston trainer Willie Stephenson, Michael Scudamore was approached to ride his stable's entry, the eight-year-old OXO. In what turned out to be one of the epic Aintree stories, the race became a dual between Tim Brookshaw on the Liverpool specialist Wyndburgh and Michael with newcomer OXO. Although many considered it an unequal struggle for Tim after his stirrup iron broke at Becher's second time round, such was the man's outstanding ability he rode virtually bareback from there on and that final slog home from the Canal Turn saw sporting endeavour at its finest. With both riders talking to each other over those exacting fences, it was an example to all of what true comradeship really means. With his race seemingly well won, OXO hit the last fence hard and only a superb horseman like Scudamore could have ever hoped to survive. Recovering with a skill to be envied by all, Michael made his run for home and the victory he had longed for. Incredibly, under such circumstances, Tim Brookshaw rallied his mount, digging deep into every reserve of energy within their beings and yard by yard they gained on the leader. Holding on tenaciously over the final lung-bursting yards, OXO passed the post one and a half lengths to the good. The first to congratulate Michael was none other than the man he defeated, Tim Brookshaw. Anyone privileged to have witnessed that heroic finish can honestly say they saw sportsmanship at its highest level. The Grand National itself was that day the principal beneficiary.

With 45 winners to his credit that year, Michael Scudamore again finished among the leading jockeys but, ironically, when he partnered Wyndburgh in the race the following year, they came down at Becher's Brook on the first circuit.

In 1961 he won the Mildmay Memorial Steeplechase with Mac Joy, but when reunited with OXO in that year's National Becher's was again as far as he got, having to pull up his mount on the second circuit. With Chavara in 1962 he called it a day at the 26th fence and the following year, after a splendid display to win the Topham Trophy 'Chase over the big fences on the opening day with Barberyn, he guided the ageing O'Malley Point round into 19th place two days later in the National.

Failing to complete the course in his next three attempts — with Time in 1964, Bold Biri in 1965 and Greek Scholar in 1966 — brought the curtain down on a remarkable man's 15-year contribution to the legend which embodies Aintree's supreme test.

Despite what in racing is considered advancing years, at 34 Michael was still a formidable opponent in any race and in his last two seasons he had topped 40 wins in each. With eight victories already behind him in the current campaign, his journey to Wolverhampton on 1 November 1966 felt just like any other day at the races. Little could he have known it was to be his last as a competitive horseman.

The horse he rode that day in a hurdle race, Snakestone, slipped up on the flat, leaving the jockey directly in the path of the following bunch. Having suffered far more serious disruptions in the course of a race, Michael felt two separate kicks; one in the chest, the other agonisingly in his face. His horrendous injuries where such that his life as a jockey was at an end.

After a long and painful recovery, he became a trainer at Hoarwithy in Herefordshire and for a change was able to spend more time with his family. He achieved some success as a trainer but it was subsequently the fame of his son Peter which revived memories of his former brilliance on the racecourse. At the time OXO carried him to victory at Aintree, his son was only nine months old and the pledge he made to buy Peter a pony from his earnings was duly kept. Peter Scudamore learned well from a master of his craft, going on to become champion jockey eight times in a very illustrious career.

Peter may well have outdone his father, whose closest tilt at the jockeys' crown only brought a second placing, but the nearest he came to emulating Michael at Aintree was in finishing third in the 1985 Grand National with Corbiere.

In the first Aintree showpiece of the twenty-first century a new generation of Scudamores registered their National intentions when Peter's very talented son Tom followed a hallowed family path by riding Martin Pipe's Northern Starlight in the big race.

Both Michael and Peter Scudamore are deserving of the pride they obviously felt that day, and of the contribution they have made to steeplechasing in general and the Grand National in particular. One can only imagine the joy they will experience on the day Tom adds his name to Aintree's Roll of Honour.

Gerald Scott

As a 16 year old, Gerry Scott took the bold step of applying to Middleham trainer Neville Crump for a position as an apprentice jockey. One can but imagine the trepidation he must have felt while awaiting a response from a man very often regarded as austere on the turf.

Reared in the world of point-to-pointing at home in Durham, his parents ran a pub and from his earliest days Gerry was accustomed to horses being a major part of his life. His father held a permit to train and from such a background Captain Crump could at least expect someone who could sit on a horse correctly. The young man's appointment to the staff at Warwick House in 1954 was a relief to his anxiety but more importantly, though no one could have known it at the time, it was to be another wonderful episode in the prestige of the Master of Middleham.

Mucking-out and bulling-up gear in the tack room, all became a daily way of life for Gerry Scott for a longer time than he could have expected but it all proved more than worth it when he rode his first winner at Sedgefield in early March 1956. In the humble Grove Handicap Hurdle, worth a mere £102 to the winning owner, Gerry gave Kiddleywink a masterly ride to secure the race by a length and a half at very nice odds of 20–1. In November this mare provided his first action at Aintree, where they finished unplaced in the November Handicap Hurdle. One of his earliest winners for his own stable came when dead-heating aboard Blackpool with the David Nicholson-ridden Royal Task at Sandown.

Under the caring tutorage of stable jockey Arthur Thompson, the young hopeful found kindness, consideration, invaluable advice and, most of all, a level of inspiration impossible to measure. Another regular stable jockey, Johnny East, also provided generous support at this period in the young man's life but most of all it was the Captain himself who imbued in Gerry Scott that self-belief, awareness of dignity and the will to rise above all adversities, which were to become such an essential part of his life.

To many, the arrival of the bay gelding Merryman II at Middleham hardly raised an eyebrow. The son of Carnival Boy, who had been bred by the Marquess of Linlithgow, was to many 'just another very good hunter 'chaser'. Quite the reverse was soon to be realised.

Owned by Miss Winifred Wallace, who herself broke the horse before riding him to three point-to-point wins, Merryman II flourished under the care of Neville Crump who planned to run the white-faced gelding in the next Liverpool Foxhunters' 'Chase. It was during that 1958–59 season that Gerry Scott first came to prominence on the northern racetracks, and at Wetherby in February, somewhat prophetically, he gained his fourth success with Rock's Cross in the Grand National Trial 'Chase.

With Johnny East booked to partner John Jacques for the Crump stable in the National, Gerry gladly accepted a spare ride in the race on the ten-year-old Surprise Packet, together with an engagement to compete in the Topham Trophy 'Chase on Aintree's opening day. His introduction to the big fences came to an abrupt end in that event when his mount Idlewood blundered their chance away at the Chair, but an hour later he had the satisfaction of seeing Merryman II make a procession of the Foxhunters' 'Chase in the hands of an amateur with the same surname as his. Though totally unrelated, Mr C. Scott and Gerry Scott both enjoyed their finest racing moments astride the powerful former point-to-pointer Merryman II.

On a perfect spring afternoon, Surprise Packet made a nonsense of his 100–1 starting price, giving Gerry the thrill of his life with a grand display of jumping at the head the Grand National field. Setting a cracking pace from the start, they met each fence perfectly and passing the stands at the end of the first circuit still led the way. Back out in the country, OXO and Wyndburgh moved into contention. Beginning to tire, Surprise Packet brought an end to a fine performance when coming down at the second Becher's.

After winning the Wetherby Handicap 'Chase on San Lorenzo at the end of March, Gerry Scott looked forward to his most important appointment so far: partnering Merryman II in the Scottish Grand National at Bogside on the third Saturday in April. In the first race that day his old friend, the hurdler Kiddleywink, carried him into second place two lengths behind George Milburn on Dunstan. In the principal event Gerry went one better, with Merryman II jumping out of his skin all the way and, after taking command three fences out, romping away for a 12-length victory. Trailing in a long way behind them were such seasoned performers as Punch Bowl Hotel, Pendle Lady, Done Up and the runner-up in the most recent Liverpool National, Wyndburgh.

With his whole preparation for the 1959–60 season centred around just one race, the Grand National at Aintree, Merryman II opened his account with a third place behind his stablemate John Jacques and Polished Steel at Kelso in October 1959. This was followed in December with a return to Liverpool for the Christmas Cracker Stakes 'Chase and even though this was only over the lesser obstacles of the Mildmay course, few could have been pleased with the outcome. After making the early pace, Merryman II fell at the 14th fence, with the eventual winner being the horse he had beaten out of sight at Bogside, Wyndburgh.

Starting the 2–1 favourite for the Rhymney Breweries 'Chase at Chepstow in December, things seemed far from right when they finished fifth after tiring in the closing stages. Making a wise decision, Captain Crump sent the horse to the veterinary college in Edinburgh, where it was discovered he had an inflamed bone in a foreleg. Their recommendation of a long period of rest was hardly practicable under the circumstances, yet somehow a combination of treatment and relaxation provided the cure. Desperate to get one last race into the gelding before the supreme test, Neville Crump must have suffered terribly in deciding when and where this was to be. The 'where' turned out to be Manchester; the 'when', the Hearts of Oak Handicap 'Chase – just 28 days before that crucial Liverpool engagement.

Given a considerate yet determined ride by Gerry, Merryman II jumped well to come up with a strong run from the penultimate fence and finish a very good third, beaten a neck and three-quarters of a length by the fitter O'Malley Point and the Cheshire-trained Badanloch.

For all at Middleham, it was a reassuring performance but little over a week before the vital Aintree appointment another serious problem arose. After winning a maiden hurdle at Doncaster on Quirinus, Gerry Scott fell three from home later that afternoon when challenging with True Cottage in the Wheatley Park Novices 'Chase, breaking his collarbone in two places.

In a desperate attempt to regain fitness, the distressed jockey attended a physiotherapist twice a day for heat treatment and when expressing his intention of riding in the Grand National, was told in no uncertain terms that he must be mad to even consider such a thing. In what must have appeared a forlorn battle, Gerry continued to receive treatment right through to the start of the Aintree meeting. With time running out, he telephoned Captain Crump for advice. With generous loyalty, the trainer invited him to ride two of his hurdlers at Liverpool the following day and then, less than 24 hours before the National, see how he felt.

After finishing down the course on Quirinus in the Lancashire Hurdle that Friday afternoon, he was wracked with pain but persevered later with Shimmering Gold in the Coronation Hurdle without ever troubling the leaders. Informing Neville Crump that the last ride hadn't felt too bad, the

Captain understandably asked him to submit to an examination by three racecourse doctors at the end of that day's sport. Gritting his teeth and forcing himself to smile, Gerry Scott survived the prodding and probing of the medical men and, despite one declaring it was impossible for him to compete, the other two nodded and passed him fit. Even then the final decision had to be approved by his guv'nor and, to the jockey's great relief, the Middleham trainer very generously agreed to his riding Merryman II in the National.

For the first time in the history of the great event, the entire contest was to be televised by the BBC and, although this brought the action and drama into the living-rooms of most, the usual crowds of spectators were only marginally smaller than normal. With old favourites such as Mr What and Wyndburgh among the 26 runners, betting reached its customary fever pitch as the final moments ticked by – but at 'the off' Merryman II was the firm favourite at 13–2.

Cutting out the early pace, Tea Fiend took them along, closely followed by Green Drill, Badanloch, Mr What, Cannobie Lee and Merryman II but uncharacteristically, Wyndburgh came down at Becher's Brook together with Knoxtown. At the next, the smallest fence on the course, the favourite made a dreadful mistake, coming down almost on his nose, but recovering brilliantly. The partnership remained intact and little ground was lost. There were still 20 left in the race as they passed the stands, with Tea Fiend and Gerry Madden still showing the way to Merryman II, Badanloch, Green Drill, Clear Profit and Mr What. After Mr What exited at the second Becher's, the contest became a virtual match between Merryman II and Lord Leverhulme's Badanloch, the pair gradually drawing further and further away from the remainder. Well clear by the time the last was reached, the favourite landed safely to gallop away to a 15-length victory over Badanloch, with Clear Profit, Tea Fiend and Sabaria the closest of the other six finishers.

The smiles of the winner's owner, trainer and jockey when led back to rapturous applause belied the pain and anxiety of the preceding days and for Gerry Scott, the joy felt was increased with the knowledge that he had achieved for his loyal trainer a third Grand National success. Having successfully brought home the first clear favourite to win the race in 33 years while still only 22, Gerry looked forward to a career full of promise and the opportunity of renewing his winning ways with Merryman II.

Sadly it was not to be. A cruel series of leg breaks prevented him from rising to the very top of his profession and in both the following years he was forced to watch Merryman II piloted into second place by Derek Ancil and then 13th position under Dave Dick. Back in the saddle by the autumn of 1962, Gerry teamed up with Colonel Lord Joicey's Springbok to win at

Hexham before making the long trip to Newbury in November to ride him in the valuable Hennessy Gold Cup. Trainer Neville Crump was doubly represented by both Springbok and the David Nicholson-ridden Rough Tweed, and in a tremendously exciting race the result lay between the two of them. In one of the closest finishes ever seen in this contest, Gerry rode Springbok out brilliantly to get up in the final strides and win by a head.

At Aintree the following March the sole representative of Neville Crump in the National was Springbok with Gerry Scott again in the saddle. Such was the reputation of this combination, they were sent off 10–1 favourites in a field of 47 runners.

Despite the soft going it was a comparatively trouble-free event, with 22 eventually completing the course. Although well in contention at the penultimate fence, Springbok was beaten for speed in the closing stages to finish an honourable fifth behind Ayala, Carrickbeg, Hawa's Song and Team Spirit. It was a similar story 12 months later in 1964, with Gerry Scott and Springbok on that occasion gaining sixth place behind the winner Team Spirit, but in the interim period the jockey unknowingly made a curious piece of turf history. Riding another old equine friend, Rough Tweed, in April 1963, they won the very last running of the Great Lancashire Steeplechase at Manchester. Some months afterwards the surprise announcement came that the racecourse was to close and would never be used as such again.

Missing the National again in 1965 through yet another injury, Gerry Scott returned to the scene of his greatest triumph 12 months later, to lift everyone's spirits with a superb display of riding. Giving the eight-year-old Forest Prince classic guidance from the saddle throughout the lengthy journey, they came back onto the racecourse for the final time in the lead and still going well. It was only at the second-last fence that the lightly weighted outsider Anglo drew up close, yet within seconds the result was decided. Running on strongly up the finishing straight, Anglo won very comfortably from the favourite Freddie, with Gerry back in third place with Forest Prince.

Sadly there was just one last Grand National which featured that brave but unfortunate, totally unassuming, thoroughly decent man, Gerry Scott. That final ride on the outsider Phemius in the 1968 National ended when he spared his mount any further exhaustion by pulling him up after the second Valentine's Brook. As with every horse he rode, Gerry had given his all and he never forgot that the welfare of the animal beneath him always had to come first.

A freak accident returning from the gallops one morning at Middleham left him with a skull cracked so badly that the doctors forbade him from ever riding again. It was only fitting therefore that Gerry Scott – a credit to his profession – was appointed by the Jockey Club as a racing official in 1973.

Eventually becoming a starter, he again made history in 1996, when becoming the only Grand National-winning jockey ever to start the great race. As always, he performed his task immaculately.

Henry Robert Beasley

Bobby Beasley was born in Ireland in 1936 into one of the most famous racing clans in the history of the sport and as such it was only to be expected that his future should revolve around horse racing.

It was in the late 1870s that the renowned Irish 'amateur' Beasley brothers made their first of many assaults on the Grand National, which in a period of 14 years brought them four wins, six seconds and two thirds in the race. Such was their fervour that in 1879 four of the 18 riders competing were Beasley brothers. After the 1892 National, when Willie Beasley finished fifth on Flying Column and brother Harry failed to get round, it was to be another century, another age and a vastly different world, before the illustrious surname appeared again among the list of probable runners and riders for the Aintree spectacular.

No matter how famous one's antecedents may have been, the very essence of the racing world demands that all wishing to pursue a career competing within it have to start at the bottom and this dictate was to apply to the young Bobby Beasley as to all others. The demanding chores of a stable lad toughened and prepared the young hopeful for the ups and downs that his future life would bring, but with an inherent determination Bobby stuck to his task.

His first success came at the age of 16 in a flat race for amateurs over two miles at Leopardstown in May 1952. Riding a four year old named Touareg, Bobby brought his 10–1 mount with a sustained late challenge to win the contest, beating such future National Hunt personalities as Tom Taaffe and Francis Flood. His style, strength and intense will to win was such that he was soon in demand by trainers throughout his native land. In 1957 he won his first Galway Plate with Knight Errant for Wicklow trainer Paddy Sleator. Further success in this event was to follow with Sparkling Flame, Clipador and Blunt's Cross. The four-mile Conyngham Cup Steeplechase also fell to him, again for Paddy Sleator, with Fugal Maid in 1960.

Following in the footsteps of his ancestors, he made frequent raids across the Irish Sea to capture some of the principal events there and in 1957 had his first encounter with Aintree, finishing tenth with Sandy Jane II in the Grand National. In 1959 he won the Cheltenham Gold Cup on the Dan Morgan-trained Roddy Owen and the following year he returned to that venue to produce a stunning late challenge and win the Champion Hurdle with Another Flash.

It was shortly after this victory that, in April 1960, he married Shirley Ann, the daughter of another legendary Irish jockey, Arthur Thompson. By now a force to be reckoned with on racecourses everywhere, his services were in constant demand. When interviewed around this time and asked what he still wished to attain in racing, his reply came naturally and with conviction. He said,

> My ambition is to win the Grand National and keep up the family tradition. My grandfather won it twice, my uncle three times and my father-in-law twice. In addition my father was champion flat jockey of Eire twice. There is a lot to live up to, you know?

Leading British trainer Fred Rimell, already a National winner with ESB in 1956, required a strong, purposeful jockey to ride one of his two entries in the 1961 Liverpool showpiece. Fully appreciating all he had seen of the lanky young Irishman, he reached the astute conclusion that Bobby was tailor-made to partner his vibrant grey gelding Nicolaus Silver, the recent winner of the Kim Muir Memorial 'Chase at Cheltenham.

Overjoyed at being given another chance to sample all the thrills his ancestors had known so well, the 25 year old had no hesitation in accepting the ride.

Some strange coincidence can always be found connected with any Grand National and in 1961 there was one connected to that controversial race five years earlier, when Fred Rimell's ESB was handed the race on a plate, through the late slip-up by Devon Loch. In that year, 1956, a member of the Soviet Union's government, Georgi Malenkov, was the guest of Mrs Mirabel Topham, Aintree's owner and Managing Director. Impressed by what he had witnessed, and at a time when international politics was a popular and ongoing pastime, the USSR decided to launch their own assault on the event recognised worldwide as the supreme test of horse and rider. It took five years but, with typical Russian firmness, the 1961 Aintree marathon had two Russian horses among the 35 entries which faced the starter. It was to be Fred Rimell's representative that showed them all the way home.

With such 'chasing notables as Merryman II, Mr What, OXO, Wyndburgh and Badanloch in the line-up, Nicolaus Silver was neglected in the betting at 28–1, as too were both Russian contenders, Reljef and Grifel, who were assigned the derogatory starting price of 100–1.

From a good start Beasley settled his mount immediately, his main concern in the early stages being to avoid the interference of loose and falling horses. Fresh Winds made most of the early running, closely followed by Fred Winter on Kilmore, the old stagers Wyndburgh, Mr What, Badanloch, the favourite Jonjo and Nicolaus Silver. At the end of the first circuit both Russian horses had called it a day and from here on Bobby Beasley rode the race of his life, gradually placing his mount into a challenging position. After jumping Becher's for the final time, he made a forward move towards the leader, last year's hero Merryman II, and from Valentine's Brook back to the racecourse this pair held command. Taking the lead at the second last fence, Nicolaus Silver maintained his advantage to race clear and win by five lengths, Merryman II, with O'Malley Point, Scottish Flight, Kilmore and Wyndburgh the next of the 14 who finished.

Since the beginning of mankind, history has had an uncanny habit of repeating itself, yet never in a more delightful way than on that day in 1961 when Bobby Beasley emulated his grandfather's feat of 70 years before with Come Away in winning the Grand National in a manner that the great gentleman Harry would have been proud of.

Barely a month later, a heroic effort to add Sandown's Whitbread Gold Cup to his tally failed by four lengths when the grey finished second to the previous year's Cheltenham Gold Cup winner Pas Seul. In what was a very competitive field and on a right-handed course which did not suit him, Nicolaus Silver put on a splendid display and in 1962, again partnered by Bobby Beasley, came seventh in the big Aintree contest. Emphasising his liking for the big Liverpool fences, Nicolaus Silver, with Bobby again in the plate, completed a clear round to finish tenth behind the surprise winner Ayala, 12 months later in 1963.

Early in 1964 Bobby provided Her Majesty the Queen Mother with her 100th winner when winning on Gay Record and in the same year came down at the Chair with Lizawake in the National. During these illustrious endeavours in England, he still found time to hold racegoers in his homeland enthralled by winning a Thyestes 'Chase and the Leopardstown Steeplechase no less than three times.

What was generally agreed to be one of the finest contests seen over the National fences took place some six months after Bobby Beasley's historic success at Aintree. In a top-class field for Aintree's Grand Sefton 'Chase, Nicolaus Silver made light of his task by winning quite easily. Any doubt concerning the brave grey's commitment to steeplechasing was removed at Doncaster in February 1962 when he completely dominated the Great Yorkshire Steeplechase. Bobby Beasley piloted him to a comfortable victory over Cocky Consort and Springbok. He finished second that season behind Stan Mellor in the jockeys' table with 65 winners and, dividing his services between trainers Fred Rimell and Paddy Sleator, he was never short of rides. It was, however, around this time that the highly talented Irishman began having serious problems within his private life, to such an extent that he began drinking to excess. Securing an excellent position as jockey to the newly established Lambourn trainer Fred Winter appeared to present fresh opportunities for him, but sadly his addiction to alcohol increased.

Forced by his worsening illness to retire from racing, Bobby Beasley returned to Ireland where, when at his lowest ebb, he sought the aid of Alcoholics Anonymous. With great courage and incisive self-examination, in his book *Second Start* Bobby Beasley describes his inner turmoil, his constant questioning of his right to be and his commitment to restoring his purpose for existence in a way only someone who has been to hell and back can. Displaying the same bravery, determination and overpowering will to win as he always did on the racecourse, Bobby fought and conquered alcoholism slowly but surely and then began trying to put his life together again. Through a long and painful process he eventually became an insurance salesman, yet somehow the memories of the glory days astride a good jumper at Aintree or Cheltenham remained within him.

Gradually Bobby ventured back to the familiar sounds and smells of a racing stable, at first mucking out and eventually assisting Stuart Barratt in the training of his horses at Portmarnock. After shedding two and a half stone in weight he made his racecourse reappearance at Limerick on a horse called Gordon and although unplaced that day, they finished third the next week at Thurles. A win aboard Paddy Murphy's Norwegian Flag at Leopardstown, followed later that day with a fourth place on Lord Fingall's No Other in the Leopardstown 'Chase, brought Bobby back onto the sports pages. After winning the John Jameson Cup at Punchestown with Dim Wit, a leading Irish journalist enthusiastically wrote, 'Now it can be truly said that Bobby Beasley has completed a brilliant comeback to race riding.' While only having been active for one third of that season, he still finished the term with 21 winners. Now fully occupied and enjoying his return to the turf, offers to ride came thick and fast from trainers all over Ireland and when a certain old friend, the legendary Pat Taaffe, offered him the mount on the highly promising young hurdler Captain Christy, the remarkable final chapter to his career began.

During the course of that 1972–73 campaign, Captain Christy won four of his six races, including the very valuable Irish Sweeps Hurdle and the Scottish Champion Hurdle at Ayr in which he and Bobby shattered the track record. They were also a good third in Cheltenham's Champion Hurdle behind the very good Comedy of Errors, which was trained by Bobby's former guv'nor Fred Rimell.

The following term their attention was directed at steeplechasing and initially Captain Christy appeared a little uncertain. With jockey Beasley's sympathetic handling, though, the gelding improved with every race, developing into one of the most thrilling jumpers seen for years. Of the six races he won that season, the important Power Gold Cup in Ireland was but a prelude to one of the finest examples of riding ever witnessed at Prestbury Park. Bobby Beasley unexpectedly held his mount up for most of the Cheltenham Gold Cup trip and when going to the front approaching the final fence, was full of running. Despite an error at that obstacle, which was cleverly corrected by his pilot, Captain Christy romped home the five-length winner from The Dikler and Game Spirit. Fifteen years after winning the race on Roddy Owen, Bobby Beasley had at last restored his reputation as one of the most brilliant jockeys ever to grace any racecourse. In his own words, 'That Cheltenham Gold Cup win was more than just what it meant in terms of a racing achievement. It had so much to do with getting one's pride back for the family.'

He finally hung up his boots for good at the end of that dignity-restoring season and, as if shouting at the devil, he ran a pub in the south of England for many years. Now living in Sandhurst, he helps to run a vineyard. A man who for so many years excelled at his craft, thrilled punters and filled so many of their pockets, has mercifully won his final supreme test and earned the peace of mind and respect he so richly deserves. He has not touched alcohol for over 30 years.

Pat Buckley

Born in July 1943, Pat Buckley became apprenticed to that brilliant handler of jumpers Captain Neville Crump in November 1957 and gained much valuable advice from the stable jockeys Gerry Scott and Johnny East.

In his very first ride for the Warwick House yard in March 1961 (unusually for a beginner, this was also a steeplechase) Pat performed splendidly to win on the ageing gelding Blue Moth by four lengths in the Hearts of Oak 'Chase at Manchester. Trailing in behind the pair were such accomplished riders as Paddy Farrell, Stan Mellor, Mickey Batchelor and John East, with the equally well-known staying jumpers Wyndburgh, Tea Fiend, Polished Steel and Glorious Twelfth.

With Gerry Scott unable to ride in the 1962 Grand National through injury, Pat, while still only 18 years of age, took the mount on the stable's second string Springbok. Because of his youthfulness he attracted much attention in the press. On a day of sleet and mud at Aintree, of the 32 runners, Springbok was the only casualty at the very first jump.

Restored to fitness and again riding winners, Gerry Scott rode Springbok in the 1963 National and, as this was Captain Crump's only runner in the race,

Pat Buckley gratefully accepted a chance ride on a rank outsider, Ayala. Trained at Lambourn in Berkshire by Keith Piggott, the father of champion flat-race jockey Lester, the nine year old had been completely useless on the flat. After switching to National Hunt racing he managed, somehow, to capture three prizes over no further than two and a half miles in the 1960–61 season. After two dismal displays during the 1962–63 term, Ayala finally came good some ten days before his Aintree appointment, when winning Worcester's Royal Porcelain Handicap 'Chase by four lengths from rather mediocre opposition.

Of the 47 runners at Liverpool on the day, it was Gerry Scott's partner Springbok who commanded most attention in the betting, going off the 10–1 favourite ahead of the other best-backed fancies Kilmore, Team Spirit, Loving Record and another Yorkshire-trained entry, Dagmar Gittell. On soft going the start was delayed for some six minutes but once on their way the runners made that cavalry-like charge across the Melling Road out into the country. Magic Tricks came down at the first, Look Happy at the next and the fourth fence brought down both Solonace and Wartown. More than half of those who began the contest were still in the hunt clearing the Water and among the leaders were Chavara, Loyal Tan, French Lawyer and Springbok. Approaching the second-last fence Carrickbeg, Hawa's Song, Springbok, Team Spirit and Ayala were all there with a chance and going into the final obstacle Pat Buckley shouted to the amateur John Lawrence on Carrickbeg, 'Go on John, you've got it won.' Carrickbeg did indeed land clear over the last fence and surged away looking all over the winner but Ayala stayed on magnificently and when the leader faltered with barely 50 yards left to run, Buckley seized his chance and raced past to win by three-quarters of a length. Hawa's Song was third, in front of Team Spirit, Springbok, Kilmore and film star Gregory Peck's striking grey Owen's Sedge.

At Sandown Park four weeks later, Pat Buckley crowned a memorable month of his life by riding Hoodwinked to a five-length success in the Whitbread Gold Cup to provide his boss, Neville Crump, with another major victory. The trainer's other two runners, Springbok and Rough Tweed, finished some way behind the winner.

Himself beset by injuries, Pat encountered something of a lean spell during the next couple of years, although in 1964 he scored a notable double when partnering Dormant to win both the Mildmay Memorial Steeplechase and the Whitbread Gold Cup for the Middleham stable of Neville Crump, in the latter defeating the mighty Mill House. So severely had he been forced to fast in order to make the weight of 9st 7lb for this event, he could hardly stand to receive his trophy from the Queen Mother after weighing-in.

His next attempt at the National came in 1966 when his mount Rough

Tweed fell at the third, the first open ditch, and 12 months later he got snarled up in the chaos at the 23rd fence when Limeking was brought down. Still representing Captain Crump, he finished fourth with his Rutherfords in 1968 and a few weeks later won the Scottish Grand National with the stable's Arcturus.

Aboard the same horse at Liverpool in 1969, Pat survived some hairy moments during the course of the National to get round in sixth place behind the winner Highland Wedding. He was brought down at the third with the seven-year-old Permit the next year and after missing the following year's race he fell at the 17th with Just a Gamble in 1972.

His final two attempts to repeat that wonderful experience with Ayala came in the first two years of Red Rum's prominence in the event. Having been brought down at the Chair on Canharis in 1973, Pat Buckley's swansong came 12 months later when safely piloting San-Feliu round into ninth place.

A very severe injury led to Pat's retirement in 1976 and he eventually became employed by the Sultan of Oman to train his horses. Since taking up that appointment he has made several visits to Aintree, where he has always enjoyed reminiscing with his old friend and mentor, Gerry Scott.

FOUR

George William Robinson

Willie Robinson was born in August 1934 in Southern Ireland and, without serving as an apprentice, rode as an amateur before turning professional. He remained, above all else, a superb horseman. Always of slight stature, his weight stayed around the 9st mark for most of his career.

His first winner was Reinstated at Navan in June 1955 on the flat, but at the beginning of the next jump season he rode Greek Sontoi to victory in a two-mile steeplechase at Waterford and Tramore's August fixture. This success was quickly followed by wins on Inquisitive Culleen at Wexford, Cullenroi at Naas and Winmar's Star in the Kildangan Plate, again at Naas.

With encouraging regularity, the winning streak continued to flow thanks to victories with Silvakhan, The Drummer, Aesculus, Duffle Coat and Zonda. Most impressive of all, though, was Willie's triumph in the prestigious Leopardstown 'Chase when holding on with Nibot to win by a short-head and beating such outstanding professionals as Eddie McKenzie, Pat Taaffe and Cathal Finnegan. At Kilbeggan in the middle of May his first double victory was gained when bringing home Zonda and Recovery in their respective races within half an hour of each other. His final appearance among the unpaid ranks came ten days later at Sligo, where he fell in the Connaught Plate with Southern Money.

Quickly off the mark as a professional, Willie Robinson won his first race at his fifth attempt, with French Sky at Bellewstown on the third day of the new season, repeating the process the next day at Dundalk with his old friend Zonda. The highlight of that first term riding for hire was his tremendous win on Kilballyown in the 1957 Irish Grand National at Fairyhouse.

By now completely established as a highly competent jockey, Willie made his first attempt at Aintree glory in the 1958 Grand National aboard the eight-year-old Longmead but it was a brief encounter. They came down at the second fence. Sixty-seven days later he returned to England to give a perfect demonstration of his versatility by finishing second in the Epsom Derby on the 100–1 outsider Paddy's Point, behind Hard Ridden with Charlie Smirke. In his naturally unassuming way, he flew back to Ireland that evening to ride a novice 'chaser the following day at Naas.

Subsequently retained by the irrepressible jockey-turned-trainer Dan Moore (who in 1938 came within a whisker of winning the Grand National with Royal Danieli when caught on the line by Battleship), Willie Robinson had gained one of the most envied positions on the Irish turf. Settling in well at Ratoath in County Meath, the new stable jockey immediately struck an affectionate rapport with a tiny bay gelding named Team Spirit. Their association was to last many years, through which together they would know complete satisfaction, absolute dejection and, eventually, that elusive moment of finding the reason for their being.

Having already won four hurdle races, it soon became obvious to all that Team Spirit's forte lay in competition over the major obstacles and in 1960 this assumption was realised when he won the Mildmay Memorial 'Chase at Sandown Park and followed it up next time out with a sparkling performance to take the Hurst Park National Trial 'Chase. Although still but an eight year old, the decision was taken to have a tilt at that year's Aintree showpiece and in Liverpool's last year with the old-style upright fences Team Spirit ran well until falling at Becher's Brook second time round. The following year, 1961, they finished ninth in the National and the jockey began to believe that Team Spirit could one day make his mark at that historic racecourse.

Temporarily recruited by Lambourn trainer Fulke Walwyn in November 1961, Willie Robinson took the mount on that man's representative, Mandarin, in the three-and-a-quarter mile Hennessy Gold Cup at Newbury. Willie gave the future Cheltenham Gold Cup winner a copybook ride and they won comfortably from a selection of the finest middle-distance jumpers in the land.

Winning the Champion Hurdle at Cheltenham on Fulke Walwyn's Anzio in 1962 set the jockey up well for another go at that elusive Grand National prize, with what he now considered his soulmate, Team Spirit. This time they did not get beyond the 19th fence and many began to believe that the little Irish-bred gelding would always find the supreme test at Aintree too great. Unexpectedly, at the suggestion of Dan Moore, Team Spirit was sent off to be trained by Fulke Walwyn and around this time the transfer became more meaningful with Willie Robinson also becoming first jockey at the trainer's Lambourn base.

With an abundance of top-class horses awaiting his partnership, Robinson had an impressive surfeit of highly talented horses at his disposal, probably none more so than an up-and-coming exciting prospect named Mill House. At only five years of age this gelding was taking on and defeating some of the most notable 'chasers in the land and with such an excellent jockey as Willie Robinson aboard they began to appear invincible.

On 13 March 1963, Mill House started 7–2 favourite for the Cheltenham Gold Cup and in the minds of many was at false odds. With such hardened and proven exponents of the sublime art of steeplechasing in opposition, it was felt that Mill House was the product of hype and wishful thinking. Fortria, Frenchman's Cove, Nicolaus Silver, Rough Tweed and Olympia, for instance, all had many years more experience than Robinson's mount. Yet in this most serious of occupations, that old adage that 'handsome is as handsome does' was never more truly proven. Mill House and his jockey simply toyed with their opposition and came home a very convincing winner by 12 lengths from the Pat Taaffe-ridden Fortria.

At the end of that month, Willie again faced the Aintree starter with the now 11-year-old Team Spirit and there were more than just a few who considered the horse's best days were past. Always a race of surprises, that year's Grand National produced more than its usual supply but Team Spirit gave the performance of a lifetime. Finding hidden reserves of energy in the closing stages, he ran on strongly at the end of the contest to finish fourth, less than 12 lengths behind the shock winner Ayala.

Willie Robinson finished that season tenth in the jockeys' championship with 30 winners and looked forward to a new term with enthusiasm and optimism. At Cheltenham in October 1963 he partnered the former Champion Hurdler Anzio to his first success over fences in the Lydney Novices 'Chase and later in the month followed it up with a runaway win on the gelding in Newbury's Halloween Novices 'Chase. Back at Liverpool on 2 November with Team Spirit, they came from a long way back in the Grand Sefton over the big fences to overtake the Queen Mother's horse Silver Dome and win by five lengths.

A highly profitable weekend for the Fulke Walwyn team was gained some four weeks later with Willie riding Irish Imp and the exciting three-year-old Kirriemuir to victory on the first day of the Newbury autumn fixture. The next day, the jockey was reunited again with Mill House in the Hennessy Gold Cup at Newbury. With top weight of 12st, they made light of their task with a riveting exhibition of jumping to win by eight lengths with plenty in hand from Happy Spring and a promising newcomer from Ireland named Arkle. On Boxing Day at Kempton another fluent display brought the pair victory by 20 lengths in the King George II Chase and after Mill House later won the

Gainsborough 'Chase at Sandown he became a short-priced favourite to repeat his Gold Cup success at Cheltenham during the first week in March.

Finishing a good third on the juvenile Kirriemuir in the Champion Hurdle, Willie later that afternoon won the Grand Annual Challenge Cup with Richard Of Bordeaux and things appeared to be going exactly to plan for the Gold Cup less than 24 hours later. Since being beaten in the Hennessy Gold Cup, Ireland's champion Arkle had won his last three races in his homeland, including the Thyestes' Chase and the important Leopardstown Steeplechase. The race developed into a veritable dual between the two impressive animals, Mill House setting the pace and jumping with his customary flair, but with Pat Taaffe always well in touch on Arkle. Going to the front, though, after clearing the second last, the Irish horse produced the better turn of foot to stride away and win by five lengths. As time would soon tell, Mill House coming only second was no disgrace, for Arkle became the greatest 'chaser of his age and proceeded to win a hat-trick of victories in the Cheltenham Gold Cup.

Naturally disappointed by the defeat of their stable star, Fulke Walwyn and his jockey concentrated their efforts into finalising the preparation of the horses destined to compete at Liverpool. With their old, worthy Team Spirit now a 12 year old, it was to be his fifth and probably last attempt at National supremacy – but with his success in the Grand Sefton still fresh in their minds and his fitness at its finest, hopes remained high.

Their confidence received a boost when Willie gave Dionysus III a superb ride to win Ainree's Coronation Hurdle the afternoon before the great test and when he won the opening event on the day itself, the Liverpool Hurdle with Sempervivum, both trainer and jockey could barely dare to contemplate what might follow. The Grand National that year was considered so wide open that there were four co-favourites all on the 100–7 mark. When the race began though, four minutes late, all thoughts of the odds even against getting round were at once dismissed from the minds of the riders. At the first fence one of the best fancied, Flying Wild, fell and Roy Edwards took Peacetown immediately to the front. Baxier, Merganser and Purple Silk remained close to the leader jumping Becher's, where the well-backed Beau Normand blundered his chance away. Peacetown still led over the Water Jump, followed by Purple Silk, Team Spirit, Time and Reproduction. With no change in the leading positions at the second Canal Turn, Purple Silk, with John Kenneally up, seemed to be going much the better of any in the firing line and when Peacetown made a mistake at the fourth from home, he moved closer still to the leader. The riderless Lizawake led over the last fence and with Peacetown beginning to feel the strain, the strongly ridden Purple Silk struck the front looking all over the winner. Then, from some way off the pace, Willie

Robinson produced a run from his mount reminiscent of his challenge on Paddy's Point in the Derby six years before. Snatching victory from defeat in the very last strides, Willie and Team Spirit passed the post to win the Grand National at their fifth attempt, half a length ahead of the brave Purple Silk. Peacetown was six lengths back in third place, followed home by Eternal, Pontin-Go, Springbok and nine others.

It was a tremendous accomplishment for all involved: the brave Team Spirit giving his all after five long years of persistent endeavour to win so gamely; Willie Robinson remaining faithful to the gelding he partnered for two different trainers, and Fulke Walwyn saddling the winner of the race he won as an amateur rider 28 years before.

In the last major National Hunt race of the season, the Whitbread Gold Cup at Sandown, Mill House and Willie Robinson again jumped splendidly throughout, only to tie up close to home and be beaten by Yorkshire-trained and 3st-lighter-weighted Dormant. Finishing the campaign with 49 winners, Willie ended up in fifth place behind champion jockey Josh Gifford, his highest position yet.

At Newbury, midway through the next term, Mill House made his reappearance in the Hennessy Gold Cup, this time being trounced into fourth place very emphatically by the winner Arkle. Obviously in need of the race, Mill House continued with his preparation for another joust with the brilliant Irish horse in the Gold Cup, winning his subsequent two events, the Mandarin 'Chase at Newbury and the Gainsborough at Sandown.

Two victories for Irish challengers on the opening day at Cheltenham, rapidly added to by another on the second, lifted the spirits of those across the Irish Sea incredibly but the Walwyn camp also gained a reason for optimism. In the Champion Hurdle, comprising the finest practitioners of the trade, Willie Robinson conjured up a fantastic well-timed late run with last year's third-placed Kirriemuir to cause a shock victory at 50–1. For all that, the superiority of Arkle the day after was undeniable when he drew clear approaching the final fence to win by a 20-length margin from Mill House.

With his own stable unrepresented in the 1965 Grand National, Robinson accepted the ride on neighbouring trainer Keith Piggott's Leedsy in the race, only to fall at the 18th and 12 months later, when partnering Fulke Walwyn's Popham Down, came down at Becher's Brook first time round.

A bystander during the tumultuous 1967 event, Willie guided round the Irish-trained Quintin Bay in 1968 to complete the National in 17th place. Although rides were by now becoming difficult to find, he did that year win his third Hennessy Gold Cup on the 20–1 shot Man Of The West and in his homeland he won the Galway Plate with Terrosian.

His final participation in the Grand National was in 1970, at the age of 36, aboard the similarly ageing The Fossa who refused at Becher's second time round. The winning jockey on that occasion was Willie's old adversary and former partner of Arkle, Pat Taaffe, who, after gaining that second big Liverpool victory on Gay Trip, at once announced his retirement.

One of the classic examples of that rare combination of horseman and jockey, Willie Robinson also retired within weeks of that final day at Aintree and returned to Ireland to enjoy a slightly more relaxing life of hunting and showjumping.

Crompton (Tommy) Smith

It was in 1964, shortly after Team Spirit and Willie Robinson had won the Grand National, that the most famous steeplechase on earth heard a death knell which was to take 20 years to eventually silence. Coincidence, irony and the totally unexpected have, since the National's earliest days, been very regular components of what many refer to as the romance of the race and in 1964 circumstances developed which were to fully exemplify this.

Having experienced for the last time the rigours and demands of the great race with Kilmore, the four-times champion jockey Fred Winter retired from the saddle to become a racehorse trainer at Lambourn in Berkshire. Training is often as perilous an occupation as is racing and Fred fully realised that it took many years for anybody to make the grade in his newly chosen profession – and that only a handful ever reached the top.

Around the same time, across the Atlantic, a 27-year-old amateur rider named Crompton Smith was pondering over the idea of sending a horse he had twice ridden to victory in the Maryland Hunt Cup – Jay Trump – eastwards towards Europe to be prepared for a tilt at the Grand National. Having a famous racing cousin in Ireland by the name of Dan Moore, the American initially felt that he should be the obvious choice until a friend suggested he seek the advice of Fred Winter. Unaware the former champion jockey had just become a trainer, Smith rang Fred inviting his recommendations concerning the most advantageous destination for his horse.

A surprised yet delighted Fred Winter had only three horses at his Uplands Stables at that particular time and the prospect of handling a qualified Grand National contestant in his first season was an opportunity too good to miss. Outlining the massive task ahead, he informed the American that the best course of action would be for him to prepare the horse, and possibly Tommy Smith himself, at Lambourn, where he was in a position to provide more individual attention than could be offered at larger establishments. It was precisely the suggestion the American had hoped for and arrangements were at once set in place for horse and jockey to take up residence at Lambourn in July 1964.

Young Crompton Smith's fascination with steeplechasing and the Grand National was inherited from his grandfather, Harry Worcester Smith, a very wealthy mill owner from Massachusetts. Increasing his wealth by inventing an automatic colour-weaving loom, Harry, at the age of 45, decided to sell all his business assets and patents and indulge himself completely in the pastime he had nurtured for so long – hunting and steeplechasing. The millionaire's prime ambition was to win the Grand National at Aintree but when failing health prevented this, the quest was handed to his son, Crompton, a highly talented cross-country rider. Sadly, though, yet again, Harry's project was thwarted when Crompton broke his leg so badly in a riding accident that he was unable to ever compete over fences. It was almost a quarter of a century before the dream of Aintree glory was rekindled for the old gentleman, with the birth of a grandson, Crompton Smith junior. To distinguish between the two Crompton Smiths, the younger was nicknamed 'Tommy' from an early age by all members of the family. One of the boy's earliest memories is of his grandfather Harry showing him a large illustrated map of the Grand National course, which took pride of place above the fireplace of the family home at Middleburg, Virginia. Introduced to hunting at just three years of age, the boy was far from enamoured by the activity and suffered a great deal of teasing from the old man.

Upon the death of Harry Worcester Smith at the age of 80 in 1945, the family fortune diminished at an alarming rate and, amid great anxiety, his mother and father divorced. It was not until Tommy's mother Margot remarried that Crompton Smith junior found renewed interest in horses and jumping, thanks largely to the persuasion of his stepfather. He rode in his first point-to-point when he was 20 and despite falling three times during the course of the contest, persevered with determination and the following year he won the first of his four Maryland Hunt Cups.

Mrs Mary Stephenson, a long-standing friend of his mother's, immediately asked Tommy to find her a horse which could carry her colours to victory in the Hunt Cup and, enthralled at the prospect, he began what was to prove a lengthy search. His eventual purchase with $2,000 of his patron's money was the bay gelding Jay Trump, utterly useless on the flat and confirmed by many as 'an absolute rogue'. A ladies' point-to-point was chosen as his first race over obstacles but to everyone's dismay, Jay Trump was beaten 60 lengths by the only other contestant.

From that moment on Mrs Stephenson refused to allow anyone but Tommy Smith to ride her horse and a week later a remarkable transformation was witnessed when Jay Trump won a steeplechase among the beautiful Blue Ridge Mountains. It was at once very clear that the horse and his rider had a unique understanding of each other and together they presented a somewhat remarkable partnership. In April 1963 they won their first Maryland Hunt Cup, breaking the course time record and a year later they repeated the win on soft ground which the horse detested. Two other important local 'chase victories followed, after which the decision was taken to venture to Aintree.

Returning from his honeymoon in the middle of July, Tommy Crompton Smith threw himself into the task of organising transport across the Atlantic for his wife Frances, himself, and the reason for the trip, Jay Trump. A last-minute problem arose when the stall arranged by Pan-Am aboard the maiden flight of their new 707 jet was discovered to be far too small and the plane left Kennedy International Airport without them. After a two-day delay for horse and rider, BOAC came to the rescue by providing a specially built stall inside one of their aircraft. After 18 hours in the air, they landed at Heathrow to be met by Mrs Frances Smith and a Lambourn horsebox.

At long last the next phase of the project could begin: the difficult task of acclimatising both newcomers to the vagaries of the English weather, its racing and, most of all, the vast differences between American-type obstacles and those they would encounter in England. After Fred Winter and his 'guest' ironed out some early differences between each other on the gallops, they worked long and earnestly as a team, with their principal priority the fitness and welfare of Jay Trump.

Having meticulously mapped out a plan of campaign, Fred Winter introduced the 'Yankee challengers' to the racecourse for their first taste of English jumping at Sandown Park in October 1964 in the appropriately named Autumn Trial 'Chase. Jumping well throughout, Jay Trump was sent to the front approaching the second last, before running on to a convincing five-length victory over Comforting Wave and Can Go. Nobody had a broader smile on their face after the race than Fred Winter, thrilled at the smooth performance of both his pupils, before chuckling with the belated realisation that they had just provided him with his first winner as a trainer. It was a similar story a month later in Windsor's Brocas 'Chase, again over three miles. Tommy Smith sent his mount into the lead at the penultimate fence to go on and win by a length and a half from Monsieur Trois Etoiles and Mrs Bessemer. Fred knew the rules concerning the system of handicapping for Aintree's great race better than anybody; in order to be weighted fairly in accordance with known form, all runners not from England or Ireland that year had to run three times in this country before 6 January 1965. If it had not been for this stipulation, Fred would most certainly not have allowed Jay Trump to take part in the King George VI 'Chase on Boxing Day at Kempton

Park, such was the state of the ground. On the day four meetings were abandoned as a result of severe frost and many racegoers believed Kempton should have been added to that number. Because of the treacherous ground there were, as expected, a flood of non-runners and Jay Trump found himself with only one opponent in the race – but what an opponent it was: the superb chestnut son of the Derby winner, Airborne, the powerful Frenchman's Cove. Making all the running, though, it was the home team which won the day, with Stan Mellor pushing out his mount to completely outpace Jay Trump. Frenchman's Cove won by an unextended ten lengths.

Despite the disappointment, trainer Fred Winter was satisfied most of all that horse and rider were unharmed and that they would not be forced to carry top weight at Aintree. At Newbury in February they found going much more to the liking of Jay Trump, who, in spite of being burdened with top weight of 12st 5lb, gave another workmanlike performance to win the Harwell Amateur Riders' 'Chase. The perfect horsemanship of Tommy Smith had been noticed by a number of shrewd observers and plenty of offers on mounts for other stables came his way, yet he resolutely turned them all down. His gaze lay in one direction only – Aintree on the last Saturday in March, with the horse which had become such a vital part of him, and with it the memory of an old man called Harry who first informed him of the grandeur of the Grand National.

Without warning, and to the horror of all in racing, equine flu suddenly broke out. Numerous stables were affected and, defying all the precautions taken, Fred Winter's Uplands yard also became a victim. One by one his horses developed the symptoms: runny noses, lethargy and a general malaise which completely destroyed their training schedule. With tremendous foresight, Fred completely isolated Jay Trump and Tommy Smith from the remainder of his inmates, banishing them to a new barn to the rear of the yard. There remained just 18 days to go to the appointment they had all laboured so enthusiastically for, Aintree's supreme test.

Mercifully still clear of the dreaded virus, Jay Trump went to Worcester for the Royal Porcelain Handicap 'Chase on 17 March and appeared to be far from his usual alert self. A lacklustre display by their standards gained Tommy and Jay Trump only fifth place behind Johnny Haine on Meon Valley and they returned to Lambourn with just ten days left before facing the sole purpose for leaving America.

With no let-up on the gallops, Fred Winter concentrated on just keeping the horse free from the virus, fit and well, content with the proof already shown that Jay Trump could both jump and stay. In the evenings followed long hours of tuition for the rider, with Fred showing again and again newsreel films of past Nationals, pointing out incidents to watch out for, particular danger spots to beware of but most importantly the most economical route to take.

On the morning of the race the instruction continued, with the trainer walking every inch of the course with Crompton Smith, imparting his vast knowledge to the young American who listened with intent concentration and utter respect.

Of the 47 runners, Scottish-trained Freddie was the short-priced favourite at 7–2 from the Queen Mother's The Rip on the 9–1 mark and Kapeno coupled with Rondetto at 100–8. Right behind these in the market came Jay Trump, Vultrix and Leedsy.

With only a three-minute delay the starter despatched the runners to a good start and Phebu took them along, closely followed by Peacetown, L'Empereur and Pat McCarron with Freddie. At Becher's, where Nedsmar and Forgotten Dreams fell, Ruby Glen, Barleycroft and Crobeg were brought down too. Jay Trump was well to the rear but was coping with the unique obstacles very well. Carrying out Fred Winter's instructions to the letter, Tommy Smith manoeuvred his mount perfectly at the Canal Turn, meeting it spot-on and gaining valuable lengths with a perfect leap. Jumping flawlessly, Jay Trump crossed the Melling Road to return to the racecourse and the end of the first circuit well within sight of the leaders. The leader Phebu fell at the 13th, joining a pack of riderless horses which became a threat to them all. Tommy Smith, with all his experience of riding over obstacles, had never been a part of such an assortment of dangers in any contest. Horses falling in front and alongside him, loose horses darting this way and that, and after every splendid leap, another dangerously unusual obstacle. Over the Water, the leaders were Rondetto, Peacetown, Freddie, Kapeno, the Royal runner The Rip, and some way to their rear, Jay Trump. There was little change in the order at the 19th except that Phebu had by now forced his way to the head of affairs, even without the aid of a jockey. A difficult moment came at the next fence when another horse bumped into Jay Trump but, hardly breaking his stride, the American challenger raced on perfectly balanced and, with another good jump at Becher's Brook, began to make ground on the leaders. With an absolutely superb leap at the Canal Turn, Jay Trump was suddenly up in the forefront of the action and when Kapeno fell directly in front of him at the fence after Valentine's, it was the horse himself who avoided a collision with a perfect mid-air swerve. With just two fences left, the race was really on in earnest with Freddie holding a marginal advantage over the American combination and already sensing a classic duel to the finish, the roars of the crowd were probably heard at the Pier Head. Freddie and Jay Trump raced side by side into the final fence and, meeting it all wrong, Tommy Smith felt certain his mount would come down. Jay Trump, however, jumped through rather than over the obstacle and, having gained a length advantage over his rival, raced on up that cruelly long run to the winning post. Still just in front at the elbow, Freddie suddenly issued his challenge and drawing closer with every stride Tommy Smith reacted as all jockeys instinctively would. Drawing his whip, he gave his mount two slaps on the quarters and then another, at which Jay Trump began swishing his tail in an obvious sign of disapproval. Realising at once that his mount was even now – after such a long and hazardous trip – giving his all, Tommy wisely sat down to ride a finish with just hands, heels and the passion of this incredible moment his life was built around. The response was immediate, as Jay Trump took a fresh hold of his bit and stayed on courageously to withstand the final surge of an equally brave Freddie, to win by three-quarters of a length. Twenty lengths behind came Mr Jones, Rainbow Battle, Vultrix, L'Empereur and, after the Queen Mother's The Rip, seven other determined survivors.

That impossible dream of Harry Worcester Smith's so long ago had become reality through the fanatical dedication of a grandson's talent and commitment, the invaluable tutelage of a legendary jockey-turned-trainer and the indefatigable spirit of a noble creature named Jay Trump.

On the crest of a tidal wave of euphoria and with their champion steeplechaser none the worse for his Aintree exertions, the decision was taken to capture another glittering European prize, the Grande Steeplechase de Paris. Coping remarkably well with the tricky fences on Auteuil's confusing figure-of-eight course, Jay Trump jumped fluently all the way to be well within striking distance of the leaders in the closing stages. His rider, though, was so drained of energy after having to shed 16lb in order to make the weight, that he was unable to ride a resolute finish and they finished third, two and half lengths behind the winner Hyeres III.

The successful partnership of Smith and Winter came to an end after the Paris contest, with Jay Trump returning home to America for an attempt at a third Maryland Hunt Cup victory. Fred and his wife Diana were invited as VIP guests to the event and were as overjoyed as everyone else when Tommy and his partner made it a hat-trick of wins in the hazardous timber classic.

Crompton 'Tommy' Smith retired from the saddle and, no doubt influenced by his spell with Fred Winter at Lambourn, became a trainer of racehorses himself in the United States.

Timothy Norman

Born in the West Country in March 1944, Tim Norman began riding as an amateur when still a teenager, winning his first race shortly after his 17th birthday in 1961, aboard the Chris Nesfield-trained mare June Mary.

The event, the Norfolk Challenge Cup, an amateur riders' 'chase over two and a quarter miles at Fontwell, was of little consequence to any except those contesting it, yet the cool manner in which the youngster timed his challenge before coming home three lengths clear showed great promise. It was also significant, to some shrewd observers, that among those behind him were such experienced performers as Bob McCreery, Gay Kindersley and Guy Harwood. It was well into the next season before he scored his second success, again for the Kent yard of Chris Nesfield, though this time aboard the eight-year-old Caca Dora and by the end of that term he achieved two other successes with Aquila and Birthday Present.

He began the 1962–63 campaign still an amateur entitled to a 7lb allowance and during this period other trainers became aware of his abilities. George Spann, the Lambourn handler, was well pleased with the manner in which young Tim rode his Flaming Toy to victory in the Gotham Novices Hurdle at Nottingham in October, as too was another Kent trainer named Neaves two days later at Plumpton. Making all the running on Do Or Die in a handicap hurdle at Plumpton, Tim won with plenty in hand by one and a half lengths, again with such famous names as David Mould, Josh Gifford and David Nicholson some way behind. That weekend Tim took his first glimpse of the Aintree racecourse when finishing a respectable fifth in the Prospect Hurdle with Resource. Shortly afterwards he rode his first winner for the famous trainer Keith Piggott on Royal Charter at Birmingham. Back at Liverpool in December, he finished third in the Mistletoe Novices Hurdle on Flaming Toy and shortly afterwards decided to turn professional. His final two winning rides of that season, on Cuban Tan and My Beauty, brought his total to a pleasing seven, but many within the game were already predicting a busier future for the up-and-coming jockey.

They were not far wrong either, for beginning with a neck victory on Boherluska at Newton Abbot in August 1963, Tim Norman rode his 20th and final winner of that season with Eastern Warrior at Stratford on 23 May 1964. Without question the most important victory of these wins was the George Duller Handicap Hurdle over three miles at the Cheltenham National Hunt fixture in March aboard the 25–1 shot Do Or Die. A little over a fortnight later he celebrated his 20th birthday.

Following much the same pattern as most had recently, Certain Danger got him off to a good start virtually from 'the off' when the new jumping term began, coming up with a strong run in the closing stages of the Sidmouth 'Chase at Devon and Exeter to beat the favourite Honey End and champion jockey Josh Gifford. Sharing his 18 victories that year were such stalwarts as

Wily Oriental, Certain Justice, Leedsy, Harlow Wood, Risky and Another Scot. It was Another Scot who provided Tim with five wins throughout the campaign, the last being at 20–1 at Ascot, when behind them in fifth place was the Eddie Harty-ridden favourite, Anglo. Nobody, including Tim, could have guessed that this beaten favourite would figure so prominently in the young jockey's future activities.

The 1965–66 season began much the same as always in the south-west with a carefree holiday mood enveloping competitors as well as spectators. For Tim Norman, it was the beginning of a period which would change his life forever and, in so doing, would elevate him to the exalted position of a 'king for a day'.

Fontwell again was the scene of his initial success that season, as he came from behind yet again to pounce at the last flight of hurdles and win on the outsider Jamie Stuart, who had been saddled by the man who gave him his first chance, trainer Chris Nesfield.

In December 1965 Fred Winter chose Tim Norman to ride the chestnut gelding Anglo in the Fairlawne Handicap 'Chase at Windsor, since the previous year's Grand National-winning trainer was temporarily without an available jockey. Formerly named Flag Of Convenience and owned jointly by Stuart Levy and Nat Cohen, the men responsible for the 'Carry On' films, the horse had been totally unsuccessful on the flat and, after showing some promise over hurdles, became extremely inconsistent. Giving the gelding his usual considerate handling, Tim guided him to a comfortable six-length win at Windsor and, impressed by the jockey's aptitude, trainer Winter made sure Tim rode his horse whenever possible. Another Windsor appointment followed for Anglo, with the same jockey in charge, and the pair gained second place behind the very useful Queen Mother-owned Oedipe, with such notable jumpers as Dormant, Rondetto and Carrickbeg bringing up the rear. Coming runner-up again behind Chris Nesfield's Kilburn at Ascot convinced the owners to let Anglo's entry in the forthcoming Grand National stand and, satisfied that the combination of horse and rider was appropriate, the trainer was happy to let fate take its course. Their final race before the really big one was at Kempton Park on 12 March 1966 and, although never threatening the leaders, Anglo and Tim finished fourth behind Kapeno, Highland Wedding and Popham Down.

A fortnight later Grand National day arrived with its usual media ballyhoo and predictions, yet what most missed was the similarity of the contest with the one 12 months earlier. Again there were 47 contestants with the pride of Scotland, Freddie, again a short-priced favourite. A man revered in the world of horse racing, Fred Winter was attempting a double victory – this time with an apparent no-hoper. Ignored in the betting at 50–1, Anglo, a flat-race cast-off, was in many people's estimation merely there to make up the numbers. Any 'experts' looking for something to upset the favourite chose between What A Myth, Highland Wedding, Forest Prince, Vultrix or Kapeno but what they forgot was that the Grand National is a law unto itself; a place where anything can – and usually does – happen.

The last few days before the down-to-earth business of riding in the National is, by anybody's stretch of imagination, a time fraught with self-doubt and a tension that has been described by some from earlier generations as similar to waiting to go 'over the top' in the Great War. For Tim Norman, all the doubt, fears and uncertainty of what lay ahead on that spring Saturday afternoon were swept away less than 24 hours before the race. While driving back to his digs at the end of Friday's racing, the vehicle he was in became involved in a collision barely two miles from Aintree racecourse. Along with his companions, he was cut from the wreckage and when he arrived at the racecourse the following morning his face was a mass of stitches. Hardly the visage one would wish for if one was miraculously required for a television interview – although he felt there was little likelihood of that.

After returning from finishing ninth in the opening event (the Liverpool Hurdle with Bob Turnell's Spring Cruise) Tim, like his colleagues, sweated away the next two hours questioning his ability and resolve until the long-awaited moment when the 'jockeys out' bell sounded. Once in the saddle, everyone knew that the task ahead allowed no time for nerves, doubt or fear, and that, along with the horse beneath them, they survived on their own merits.

With a delay of only two minutes, the starter despatched the big field to the joyful roar from a mass of spectators who little realised the true desire, commitment and dedication to a purpose they were witnessing. For the first time in many years there were no casualties at either of the first two obstacles and the first open ditch claimed but one, Pat Buckley on Rough Tweed. Packed Home, Popham Down and Groomsman fell victims to Becher's Brook but unusually the first circuit was completed with most of the field still intact. With Forest Prince blazing a trail at the head of affairs, Loving Record, Harry Black, Freddie and Quintin Bay were all to the fore until well into the final circuit. Tim Norman kept Anglo clear of the customary early trouble, concentrating on giving his mount as clear a round as possible until the pace settled down, but he began making progress after jumping the 19th. The front-runner Forest Prince jumped perfectly all the way and, coming back to the racecourse with just two jumps left, looked to have the race at his mercy. It was at this point, though, that Tim brought Anglo through into a challenging position and, jumping to the front at the penultimate fence, ran on with surprising vitality. Drawing well clear from the opposition after clearing the final fence, Anglo simply romped home to a 20-length victory over the staying-on Freddie and the gallant Forest Prince. They were followed home by The Fossa, Jim's Tavern, Quintin Bay, Norther, Highland Wedding and four others. The fact that this was another Grand National for Fred Winter in only his second year as a trainer somewhat overshadowed the excellent performance by the man in the saddle, Tim Norman, but the delight in the young man's eyes when interviewed showed not the slightest preoccupation with anything but the fact that he had conquered the most demanding test his profession could ever offer.

At Chepstow, some three weeks after that unforgettable day at Aintree, Tim in a sense returned to his roots, when riding Chris Nesfield's Kilburn to a very impressive victory in the Welsh Grand National.

It was a mere matter of statistics to Tim when, at the end of the season, he gained his highest number of winners ever, 28 in all, for he knew too well that nothing again could ever come close in comparison to that one single moment when everyone at Aintree, and far beyond, knew his name.

It was Kilburn he joined up with in the 1967 National but the partnership became unstuck at the 19th and the following year he made an early exit at the first fence with Fort Ord.

An unfortunate series of injuries over the next few years kept Tim out of the saddle for long periods and his last ride in the National was astride Frank Cundell's Rough Silk in 1973. They were baulked by two loose horses at the 19th, at which point he considerately pulled his mount up.

After hanging up his boots, the ever-genial Tim Norman became head of a building company in Wiltshire, though for many years before this his address remained 'Anglo', Mill Lane, Lambourn, Berkshire.

John Anthony Buckingham

It was not until 1955 that John Buckingham's future became directed towards the world of horse racing and only then as a result of his mother taking up employment with Mr and Mrs Edward Courage at their large estate near Banbury. Like many youngsters leaving school, John had no idea what kind of job he wanted but when discovering that a couple of vacancies existed at his mum's place of work John duly applied for a position and to his relief secured one.

Being assigned to stable work suited the youngster more than the alternative of looking after sheep and although at first scared of venturing into a stable occupied by a horse, he was eventually cajoled and coaxed into mastering his trepidation. Those in charge at the Courage stables, Tom and

Jack Morgan, taught him to ride and the 15 year old was soon travelling to race meetings to help with the tack and lead the horses around the paddock.

Quickly adapting to his new environment and duties, John was soon assisting in the breaking-in of young horses and by the spring of 1956 he was elevated to the important role of riding work on racehorses and schooling them over hurdles.

The feel of the horse, its way and its nobility all now gripped John Buckingham. He found enthusiasm he'd never imagined and from the still recent days of being scared in their company he developed into a fine young horseman. His sights were now firmly set on becoming a jockey and in April 1957, Edward Courage entrusted John with the care of his Royal Oak in the Chipping Norton Hurdle at Stratford. They finished down the course behind the winner Royal Troubador but returned unscathed and teamed up again for three more contests before the end of that term, one at Southwell and the other two back at Stratford. His great moment came at the 16th attempt, in the Burgage Hurdle over two miles at Southwell in March 1959. Making headway from the halfway stage, he took the lead with the four-year-old Sahagun at the second-last and ran on well to win by seven lengths from the two favourites, Merry Joker and Rose's Reject.

With David Nicholson riding regularly for Edward Courage's Edgcote establishment, John Buckingham received superb advice concerning the art of race riding and during the 1959–60 season he rode three winners in the famous maroon and yellow-halved Courage colours. Over the next couple of years the young rider's technique improved greatly and among those he rode to victory in the 1961–62 campaign were Lira, Neapolitan Lou, The Mexican, Noble Pierre and Woodcutter's Samba. At Southwell in mid-May, the last of these and Neapolitan Lou provided John Buckingham with his first double victory in taking the three-mile Upton 'Chase and then the Rolleston Handicap Hurdle over two and half miles.

His first two successes of the next jumping period were aboard the ageing gelding Chiel at Newton Abbot and at Uttoxeter for the first time he carried another owner's colours to victory, those of the Warwick trainer Mr H.G. Smith.

On the first day of November 1962, John lined up at the start of the November Handicap Hurdle at Aintree with his old friend Neapolitan Lou, the 33–1 outsider of 14 runners. Prominent throughout the trip, they were beaten for pace in the closing stages, yet they finished a creditable third behind the favourite Silver Green. Returning to Liverpool a month later, John finished third with Lira on the Wednesday before coming second with Neapolitan Lou the next day in the Matrimony Handicap Hurdle.

It was this brave little mare who became the mainstay of a somewhat lean period for the jockey the following year, when she carried Buckingham to two victories before putting up a splendid performance in the Liverpool Handicap Hurdle at Aintree on Grand National Day 1964. They finished in fifth place, barely five lengths behind the extremely smart Willie Robinson-ridden Sempervivum. Some 90 minutes later, Robinson made it an unforgettable double when getting Team Spirit up in the final strides to win the National.

Edward Courage, a member of the brewing family, bred and trained some brilliant jumpers at Edgcote and was a tremendous supporter of National Hunt racing all his life, despite being confined to a wheelchair through an attack of poliomyelitis in 1938. Among the many contributions he made to racing was the breeding of such fine staying mares as Tiberetta (who was placed three times in the Grand National in the late 1950s) and Tiberina. Both these exceptional steeplechasers passed on their outstanding ability to their many offspring when retired to stud. A more ideal place for anyone to begin a career in steeplechasing than Mr Courage's Banbury establishment would be very difficult to find and John Buckingham is always the first to admit his good fortune in becoming a member of the Edgcote team.

The rising star of National Hunt racing in 1962 was the Gloucestershire jockey Terry Biddlecombe and before being retained by Kinnersley trainer Fred Rimell, he often rode in the Courage colours. With a calm and realistic acceptance of the fact that the more experienced riders were always going to partner the stable's runners in important events, John Buckingham contented himself with whatever opportunities came his way and during the 1964–65 campaign his five wins came from just Neapolitan Lou and Lira. It was around this time that John began riding out a young son of Tiberina named San Angelo and the gelding remains his favourite horse of the many he partnered. After introducing the horse to the racecourse in Nottingham's Stayers Handicap Hurdle in October 1965, and later taking him into second place in his first 'chase at Doncaster, Terry Biddlecombe took over the mount. Terry rode San Angelo to three rapid victories including one over Aintree's Mildmay fences in the next couple of months but John would renew acquaintanceship with his favourite at a later date, in a year when both the horse and he would be older and wiser.

On the opening day of Aintree's Grand National meeting in March 1966, John Buckingham came agonisingly close to winning his first race at the world-famous venue, when partnering a full-brother of San Angelo. In Division One of the very well-contested Lancashire Hurdle, with a well-timed run after the final flight, he brought the four-year-old Saccone to get within three lengths of the winner, The Spaniard. In action again in little over an hour, he rode

Happy Henry over the National fences in the Topham Trophy Steeplechase for trainer Donald Charlesworth and although failing to complete the trip, he could at last say he'd been over 'the big ones'. Back again in the maroon-and-yellow colours of Edward Courage, the next day John took his mount Attribute to the start of a race specially laid on by the Liverpool Executive to mark an important milestone in the history of the 'sport of kings'. The National Hunt Centenary Year Mildmay 'Chase commemorated the occasion a century before, when such men as Benedict John Angell, Lord Coventry, Captain James Little and Lord Poulett finally introduced a governing body to control 'cross-country racing'. Attribute and John finished eighth of the 20 runners.

That season ended with Terry Biddlecombe winning his second jockeys' championship, his nearest rivals being Stan Mellor, David Mould, Bobby Beasley and David Nicholson, but with the new term underway John Buckingham won a prize way beyond the value of any to be gained from riding horses. In September he married Ann after a two-year courtship and settled in a new house in Chipping Warden, which they called Sahagun as a reminder of the horse which provided his first sweet taste of success.

By now resigned, yet totally committed, to a career which would never see him among the leading lights of his profession, John, like so many other jockeys, got on with the job in hand, grateful for any rides which came his way and overjoyed should any of them be something out of the ordinary. With but one ride booked for the Cheltenham National Hunt meeting in the middle of March 1967, many others would have been a little dismayed but John was delighted, for one simple but very personal reason. The race was the prestigious Cheltenham Grand Annual Challenge Cup, the last event on Champion Hurdle day, and his companion was to be the horse which meant so much to him – San Angelo. It was a long wait in the jockeys' room for John Buckingham that day but once under way San Angelo answered every demand from his pilot. Always in a prominent position, they took up the running coming to the last and, fighting off the challenge of Eddie Harty on Riversdale, drew away up the hill to win most convincingly by four lengths. With the generosity of feeling only found in this most hazardous of sporting endeavours, all those he defeated in this, his most famous win, bombarded the well-known 'job jockey' John Buckingham with congratulations. Eddie Harty, Johnny Haine, Terry Biddlecombe, Ken White, Stan Mellor and Josh Gifford all endorsed his victory in the manner only a member of their brotherhood could completely appreciate.

To John, the high point of his career had been attained and he could never again expect a moment of such sheer joy and satisfaction after any other race which may have awaited him. The following afternoon Terry Biddlecombe won the Cheltenham Gold Cup on Woodland Venture for trainer Fred Rimell. Last of the seven which finished the race was a nine-year-old 500–1 chance named Foinavon.

At the beginning of April 1967, all involved in racing automatically turned their thoughts to Liverpool and the showpiece of steeplechasing, the Grand National. Among those millions, John Buckingham naturally shared their interest but from the perspective of a non-participant. He was more than content with his three booked rides for trainer Jack Peacock at Worcester races on the same day as Aintree's spectacular event, and his hope was to be able if possible to watch the big race on television between the day's commitments. Just three days before the race, while preparing to attend his uncle's funeral, John received an unexpected telephone call from the Berkshire trainer John Kempton. Obviously unaware of the sad occasion Buckingham was preparing for, Kempton immediately enquired if was available to partner his representative Foinavon in the National. Overwhelmed at such an unexpected opportunity at such a late stage, John obviously at once agreed and met Kempton the next day at Taunton when he rode his Sailaway into fifth place in a hurdle race.

It was only then that he learned that two other jockeys had turned down the offer to ride Foinavon at Aintree – Bruce Gregory and Ron Atkins – because they weren't being offered enough. The usual two hundred pounds 'present' was this time considered unrealistic by the owner, Cyril Watkins, in the belief that his horse would probably only survive a few fences. Watkins later informed John that he'd pay any extra according to how the horse performed. Just thrilled to be able to compete in the greatest race on earth was sufficient for Buckingham, who now at such a late stage was faced with the problem of finding somewhere to stay in Liverpool. Accompanied by his brother Tom, he made the journey to the north-west, glad to be able to find accommodation at a house just minutes from the racecourse at the top of Melling Road. Like no other Grand National jockey before, John spent the night before the race sleeping on two easy-chairs pushed together but considered it a small discomfort in the face of the thrill of being a part of racing's supreme test.

On the day of the race, probably slightly more disconcerting than the task facing John, was the realisation that neither the owner nor trainer had considered it worthwhile making the journey north to see their horse compete. John Kempton, the trainer of Foinavon, in fact elected to go to Worcester where he rode Three Dons to victory in the opening event.

With Aintree and its famous contest still under an enormous cloud of uncertainty regarding future activities, the venue was now reduced to but one fixture a year and the National itself still carried the tag of being 'the last one'. Yet the 1967 renewal attracted one of the most competitive fields for many years and of the 44 runners, the favourite, Honey End, had stiff opposition from such notables as Bassnet, Freddie, Anglo, The Fossa and Hollywood film star Gregory Peck's hopeful, Different Class. Almost ignored on the racecard was number 38, Foinavon, and his partner, the almost unheard of John Buckingham.

Despite constant torrential rain, the going was good, a fact evidenced by the fast pace set right from the start. The usual cavalry charge to the first fence led to three casualties, including second favourite Bassnet, yet the one who safely touched down first was the alleged no-hoper Foinavon. Soon swallowed up by the quicker trailblazers, John Buckingham concentrated his efforts on keeping his mount clear of interference in the big field. Castle Falls, Princeful, Kapeno, Rutherfords and Rondetto led the way over Becher's Brook, where already one victim of the first fence was running riderless with them. John kept his mount to the rear of Honey End, trusting that with Josh Gifford on board, that horse would be given a safer run than most and at the halfway stage Foinavon was in the mid-division some way behind the leading group. The outsider was giving his jockey a great ride, coping well with the obstacles and above all avoiding difficult situations when they appeared. There was little change in the order as the leading group took the Water Jump but as they went back into the country the tempo increased and Foinavon began losing some ground. Still at the head of the proceedings approaching Becher's for the second time, the loose horse jumped the Brook perfectly, some five lengths clear of Rutherfords, Kirtle Lad, Castle Falls and Different Class but by now Foinavon had become detached from the leading group. With so many still in the hunt, a thrilling finish looked a certainty and then, almost in the twinkling of an eye, drama at its deadliest unfolded. The wayward riderless horse cut right across the approach of those following at the precise moment they were about to jump the smallest fence on the course, the 23rd. Pandemonium erupted as riders attempted evasive action with their mounts, which only led to innumerable collisions and at one fell swoop the race came virtually to a standstill. Ahead of him as he left Becher's safely behind, John Buckingham encountered total chaos, with horses charging back towards him, running across his line of approach and jockeys frantically trying to catch their horses or remount. With commendable presence of mind, he steered Foinavon through what resembled a battlefield during a cavalry charge. Guiding his mount to the right, he amazingly found a gap amid the shambles and galloping through the mayhem, jumped the fence on the wide outside. With three loose horses surrounding them, they were soon clear of the pile-up and with a good leap at the Canal Turn shook off the riderless intruders to race on with a lead of over 100 yards. In what was a lonely and anxious trek back over the remaining obstacles, John Buckingham kept his composure, nursing Foinavon over every fence with a calm determination. Approaching the second last he was aware that his pursuers were closing rapidly, as Greek Scholar, Packed Home, Solbina, Red Alligator and Honey End raced like fury to catch the runaway outsider. It was Honey End who eventually posed the greatest threat, with Josh Gifford throwing down a concentrated challenge on the run for home. Sticking to their task bravely, Foinavon carried his rider past the post 15 lengths clear of Honey End, with Red Alligator, Greek Scholar and Packed Home the nearest of the remainder.

A rather bewildered looking John Buckingham was led back to the winner's enclosure through a shocked and disbelieving crowd, many of whom were still unaware of the winner's name. In one of the greatest upsets in the history of the race, the impossible had happened. An unknown horse and rider had triumphed over every hazard the National could render and became the only pair that day to complete a clear round without falling or being brought down. Not since the shock Grand National victory of Tipperary Tim in 1928 had such a scene of chaotic frenzy been seen on a racecourse, yet despite the circumstances, Foinavon and John Buckingham saw it all through to the exhausting end, to win fairly and squarely.

It was only when some degree of calm had been restored to Aintree later that afternoon that it was discovered the villain of the piece, that confounded loose horse at the fence after Becher's Brook had the extraordinarily appropriate name of Popham Down.

After such an incredible victory in the most spectacular circumstances, John Buckingham found himself a celebrity overnight. A letter addressed to 'The Winner, The Grand National' was handed to him in the jockeys' room halfway through the traditional champagne revelries among his colleagues. Opening it still in a rather dazed state, John discovered an invitation to appear on *Saturday Night at the London Palladium* as guest of the compére Bob Monkhouse. Back home that evening his family, friends and neighbours had laid on their 'welcome home' celebrations, a thoughtful touch being the decoration of his house which was emblazoned with flags, 'well done' signs and the words 'Buckingham Palace' painted on its façade. The latter inscription had greater meaning the following day when he rode Foinavon from the Royal Mews, in front of the real Buckingham Palace, down The Mall to be presented to the Duchess of Kent. An important member of the entourage was Susie, the tiny white goat which, as a constant companion of Foinavon, had made the long journey to and from Aintree alongside the horse.

That Grand National success was John's 11th win of an unforgettable season and his 45th since becoming a jockey but though now a part of Aintree folklore, he still went to work at Wye two days after that day of days at Liverpool, finishing down the course on his only ride of the afternoon. It was to be a full six weeks before he rode into the winner's enclosure again, at Towcester on Jolly Signal. With more rides coming his way after winning the National, John Buckingham had his busiest period yet, taking part that term in 180 races and when it ended, he looked forward to an even more active 1967–68 season.

With Edward Courage's San Angelo a candidate for the 1968 Aintree epic, John was naturally pleased to be claimed as the partner of his favourite horse but sadly it was not to be. When riding another of John Kempton's horses at Worcester in March, he fell and broke his arm, which caused him to spend the next two months on the sidelines. A mere spectator with his wife Ann at Aintree in 1968, they watched the National with eyes focused on both Foinavon and San Angelo. The former was this time partnered by Phil Harvey and was going well until brought down at the Water Jump and, with Bill Rees deputising for John, San Angelo ran a fine race to finish 12th behind the previous year's third-placed Red Alligator.

Fit and well again in time for the new season, John partnered Foinavon three times, winning on him at the third attempt at Devon and Exeter and in all the jockey notched up 20 winners before the curtain fell on that term. Feeling glum about being without a mount in the 1969 National, trainer Bob Turnell rang John just a week before the race to offer him the ride on his Limeburner. Like his winning Aintree horse, this chestnut gelding was making a first appearance over the big fences; but after acquainting himself early on with the peculiarities of the course, Limeburner jumped very well for the remainder of the journey. John in turn gave the horse a super ride to finish in 12th place behind the seasoned performer Highland Wedding.

After inexplicably losing the ride on Spanish Steps, a horse John had schooled, who rode to victory in both his first hurdle and 'chase successes, he decided to turn freelance the following year and in his second outing as such won a two-and-a-half-mile 'chase at Newton Abbot aboard Silver Lily. Back in the Courage colours on San Angelo at Sandown he romped home impressively, yet sadly it was the last time the combination was ever seen on a racecourse. Securing the National ride on Mr Courage's Pride Of Kentucky and on ground completely against them, they gave a splendid display to finish sixth behind the very good Gay Trip.

Aware that his career was coming to an end, John Buckingham frantically wracked his brain for a clue as to how he was going to survive financially away from the sport he had served so diligently. His final appearance in the Grand National was aboard Limeburner again in 1971. After jumping perfectly the whole way, they were in front jumping the Canal Turn for the last time. Well in contention at the penultimate fence alongside the Irish challenger Black Secret, Limeburner crumpled on landing and although John remounted him, their chance had gone. They finished 11th and last behind the winner Specify and, after riding in his last race at Wetherby in May, John reluctantly called it a day.

Unbeknown to Buckingham, his mates in the jockeys' room, aware of his imminent retirement, had made overtures to the Jockeys' Association suggesting that they needed an extra valet and as a result John Buckingham began his new career on the racecourse at the start of the 1971–72 National Hunt season. Initially he worked in partnership with former jockey Steve Rooney preparing and dressing jockeys and cleaning all their equipment. When that association ended after a couple of years, John's brother Tommy became his partner and for the better part of 30 years both brothers were the mainstay of riders at all the major racetracks – comforting and advising the newcomers, acting as confidants of the famous, but above all else just being two guys who would always give help and assistance when needed.

During his life as a valet, John Buckingham sent out 15 jockeys from Aintree's historic jockeys' room to win 17 Grand Nationals; from Graham Thorner in his championship year of 1972 to Carl Llewellyn for the second of his victories in 1998. From a totally personal viewpoint, that inner sanctum they call the jockeys' room at Aintree has never been quite the same since the Buckingham partnership quietly left Aintree for good, with their well-earned retirement after the 2000 Grand National. The jokes, the leg-pulling and, above all, those precious memories – often recounted during long hours of polishing boots and saddles, emptying and refilling washing machines and sorting out countless pairs of ladies tights – are happy thoughts which will long be missed by myself and many others.

Now grandparents still living in Banbury, Ann and John Buckingham have experienced the highs and lows which life can bring so often in unequal proportions. But whatever the future may hold for them, their conduct through trials, tribulations and too-brief moments of glory is an example all could benefit from.

Brian Fletcher

One of only two men to win the Grand National three times during the twentieth century, Brian Fletcher was born in the north-east of England in 1948 of working-class people hardened to the harsh reality of surviving in a depressed employment area.

When still a pupil at Barnard Castle Grammar School, the youngster entered the perilous environs of unauthorised 'flapping' racing. Having ridden horses from an early age, he quickly improved his technique, style and will to survive. His big chance came through a surprise encounter with the Bishop Auckland racehorse trainer Denys Smith, who, impressed with the boy's enthusiasm and down-to-earth manner, offered him an apprenticeship.

In his first season at Bishop Auckland, Brian rode three winners from just 20 rides; a promising beginning for a young man still not yet 17 years old. His flair, sensitivity and cool attitude when in competition were at once observed by many of the north-country old-brigade of racegoers and at Catterick in February 1967 the 5lb-claiming jockey Brian Fletcher partnered a star of Denys Smith's yard, Red Alligator. Rather significantly, the contest was the Grand National Trial Stakes over three and a half miles and, with a confident display of horsemanship, Brian kept his mount well in touch the whole way before taking up the running three from home to pilot Red Alligator to a three-length victory over Kirtle Lad, Tamerosia and Phemius.

Exactly one month later, the partnership reappeared in the Durham National Handicap 'Chase as odds-on favourites in a field of eight and, after riding a waiting race, Brian brought the gelding, with a perfectly timed run at the second-last, to win convincingly by four lengths from Moonlight Message and Moon Shot.

With a display of supreme confidence in young Fletcher's talent, both owner John Manners and trainer Denys Smith were agreed that Brian should partner their horse in the forthcoming 1967 Grand National at Aintree. Giving his mount a superb ride round in that notorious race, Brian, like so many others, found himself caught up in the mêlée at the 23rd fence, where he suffered probably more than most. He had to put Red Alligator back into the fence three times before eventually extricating himself. Brian and his mount fought back brilliantly after losing so much ground and they finished third behind Foinavon and the favourite Honey End. Denys Smith had seen all he needed to see and the whole of Red Alligator's next campaign was set out with but one race in mind – the Grand National of 1968.

Now deprived of his riding allowance, Brian Fletcher rose strongly to the challenge during the next season, a term during which he rode the highest number of winners of his career, but more importantly it was one in which his association with Red Alligator gained a new and more determined understanding. At Hexham in September they won the Blackhill Handicap 'Chase by two lengths and fifteen from Tant Pis and the very good Freddie. After two disappointing runs without Brian Fletcher, the partnership was restored in another Grand National Trial, the Greenall Whitley at Haydock

Park just under three weeks before the real thing at Aintree. Given a very considerate ride by his jockey, Red Alligator finished fifth behind a very promising newcomer, Half Awake, and all concerned with the County Durham horse were more than satisfied.

A double at Doncaster for Brian Fletcher, with Young Ash Leaf and Autobiography, put the young jockey in the right frame of mind for Aintree and on the opening day there 24 hours later he provided a surprise 100–7 victory with Golden Duck in the Lancashire Hurdle. Both his other rides before teaming up with Red Alligator again were far less successful. Border Fury fell at Becher's in the Topham Trophy and JFK proved to be a costly favourite in the Mildmay 'Chase by coming down at the first.

Of the 45 contestants assembled at Aintree on 30 March 1968, Different Class topped the market as clear 17–2 favourite with among the next-best backed Rutherfords, Red Alligator, French Kilt and Regal John. Milling around at the start before coming under starter's orders, the bright sunshine gave a carnival atmosphere for the thousands in attendance and with the going perfect, a fast-run race was expected.

Away to a good start, the jockeys took the advice of the senior steward, taking it easy going into the first, instructions which proved wise, for only Fort Ord fell there. Princeful, The Fossa and Rutherfords made the early pace and with only Beecham departing at the first ditch, 43 approached Becher's for the first time. As usual, however, the Brook took its toll with What A Myth, Go-Pontinental, Ross Four, Chu-Teh, Valouis and Polaris Missile all exiting the contest. The last named fell directly in the path of Red Alligator yet, with incredible agility, Brian Fletcher's mount gathered himself brilliantly and cleared the scrambling Polaris Missile. Another four departed three fences later at Valentine's Brook and by this time the field was well strung out. Jumping safely so far, Red Alligator was in 12th position jumping the Chair, with The Fossa, Reynard's Heir, Rondetto, Moidore's Token and Different Class among those ahead of him. A slight mix-up at the Water Jump involving Bassnet, Foinavon, Champion Prince and Ronald's Boy reduced the field still further and, turning back into the country, Red Alligator took closer order as the tempo quickened. The second Becher's Brook was cleared without incident but Rondetto came down at the next, bringing down Chamoretta in the process and, swinging left-handed over the Canal Turn, Brian took Red Alligator smoothly into sixth place. Different Class gave his jockey David Mould and owner Gregory Peck hopes of glory when striking the front after clearing Valentine's but four from home Brian Fletcher made his move. Still jumping superbly, Red Alligator came towards the final two obstacles a certain winner bar a fall and, touching down safely at the last, drew clear away from running-on Moidore's Token and Different Class. They passed the post 20 lengths clear of these two, with Rutherfords, Valbus and Highland Wedding the nearest of the 17 to complete the course.

It was a tremendous achievement for the young jockey who, in only his third season as a professional, had won steeplechasing's supreme test at his second attempt and in such confident and brilliant style. Swallowed up by the customary bombardment of media people at the post-race press conference, Brian answered every question with refreshing modesty and, returning to the congratulations of his mates in the jockeys' room, he almost bumped into Lester Piggott, who was weighing out for the Earl of Sefton Stakes. The legendary flat-race champion went out to partner the favourite over Liverpool's stiff one-mile track, a horse by the name of Red Rum. In a tight finish, and giving away 18lb at the weights, Red Rum was beaten into second place, a short head behind the winner Alan's Pet.

Riding with renewed vigour, Brian finished the season on the crest of a wave with 70 winners, which took him into second place in the table, just five behind the champion Josh Gifford.

Quickly off the mark in the new term, the jockey enjoyed a number of wins with Most Handsome, Black Ice and Look North but with Red Alligator now firmly in the grip of the handicapper, the gelding appeared to have lost his taste for racing. At Haydock in early February, however, a glimmer of hope returned when Brian gave the gelding a superb ride in the long-distance National Trial 'Chase. Beaten by the narrowest of margins by Game Purston, a horse receiving almost a stone and a half from the former Aintree champion, the public responded by making Red Alligator clear ante-post favourite to repeat his Grand National victory. On the first day at Liverpool, the north-eastern jockey won the Lancashire Hurdle with Clever Scot and later that afternoon finished a respectable fourth over the big fences with Moonduster in the Topham Trophy. Of the 30 runners taking part in the National, the nearest in the betting to Red Alligator on the 13–2 mark were the Terry Biddlecombe-ridden Fearless Fred at 15–2, Highland Wedding at 100–9 and Bassnet on 100–8. Again giving Brian a good feeling by his jumping early on, Red Alligator became a little too deliberate from Becher's on and was towards the rear coming towards the stands at the end of the first circuit. Back on the final lap, the County Durham horse fell at the first ditch, the 19th and Brian Fletcher was near the winning post to watch Highland Wedding win from Steel Bridge and Rondetto. He ended his racing year in eighth place among the leading jockeys with 41 winners to his credit, a splendid achievement for a 21 year old.

One final ride on Red Alligator in the 1970 Grand National found Brian leading back his mount with the race not halfway through. Well up with the leaders from the start, the 1968 winner fell at the 11th, the open ditch two after the first Valentine's, and for all his connections it was a sad farewell. Red Alligator never ran again. Apart from losing the horse which had put him on the map, Brian completed another very good year, riding 44 winners, but there was little likelihood that he would ever encounter such a tough and brave horse as that which gave him his proudest racing moment. He upped his total of winners the next time to 46 but in that 1971 Grand National his mount The Inventor refused at the final ditch.

In late February 1972 at Teeside Park, Brian Fletcher's world fell apart when riding the favourite Tartuffe in a humble Novices 'Chase worth but one hundred and seventy pounds to the winning owner. Looking well set for victory, his horse crashed to the ground at the fifth fence. Brian was immediately rushed to hospital and remained unconscious for ten days. It was a freak accident, which, like so many before and since, can potentially destroy not only a jockey's career but so often their very lives. Apart from a broken arm, far more serious were the injuries to his head and after months of intense treatment Brian was eventually advised by the specialist to give up riding in the interests of his future health. It was an impossible verdict to contemplate and Brian, although aware that he was far from fit, refused the offer of the compensation due to jockeys whose careers are brought to an end through injury. Some two months later he presented himself for another examination by the specialist and was delighted when he was given a clean bill of health.

Back at his farm, with renewed hope of kick-starting his interrupted career, he soon became aware that the hardest part was still ahead of him. Many within racing sadly suspect that when a rider has suffered the kind of head injuries that Brian had, their nerve is adversely affected and are therefore reluctant to take a chance with them through the uncertain period of their rehabilitation. His first ride in public, and the first step in what could well have been just a pipe dream, came in September 1972 at his local track, Sedgefield. Up on a five year old called Walshaw Demon in the Aycliffe Novices Hurdle, and with Brian in desperate need of a confidence boost, the exercise proved fruitless for they finished a long way behind the winner Dreadnought. With his guv'nor Denys Smith giving him excellent support through this difficult time, Brian struggled on and a month to the day of making his comeback on 9 October, the jockey roared back with a vengeance. Partnering War Cry and Scorton Boy for Denys Smith at Ayr, Brian brought both hurdlers home as winners of their respective races. That fine judge of horses and horsemen, Neville Crump, was sufficiently impressed to engage Brian as deputy to Pat Buckley and at Newcastle in early November, Fletcher got the leg-up from

Captain Crump on Lord Zetland's Canharis. The former point-to-pointer was a notoriously difficult horse to ride and a bit of a chancy jumper, so being a rank outsider at 25–1 was no surprise to anyone. Despite his mount's reputation, Brian got on with him like a house on fire and making all the running in the John Eustace Smith Trophy 'Chase they romped home very comfortable winners.

Just a few days later a certain Donald McCain contacted Brian Fletcher to enquire if the jockey would be prepared to take over as regular jockey for a recent purchase of his, a gelding bred to be a flat-race sprinter named Red Rum. The most exciting period in the lives of both horse and jockey, but more particularly in the history of the Grand National, was about to begin.

Having already won his first four races of the current campaign, Red Rum carried 11st 9lb for his first appearance with Brian Fletcher as pilot. This was at Ayr in the Mauchline Handicap 'Chase over three miles and three furlongs the second week in November and after giving a brilliant exhibition of jumping, Red Rum won going away by six lengths. In the winner's enclosure after the race, Brian told the trainer, 'Mr McCain, this is without question an extremely good horse; he jumps and he stays and is a typical National horse. If you run him at Aintree I would love to ride him.'

From his Birkdale stables, Donald McCain trained a small string of horses on the nearby Southport sands, a practice many so-called 'more knowledgeable' racing men condemned, though they were soon to be made to rethink their attitudes. His major patron was an elderly Southport resident named Noel le Mare, who now had two Grand National contenders at Donald's Upper Aughton Road stables – the newcomer Red Rum and his long-time favourite, Glenkiln. Both became local celebrities in the weeks leading up to the 1973 National and the 'rookie' McCain coped surprisingly well with the attention of the media while still keeping his team of jumpers well, fit and ticking over. The mid-term break he'd planned for Red Rum was coming to an end and the final stage of his strategy was about to begin. His first race in 1973 was the Cumberland Grand National Trial at Carlisle on the last day of January and, giving his customary workmanlike performance, Red Rum finished a very close third behind the favourite Bountiful Charles and Gyleburn. Coming second next time up at Haydock Park in their National Trial shortly afterwards – behind Highland Seal and with such good horses as Gyleburn, Proud Tarquin and last year's Aintree hero Well To Do behind them – both Brian Fletcher and Don McCain were thrilled. They finished fourth, just eight lengths behind the winner Tregarron, in the Greenhall Whitley again at Haydock exactly four weeks before their most important engagement and Red Rum spent the remaining time working out every morning on Southport beach – his host of spectators consisting of admiring sightseers and expectant newshounds.

On the last day of March 1973, the moment of truth for so many arrived. As always on that special day, the atmosphere was electric, the sense of anticipation blistering and the hopes of all Merseysiders were with the underdogs from nearby Southport.

It was more than likely that the weight of money invested by the locals played a large part in Red Rum's being installed joint-favourite with the brilliant Australian champion Crisp at 10–1. Sharing top weight of 12st with the former dual Cheltenham Gold Cup winner L'Escargot, Crisp was trained by that icon of National Hunt racing Fred Winter and, like Red Rum, had been specially prepared for this, the ultimate test. L'Escargot was third-best backed at 11–1, with Ashville at 14s and Princess Camilla, Spanish Steps and an old acquaintance of Brian Fletcher's, Canharis, on the 16–1 mark.

The first race on the card was the BP Shield Handicap Hurdle won by Hasty Word in a driving finish but Brian Fletcher was less than three lengths behind in fourth place on Irish Special, a horse he chose to partner on such an important day because its trainer, Palmer, was one of the few who supported the stricken jockey when rides were scarce.

On firm going, under perfect spring-like conditions, the field was sent off only three minutes beyond the set time and Black Secret led them across Melling Road and jumped the first fence in front, with Richleau the only faller here. Setting a terrific gallop, Grey Sombrero took over at the second, staying in the lead until blundering his way over Becher's. From that point, Richard Pitman allowed Crisp to dictate affairs from the front, followed by Grey Sombrero, Black Secret, Endless Folly and Sunny Lad. In this order they soared over the Canal Turn and Valentine's Brook, with Red Rum and L'Escargot almost together to the rear of the main bunch. At the Chair Grey Sombrero came down heavily and Crisp increased his lead back out for the second circuit, with his closest pursuers Endless Folly, Sunny Lad, Rouge Autumn and Red Rum. Drawing further away from the rest with every stride, Crisp opened up a huge lead going back to Becher's and it was soon obvious that the jockeys behind felt certain that the leader would come back to them. All, that is, except Brian Fletcher, who after jumping the 19th decided that they had allowed Richard Pitman too great an advantage over them. Setting off in pursuit, he knew that Crisp would jump forever and, with so much ground to make up while negotiating the toughest fences found anywhere, realised that he and Red Rum really had their work cut out merely to get in touch with the runaway Australian. Over Becher's, the Canal Turn and Valentine's, Crisp if anything widened the gap and approaching the second last appeared completely unbeatable. Yard by torturous yard Red Rum slowly got closer but when Crisp landed over the final fence he was still fully 15 lengths ahead of the local horse. Being shouted home as the victor from a long way out, it was only at the elbow that first warning signs appeared, with Crisp suddenly seeming to just be running on the spot. It was sad to see the brave front-runner beginning to stagger like a drunken man, yet only 50 yards from the winning post he still held the advantage. Brian Fletcher worked wonders with the brave little horse beneath him, galloping on with admirable commitment and virtually in the dying strides of the race, he pushed Red Rum to the front to win by three-quarters of a length. Coming from a long way back, L'Escargot stayed on to finish a distant third, with Spanish Steps, Rouge Autumn and Hurricane Rock the best of the rest.

There was absolute bedlam in the winner's enclosure, with Donald McCain, Noel le Mare, Beryl McCain and head stable-lad Jackie Grainger, together with the lad who rode work on the winner, Billy Ellison, almost manically ecstatic. Brian Fletcher himself was near to tears during the press and television interviews, while continuing to insist that all the credit for such an incredible victory should go to Red Rum and his trainer. For all involved in the victory, there was increased cause for pride when it was announced that Red Rum had broken the time record for the race set by Golden Miller in 1934.

Sadly, after all the acclaim so lavishly laid on all connected with the National winner, the following day certain journalists chose to suggest that Red Rum had in fact scored a very lucky victory. Pointing out that the runner-up Crisp had conceded a full 23lb to the horse which caught him so close to home, the suggestion was obvious. It implied that Red Rum had won the National by an unfair handicapping system. All connected with the horse at once decided that the record would be put straight and that those expressing such outlandish opinions would be made to eat their own words. But before that opportunity presented itself, Brian Fletcher proved again his immense talent and resilience by completing that season in fifth place among the top jockeys with 47 winners.

In 1974 there was no Crisp to contend with in the Grand National but Red Rum was this time placed in the same position the Australian runner-up had been the year before. Now top weight himself with 12st, his preparation had followed much the same pattern as before, a 15-length victory in the Windermere Handicap 'Chase at Carlisle, another fine win at Ayr and a third in the John Eustace Smith Trophy at Newcastle. An outstanding performance in the Hennessy Gold Cup at Newbury followed, the animal's first trip south, but, obviously well acclimatised, Red Rum ran and jumped his heart out to be beaten on the line by the lighter-weighted Red Candle. By now those gentlemen of the press, so accusatory after Rummy's last National, were beginning to wonder if they had perhaps been a little hasty with their criticism. Against the advice of Brian Fletcher, the trainer went ahead with the engagement in the Brettanby Handicap 'Chase at Catterick, despite the going being bottomless and totally against Red Rum. McCain, though, was most anxious to get one final race into the horse before the National, although he agreed that if the jockey felt concerned, Brian should pull him up, with the Aintree appointment so close at hand. As it turned out the gelding confounded everyone, carrying top weight of 12st 7lb to an eight-length victory over animals he was conceding a lot of weight to.

In his last race before Aintree, the Greenall Whitley at Haydock, Red Rum was again heavily burdened by the handicapper but it was not the weight which defeated him. Jumping the first fence brilliantly behind the useful Glanford Brig, Red Rum was so accurate and fast in his leap that he passed two horses in mid-air but, unfortunately, the swerving Noble Hero collided with him and Brian Fletcher for the first time ever parted company with Red Rum. The horse continued riderless for the entire trip and, in trainer McCain's view, was better for the experience.

In 1974, 30 March was not just another day among 365, but the one which was the annual reason for risking all in the world for the thrill of the chase; a day so remote in purpose from any other in the calendar that only those who tempt the gods so regularly can completely appreciate its meaning. The favourite for the race this time was the 7–1 eight-year-old Scout, whose rider Tommy Stack had partnered Red Rum in his earlier days to a number of victories and had even for one brief spell trained the gelding. That dual champion of Cheltenham, L'Escargot, was next in the market at 17–2, followed by the 11–1 chance Red Rum. Rough House was on 14s and Spanish Steps together with Straight Vulgan were both at 15–1.

The start was delayed a few minutes while Martin Blackshaw regained control of his mount Princess Camilla, who amused the crowds with a performance of bucking and kicking, but once settled she concentrated her attention on the work at hand. Away to a good start, the 42 hopefuls charged across Melling Road to the first barrier, which only Lord Oaksey on Royal Relief failed to survive. Go-Pontinental came down at the third and after making a series of mistakes Bahia Dorada was pulled up going into Becher's Brook, which, surprisingly, all 39 remaining cleared without incident. Sunny Lad, Charles Dickens, Rough Silk and Straight Vulgan led the field over the Canal Turn but Culla Hill, Rough House and Huperade failed to cope with the sharp turn, bringing down Karacola, Argent and Deblin's Green as they fell.

With Charles Dickens taking up the running at the tenth, there was an unusually large number still well in contention returning to the racecourse and, joined by the Irish outsider Pearl of Montreal at the 14th, the two leaders headed for the Chair tracked by a whole host of rivals. A loose horse cut across the leader at the big open ditch and Andy Turnell did extremely well to keep Charles Dickens in the contest but he surrendered his position in front to Pearl of Montreal. This pair led over the Water Jump, closely followed by L'Escargot, Sunny Lad and Spanish Steps but going beautifully in tenth place was Red Rum and Brian Fletcher was having the ride of his life. Back in the country the pace increased, with Pearl Of Montreal weakening as Charles Dickens again took over, closely chased by Vulgan Town, L'Escargot, Spanish Steps, Scout and the improving Red Rum. With a perfect leap at the second Becher's, Red Rum went to the front, generating a terrific roar of approval from those in the vicinity. Closely pressed by Charles Dickens, Scout, Vulgan Town and L'Escargot, he strode out well over the Canal Turn and Valentine's on the final stretch back to the Anchor Crossing. At the plain fence five from home, Red Rum pitched badly on landing and in that split second his jockey's brilliant horsemanship was seen to perfection. Allowing his mount plenty of rein, he hardly moved in the saddle, leaving the horse to recover in his own exceptional way and get back in stride immediately. Still with a double handful approaching the second-last, Brian was fully aware of L'Escargot beginning his challenge yet completely unfazed, he continued to ride his horse with hands and heels. Touching down splendidly over the final obstacle, Red Rum increased his stride without any demands being made of him, to romp home the winner of his second successive Grand National – this time with 12st on his back so there could be no quibbles from anybody. Seven lengths behind came the gallant L'Escargot, just a short head in front of the fast-finishing Charles Dickens, with Spanish Steps fourth ahead of Rough Silk, Vulgan Town and Rouge Autumn.

As the first horse to win two Nationals on the trot since Reynoldstown in 1935 and 1936, Red Rum became the talk and toast of the nation. But amazingly there was further glory to come his way before his season's work was done. Just three weeks after that tremendous Liverpool victory, Red Rum and Brian Fletcher faced the starter in the Scottish Grand National at Ayr and in a very competitive field consisting of 16 opponents, the jockey rode one of the finest judged races of his entire career. Some way off the pace in the early part of the contest, he gradually moved Red Rum up into a challenging position on the final circuit to take up the running at the last fence and effortlessly romped away to a four-length victory over Proud Tarquin, Kildagin and Canharis.

Now a personality in his own right, the gelding found an occupation away from the racecourse when his training schedule permitted. Frequently requested to be present for opening garden fêtes, supermarkets and betting shops, he demonstrated on numerous occasions what a wonderfully intelligent and friendly character he was and he was even appointed to switch on Blackpool's illuminations.

With everyone now wondering if a Grand National hat-trick attempt would be made, Donald McCain quickly supplied the answer: a very emphatic 'yes'. Much of the programme which had proved so successful before was adopted, with the knowledge that again the horse would top the handicap with 12st. Undeterred, they began with giving Red Rum his first run of the 1974–75 term at Perth in late September when, giving two stone to Tommy Stack on Southern Lad, they finished one and a half lengths behind this pair in second place. Next time out at Ayr, Brian Fletcher turned the tables on Tommy Stack, who was this time on board Scout, with Red Rum giving a fine display of jumping to win the Joan Mackay Handicap 'Chase without being stretched. A journey south to Kempton followed and at this Red Rum showed his dislike of a right-handed course by running miserably way down the course behind the winner Rough House. Another poor result came next at his local track, Haydock Park, this time making a number of mistakes before finishing last of three, well to the rear of Fred Winter's classy Pendil. After the usual mid-season break, a revitalised Rummy gave a much improved performance when winning the Haydock Park National Trial but, returning to the Lancashire course some three weeks later, again ran disappointingly, coming a weary-looking fourth behind The Benign Bishop over three miles. With a good deal left to work on in the five weeks left before Aintree, Donald McCain carried on as normally as possible, ensuring that his dual champion retained his fitness.

Starting the 7–2 clear favourite of the 31 runners, Red Rum looked an absolute picture as he led the parade in front of the stands, again with top weight and this time conceding a full 13lb to L'Escargot. There was a delay of 15 minutes before they were at last sent on their way, whereupon the amateur-ridden Irish horse Zimulator went straight to the front, with High Ken, Glanford Brigg, Southern Quest and Manicou Bay also prominent. There was much interference nearing the halfway stage, with several loose horses darting back and forth across the leaders on the approach to the Chair. Some distance away at this point, Brian Fletcher was able to steer his mount clear of the danger ahead. Moving easily through the stragglers on the run back to Becher's, Red Rum joined issue with Glanford Brigg and Southern Quest at the head of affairs crossing the Brook. With The Dikler, Spanish Steps and L'Escargot in hot pursuit, Red Rum struck the front four from home, with L'Escargot and The Dikler right on his heels. At the final fence L'Escargot and

Red Rum touched down together but it could be clearly seen that Brian was hard at work on the favourite. Surging ahead, L'Escargot ran on to win by 15 lengths from Red Rum, who was followed past the post by Spanish Steps, The Dikler, Manicou Bay and Southern Quest.

After his fourth racecourse appearance the next season, a race at Newcastle which he had won earlier in his career, a regrettable disagreement between Donald McCain and Brian Fletcher led to the severing of a partnership which had not only been friendly and highly successful but which had re-written racing's record books. The new jockey chosen to ride Red Rum was a man who had been associated with the horse even before Ginger McCain became Red Rum's trainer, the talented Irishman Tommy Stack.

In 1976 Brian Fletcher went out for his last Grand National aboard the ten-year-old mare Eyecatcher, owned and trained by John Bosley, and as he always did around the racecourse he knew so well, the jockey gave his 28–1 mount a copybook ride. Bang up with the leaders after being gently brought through at Becher's Brook the final time, Eyecatcher battled on bravely alongside The Dikler, Spanish Steps and Red Rum over the final mile. Momentarily ahead of Red Rum coming to the last fence, Brian was well in with a good chance of winning his fourth National but on the run to the line, having given her all, his mount was unable to match the stronger Rag Trade and that unique jumping machine, Red Rum. The latter was run out of it in the last hundred yards, Rag Trade winning by two lengths, with Eyecatcher eight lengths back in third place.

Later in the year Brian Fletcher retired from racing on medical advice after suffering more head injuries and the racecourse lost a certain something with his departure. Back with his cattle in the north-east, Brian forever could reflect on the those wonderful days at Aintree when he took the world of steeplechasing through moments of splendour rarely seen. Within hours of Red Rum being buried alongside the winning post at Aintree racecourse in October 1995, Brian Fletcher and former head-lad Jackie Grainger paid their final respects to an equine giant who completely changed their lives, on the very turf they had graced so often.

FIVE

Edward Patrick Harty

Another member of that intrepid band of Irishmen who were reputed to have been born in the saddle, Eddie Harty was born on 10 June 1937, the son of Captain Cyril Harty, a highly talented amateur rider who in later life turned his skills to training horses.

During that most difficult period of the early 1920s, when the Irish Free State was attempting to become established not just throughout the world but more particularly within the whole of Ireland, Cyril Harty, a member of the famous Limerick family, was an officer of the Free State Army. Most ironically, it was as 'Captain Harty' that he won the Grand Military Cup at Punchestown in April 1922 on Santox, which was owned by Colonel Bingham of the British Army. This is, if proof were ever needed, a superb example of the magnetism of the horse transcending all, crossing all boundaries and bringing men of all persuasions and denominations together.

During a less traumatic period in the Republic of Ireland's history, Cyril Harty trained Knight's Crest to win the Irish Grand National at Fairyhouse in 1944, beating the mighty Prince Regent into second place. Young Eddie followed swiftly in his father's footsteps, becoming a rising star of the junior showjumping arena and, after riding in his first hurdle race when just 14 years old, he went on to win over 50 point-to-points.

In September 1953, when still only 16, Eddie Harty won his first race under rules, an amateur riders' steeplechase over three miles, one furlong at Newton Abbot. At this time he shared the unusual distinction of being retained as an amateur at his father's St Lawrence Manor stables near Dublin at the same time that his dad rode in an amateur capacity for the yard. Stricken temporarily with wanderlust, Harty junior went off to America around this time and worked for two years as a cowboy; a less demanding role than riding over fences on the other side of the Atlantic but one which broadened his outlook considerably.

Back home again, by now 22 years old, he won the prestigious Conyngham Cup on Take Time over four miles in 1959 and within 12 months Eddie's life entered a completely new phase. In March 1960 he gained his first sight of Aintree when partnering the County Meath trainer Jimmy Brogan's Knoxtown in the Grand National. Travelling well in the mid-division, the pair fell at the first Becher's but the thrill of the occasion was something he could never forget.

It was more by fate than design that in that same year, when offered the chance to become a professional jockey, Eddie Harty was selected to represent his country in the 1960 Olympic Games three-day event in Rome. Enjoying such a proud excursion doing what he did best, Eddie returned to Britain after finishing ninth in the Italian Games to concentrate his efforts on creating a career for himself in National Hunt racing.

Originally with fellow countryman and former champion jockey Tim Molony, he gained further valuable experience with such distinguished trainers as Fred Rimell, Fred Winter and Toby Balding. It was for Fred Rimell that Eddie had his first paid ride in the National, aboard the 50–1 shot Floater in the 1961 race but unfortunately it was a short-lived experience as they came down at the very first fence. The following year he did considerably better when, with trainer Nicholson's Cannobie Lee, he completed the course in eighth place behind Fred Winter on Kilmore. After missing the race in 1963, he gave a good showing 12 months on when guiding home Alex Kilpatrick's gelding April Rose into seventh place some way behind the winner Team Spirit.

Absent from the race the next year, Eddie Harty did, however, register an important milestone in his career when winning the Topham Trophy 'Chase on the opening day at Liverpool. Riding the favourite, Hopkiss, the Irishman provided a splendid example of how to cope with the big fences, to lead at the Canal Turn and resist the late challenge of John Leech on Spring Greeting to hold on and win by a neck.

A spell on the sidelines through injury cost him some valuable mounts during the 1965–66 period and again he did not compete in the Grand National, but he made up for it well when he was back in action for the next term. Partnering 48 winners that season, Eddie for the first time reached the top jockeys' table in eighth place behind Josh Gifford and, in spite of the chaos encountered in that year's Grand National, he escorted the Fred Winter-trained Solbina into sixth place behind the shock winner Foinavon.

Harty enjoyed a good ride round at Aintree the next year too, this time gaining tenth place with Steel Bridge behind Red Alligator, and a little over a fortnight later he rode a fine race on Glenn to win the Welsh Grand National at Chepstow.

Eddie's somewhat topsy-turvy career took an upward surge early the next season, when trainer Fred Rimell offered him the mount on Jupiter Boy in Newbury's feature race of their November meeting, the valuable Mackeson Gold Cup Handicap 'Chase over two and a half miles. In a well-contested race, featuring such future stars as Gay Trip, Specify, San Angelo, Playlord and Her Majesty the Queen Mother's Makaldar, Eddie took his mount to the front coming to the fourth-last. Staying on well, Jupiter Boy held on for a short-head victory from Specify, Moonduster and Playlord. It was the perfect fillip for the jockey, but even better awaited him at Liverpool the following March.

Two days before the Grand National, Eddie took the mount on the eight-year-old Dozo in the Topham Trophy 'Chase. Having ridden the gelding into fourth place at the recent Cheltenham Festival, he had every confidence his horse could handle Aintree's difficult obstacles. His belief was fully justified. Dozo jumped splendidly all the way and when under severe pressure in the home stretch, he gamely fought back to win by a length and a half from Bill Rees on La Ina. The winning trainer Toby Balding and the owner Mrs Wetherill were overjoyed at the success and the former was encouraged to hope that this was a foretaste of what he could hope for two days later.

Balding's sole representative in the National was the evergreen Highland Wedding, a 12 year old who had already twice completed the race, albeit some way behind both Anglo in 1966 and Red Alligator in the previous year's race. Since losing his regular partner, Owen McNally, through injury, the horse had been ridden alternately by Eddie Harty and the 3lb-claiming jockey Bob Champion, but with experience the main priority in such an exacting event as the Grand National, it was the more senior rider who was chosen for Aintree. An out-and-out stayer, who had recently won the four-mile Eider 'Chase at Newcastle for the third time, there were, however, many who thought the gelding had missed his best chance in the race.

Trying for a second victory, Red Alligator was a clear favourite at 13–2, with Fearless Fred well fancied on 15–2 and Highland Wedding the 100–9 third-best backed. Others well supported included Bassnet, Hove, Moidore's Token, Arcturus and The Beeches, though, as always, it could be said that each of the 30 competitors carried somebody's money.

Away to a great roar from the crowds, the field raced towards the first fence where they all jumped safely, as they also did at the next but the first open ditch claimed Tudor Fort and a groan from spectators at the fourth signalled the end of Fearless Fred's involvement. With Furore II showing the way to

Castle Falls, Steel Bridge, Miss Hunter, Highland Wedding and The Fossa, they approached Becher's Brook, at which only the American-ridden Peccard fell. Running well within himself, Highland Wedding was kept close to the leaders, with his jockey cleverly avoiding all dangers. Coming back from Valentine's, Castle Falls took over with the remainder close behind. Fort Sun, Kellsboro' Wood, Flosuebarb and The Fossa all took closer order coming to the Chair and just to the rear of these came Steel Bridge, Rondetto, Highland Wedding and Limeburner. Back onto the final circuit there was little change in the order until The Fossa took up the running, with Steel Bridge, Fort Sun and Highland Wedding within striking distance. Kilburn fell at Becher's and two fences later Highland Wedding went into the lead at the Canal Turn, from which point Rondetto suddenly began to look dangerous. Jumping every fence perfectly on the run back towards the Melling Road, Highland Wedding appeared much the stronger of those behind and, clearing the last fence well, Eddie Harty drew away from those chasing to win comfortably by 12 lengths from Steel Bridge, Rondetto, The Beeches, Arcturus and eight others.

The scenes in the winner's enclosure were unbelievable, with owner, trainer and jockey congratulating each other again and again. When interviewed on BBC television after weighing in, Eddie hardly gave David Coleman a chance to speak, rattling off like machine gun fire a graphic description of the whole race, which, due to the jockey's excitement and his pronounced Irish brogue, even the experienced Coleman had difficulty keeping pace with.

With Highland Wedding retired to his owner's home in Canada, Eddie Harty was more than happy with his mount for the 1970 Grand National, the bay gelding Dozo, who had given the jockey his first taste of Aintree success. Joint second-favourite at 100–8 with French Excuse, the pair stood their ground in the betting behind the most fancied contestant, the 13–2 chance Two Springs.

With the favourite out of the race after falling at the third, Dozo, Assad, Miss Hunter and Gay Trip cut out most of the early pace but when the race began in earnest on the second time round nothing appeared to be going better than Gay Trip. Holding a slight advantage after jumping Valentine's, Dozo looked to have every chance of providing a second win for his jockey but when Pat Taaffe made his move on Gay Trip at the penultimate fence the writing was on the wall. Striding away in the most commanding fashion, Gay Trip won from Vulture, Miss Hunter and the brave Dozo.

Making his ninth and final appearance in race in 1971, Eddie rode the Roddy Armytage-prepared Twigairy but the contest was a short one for the pair for they were brought down by a falling horse at the first fence.

In 1972 Eddie acquired a trainer's licence and set up his stables in his homeland at the Curragh and from there he frequently scouted many promising young jumpers to recommend to his old friend and former guv'nor, Fred Winter.

John Dennis Cook

John Cook was born in June 1937 and his parents worked at Kingsclere stables near Newbury, looking after the apprentices, so it was only natural that, being reared in such an environment, young Master Cook would develop an early interest in horse racing. Becoming an apprentice himself when leaving school, he spent five years with Evan Williams and Peter Hastings-Bass at Park House, Kingsclere, but, as so often is the case, the boy's increasing weight put an end to his dreams of becoming a flat-race jockey.

After completing his National Service in the Royal Navy, John returned to his roots but, frustrated at not being able to make a breakthrough in the area he knew so well, secured a post with a private trainer in the West Country, for whom he succeeded in riding a few National Hunt winners. With the future looking decidedly bleak, John went back to Kingsclere in the hope that perhaps something may materialise in an area where he was better known.

Devoid of any prospects at all, he placed an advert early in 1962 seeking a job which included any chance whatsoever of rides. From this initiative, he secured a position with Frank Cundell, the Aston Tirrold trainer. With a leading jockey, Stan Mellor, retained by Cundell, the young hopeful received plenty of valuable advice and guidance and at Stratford in April 1963 John Cook rode his first winner under rules. The event was the second division of the Leamington Handicap Hurdle over two and a half miles and as one with his mount, Samoan Sun, they were always upsides the leaders before going on three from home to win handsomely by two lengths from Colotor and Speaker. Again at Stratford in the closing weeks of the season, he partnered Samoan Sun to victory and this time young Cook attracted admiring glances for the strength of his efforts. After leading for most of the way, he was tackled two from home by the very good performer Owen McNally on Black Sumatra and, although headed, he fought back brilliantly to regain the advantage in the final strides and win by a short-head.

The chances of rides he had asked for in his desperate advertisement certainly came his way with Frank Cundell, as well as what every aspiring jockey longs for — winners. One of John's favourite horses, Superfine, carried him to victory twice in his second term and another good horse which treated him proud was that gallant little battler, Super Flash, who provided John with his first Cheltenham winner. An indication of the esteem in which he was held by Mr Cundell came near the season's end when he was given the leg-up on Superfine for the Whitbread Gold Cup at Sandown Park. Although finishing down the course, Cook's future looked brighter than at any time before.

A sure sign that John Cook's ability was becoming noticed came when another trainer began giving him rides and it was for this man, Les Kennard, who was based in Devon, that he steered Tillingbourne to victory at Newton Abbot in September 1964. As a result of this latest success, John lost his right to claim any weight allowance but the reward was the fact that he was now a fully fledged jockey.

In the Englemere Handicap 'Chase at Ascot in 1965, John Cook enjoyed his greatest moment so far, when giving the grey Burley Hill a superb ride to outjump and outrun Bill Rees on the Queen Mother's brilliant gelding The Rip – and win very easily by six lengths. Four decent rides at the 1966 Cheltenham National Hunt Festival were the high spot of another period which ended with 'Cookie' finishing in 11th position of the leading jockeys, with 36 winners to his credit.

Having two engagements on the opening day of the Grand National meeting at Aintree in 1967 was a useful introduction to the famous Liverpool course and after finishing way back with Tudor Chanteur in the Lancashire Hurdle he sampled the thrill of the big fences on Indian Spice in the Topham Trophy. Down the course again in this event, it was nonetheless a good prelude for his adventure two days later in the National.

For many, the mayhem encountered at the 23rd fence in the 1967 Grand National could understandably have soured a competitor's enthusiasm but, like many that day, John Cook persevered doggedly on his 66–1 outsider Ross Sea to finish a remote 15th behind what many describe as the luckiest winner of all time.

It was another three years before he had an opportunity to lay the ghost of the 'Foinavon fence' but in the meantime there were other venues, other races and, above all, a living to earn. During that time he hit the headlines with two fabulous victories with that outstanding horse Spanish Steps. In March 1969 John scored a runaway victory with Edward Courage's game gelding in the Totalisator Champion Novices 'Chase on the first day of the Cheltenham Festival. Then in November that year, he simply trounced a very high-class field to win Newbury's major steeplechase, the Hennessy Gold Cup, by a staggering 15 lengths.

With just the two mounts on the big day at Aintree in 1970, John felt quietly confident about the main one, Specify, in the National, even though he was aware that he was the fifth jockey to accompany the gelding in public during the course of that season.

After finishing unplaced on the Edward Courage-trained Tikitas in the opening event, the Liverpool Handicap Hurdle, on National day, John joined his colleagues to somehow get through the next two hours without disclosing any discomfort he was feeling. By now a seasoned professional, he accepted that this was 'just another race' but like everyone else in that shabby, character-filled room, he also knew, above all else, that at the same time it was that incomparable contest which everyone who has ridden over fences dreams of being a part of. The 'jockeys out' call came as a relief to tangled nerves. They had thoughts sacred to them alone and the deepest desire that they would all return safe and in one piece. Once in the paddock, their only consideration would, as always, be getting on with their job.

Taking extremely well to big fences, Specify jumped really well through the first circuit, touched down in fourth place behind the leading three at the Water Jump and was still well to the fore going to Becher's for the second time. Jumping the mighty fence perfectly, John Cook was horrified to see The Otter falling directly in front of him and, too late to take evasive action, he and Specify were brought down. Dreadfully disappointed at their misfortune – for the jockey felt certain they would have been involved in the finish had they stood up – 'Cookie' was determined to try again with the gelding the next year.

In the intervening 12 months Specify changed stables, being transferred by his owner, holiday camp king Fred Pontin, to the Epsom establishment of John Sutcliffe. In his first five races for the new yard he was partnered by three different jockeys. John Cook was not one of them, but in January 1971 he was engaged to ride Fred Pontin's hurdler Cala Mesquida. After a none too promising effort over two miles at Newbury that partnership was resumed a month later at the same venue in the valuable Schweppes Gold Trophy Hurdle. Producing a fantastic burst of speed on the run-in, Cala Mesquida got up in the very last stride to beat Volunteer by a head at the generous odds of 33–1.

Of the 38 gathered for the Grand National on 3 April 1971, the previous year's winner, Gay Trip, topped the betting at 8–1, ahead of Lord Jim, The Laird, The Otter and Two Springs. Unfancied due to his lack of recent form, Specify featured at 28–1 and for the first time in 12 months, John Cook was back aboard the nine year old. The usual frantic dash to the first fence ended with five horses leaving the contest almost before it had begun and among those was the most heavily backed horse, Gay Trip. The Laird and Indamelia went at the third, Battledore refused a fence later and at Becher's, Soldo, Copperless and Pride Of Kentucky also fell by the wayside. Gay Buccaneer was carried wide by a riderless horse when leading at the Canal Turn and from there on Miss Hunter took over from Flosuebarb, Smooth Dealer and

Vichysoise. Reaching the end of the first lap, the white-faced Astbury was at the head of affairs, with Flosuebarb, Smooth Dealer and Beau Bob close up but Vichysoise lost a lot of ground when badly hampered at the Chair. Early on the second circuit Beau Bob took up the running, with Ron Barry making a forward move on Sandy Sprite and Astbury, Black Secret, Specify and Bowgeeno beginning to make ground. At Becher's Brook Beau Bob unseated his rider and Money Boat took a nasty-looking fall but with Sandy Sprite and Bowgeeno now disputing the lead, the race entered a decisive stage. Despite his rider losing his irons and making a blunder at the Canal Turn, the Irish horse Black Secret moved threateningly into the picture from Valentine's Brook. Sandy Sprite held a marginal advantage over Bowgeeno jumping the second-last but both were closely attended by Black Secret, Specify and Astbury. With the five almost in line landing over the final fence, the crowds roared their approval at what looked like being the closest National finish in years. Tightly bunched rounding the elbow Sandy Sprite appeared to have gone lame, though the gallant little mare struggled on bravely and with the jockeys riding determinedly John Cook squeezed Specify through a gap between two rivals and produced a terrific burst of speed to pass Black Secret in the final 75 yards. Only a neck behind in second place came Black Secret, with Astbury third, Bowgeeno fourth and the very brave Sandy Sprite fifth. A distance of under five lengths separated the first five finishers.

It was a momentous moment for 33-year-old John Cook, who, since his childhood, had dreamed of making a name for himself in racing. After those desperate days of seeking an employer within the sport and waiting for replies to a pleading advertisement, it was a worthy tribute to his indomitable character when he was greeted in the winning enclosure as the winner of the Grand National.

Tragically, less than 12 months later, John suffered a very serious injury in a fall and was forced to retire from the sport he loved and served so well. Eventually he made a life for his family and himself in Australia but sadly, early in 1999, it was revealed that he was seriously ill. On Grand National day of that year, a card of goodwill and best wishes was signed in the jockeys' room at Aintree by all his former mates, every official present and the latest generation of riders. It was intended as more than a 'get well' message; it was a recognition of the esteem in which he was held by all who knew him, who envied his resilience and who sought one day to emulate his triumph against the odds.

In December 1999, John Dennis Cook passed away peacefully in Australia, far away from the Aintree winning post but never from the thoughts of those who knew and admired him.

Graham Edward Thorner

Born into a Somerset farming family in 1949, Graham Thorner left school at 15 and immediately obtained employment at the Letcombe Bassett stables of Captain Tim Forster.

It says much for both men that he stayed there for his entire racing life. As is usual in the jumping world, his early rides for the yard were as an amateur and as such he rode three winners during the 1966–67 season. Graham turned professional during the next steeplechasing period and enjoyed much success over the ensuing years.

In March 1968 he had his first ride at the Cheltenham National Hunt fixture while still claiming his three-pound riding allowance on Foxwell, with which he had already enjoyed two successes that year. Finishing way down the course in the George Duller Handicap Hurdle with the Somerset-trained gelding, the jockey did, however, thoroughly enjoy his first taste of one of the major jumping occasions of the year. In the closing weeks of that jumping session, Graham was given the leg-up by Captain Forster on a five year old having only its second run over the minor obstacles at Stratford. Finishing ninth of fifteen in the White Lion Novices Hurdle was not the most promising of introductions but in the future Graham Thorner was to experience happier and more memorable times with this young gelding whose name was Well To Do. He rode the horse in two events the next season without catching the judges' eyes on either occasion but wins with Draycott Moor and Timur Beg were encouraging, as was having a second engagement at the big Cheltenham meeting, this time without any claiming allowance.

It was during the 1969–70 season that his career really took off, right from the opening weeks, with such winners as Clareman, Gay Bruce, King of Tarsus and, also in September at Devon and Exeter, with a very satisfying victory on the now six-year-old Well To Do. Three mounts at the Cheltenham Festival resulted in a third place in the County Handicap Hurdle with Firebrite and on the day Gay Trip won the National at Aintree, Graham Thorner recorded his second victory within two days at Devon and Exeter on the David Gandolfo-trained Steeplejack. Finishing in eighth place in the top jockeys' league, he ended a very rewarding period with 44 winners and by now was being offered engagements from some very famous sources.

On the very first day of the 1970–71 campaign, Graham registered his intentions emphatically, travelling north to join trainer Colin Davies' horse Farmer Giles in a decisive eight-length victory in the three-mile Alford Novices 'Chase and then rounded off a profitable day by winning the Caistor Handicap 'Chase on Bryan Marshall's Clareman. Winner followed winner regularly for Thorner – Trapani's Bell, Gay Kildare, Twigairy and Bridgedown all adding to his tally as the weeks went by, and after Loup Cervier carried him into second place in the Mildmay of Flete Challenge Cup at Cheltenham's National Hunt meeting Graham's thoughts became centred on Liverpool at the beginning of April.

Four days after finishing second in that important Cheltenham event, Graham received a boost to his Liverpool aspirations when getting up in the final strides to win the Rye Handicap Steeplechase at Folkestone on Bowgeeno, for this was the horse which was to provide him with his first ride in the Grand National. It was also Captain Forster's only representative in the race and the improvement in the gelding's form lifted the whole stable's hopes.

With the previous year's winner 8–1 favourite of the 38 runners, others attracting the attention of the betting public included Lord Jim, The Laird, The Otter and Two Springs, while Bowgeeno was among those unconsidered at the bottom of the market on 66–1. Given a splendid ride by his jockey, Bowgeeno coped excellently with the fences, kept in mid-division for most of the first circuit, until moving up with the leaders at the second Canal Turn. Right in the firing line at the penultimate fence, Bowgeeno was still well there after clearing the last almost in line with four others. Beaten for speed when Specify, Black Secret and Astbury turned on the tap, Bowgeeno came fourth barely three lengths behind the winner, Specify. It was a tremendous effort for a horse and jockey both making their initial attempts at the race and both trainer Captain Forster and Graham Thorner were overjoyed with such a game showing to finish in the frame.

An extremely busy season by Graham was well rewarded, with his ending that term as champion jockey with 74 winners. For him, one of the most encouraging aspects of that impressive total was that four of those victories had been gained astride a horse he had been associated with for many years, the chestnut gelding Well To Do.

For some time considered a likely National horse by Tim Forster, Well To Do was brought along in the trainer's usual well-planned manner, with the 1972 Aintree spectacular in mind but when the owner, Mrs Heather Sumner, tragically died of cancer in June 1971, such considerations had to be put on hold. To Tim Forster's surprise, the contents of Mrs Sumner's will stipulated that Well To Do should become the property of her trainer. Understandably disturbed by this turn of events, the Captain faced a period of great uncertainty. With little more than 15 minutes to spare in which to confirm the registration of Well To Do as an entry for the Grand National, Tim Forster, still with some reservations, sent a telegram to Weatherby's which brought a gasp of relief from Graham Thorner at the prospect of partnering the horse in the National.

Brought along gently yet purposefully, Well To Do responded well to his preparation, finishing second on his first outing before scoring a runaway victory over three and a half miles in the Hogmanay 'Chase at Warwick at the end of December. From then on it was a matter of keeping the horse ticking over while avoiding the ever-present danger of injuries. On the run-up to Aintree's famous contest, Graham himself was conscious of the need to stay clear of serious accidents and at the Cheltenham National Hunt fixture he improved considerably on his placing the year before in the Mildmay of Flete Challenge Cup, when winning the race aboard Mocharabuice.

With a field of 42 for the 1972 Grand National, speculation was rife as to the outcome of the most unpredictable event of the year. The dual Cheltenham Gold Cup winner L'Escargot was a heavily supported favourite at 17–2, while others carrying large amounts of public support were Gay Trip, Cardinal Error, Black Secret and Fair Vulgan. A little over three days before the race, Well To Do was readily available in ante-post betting at 33–1, yet for some reason, money seemed to pour on the horse, reducing its price on the day of the race to less than half that, a surprising 14–1.

During constant driving rain, the race began with the usual cheers of impatient anticipation and with Fair Vulgan, Miss Hunter, Black Secret, Gay Buccaneer and L'Escargot setting the pace, expectations were high. A gasp of despair erupted when L'Escargot was baulked at the first ditch and knocked out of the contest. More interference came with a riderless horse almost carrying out the Irish horse Gay Buccaneer at the Canal Turn. After this mishap Black Secret took over from The Pantheon, Gay Trip, Miss Hunter and General Symons and with Nephin Beg, Well To Do and Astbury also well in attendance expectations rose among the multitude of spectators. At the halfway stage, a riderless horse interrupted the progress of Fair Vulgan and, although he survived the disturbance, he lost his position when headed at the 18th by Black Secret, General Symons, Bright Willow, Specify and Money Boat. The leaders encountered few problems at Becher's the second time round and two fences later at the Canal Turn, Black Secret was in command from General Symons, Well To Do and Specify. On that long slog back to that vital, punishing homestretch after the remaining fences, all that had gone before was of little consequence if the demands of what lay ahead could not be answered. With the leading group drawing steadily away from the stragglers, it was now more than just a question of survival. With a brilliantly timed challenge, Graham Thorner struck the front by the narrowest of margins at the last fence from Gay Trip, General Symons and the staying-on Black Secret, but with an exceptional renewed effort Well To Do prevailed to win by two lengths from the battling Gay Trip and the dead-heaters for third place, Black Secret and General

Symons. In one of the most closely contested climaxes to a National in years, champion jockey Graham Thorner achieved a victory of which many dream but of which most are denied.

Finishing third in the top jockeys' table with 75 winners that year was of little importance compared to his victory in the most demanding equestrian contest on earth. After missing the race in 1973, Graham came back to that most incomparable of races in 1974 when he finished in 12th place on the Edward Courage horse Quintus behind an animal already a legend in his own lifetime, the inimitable Red Rum.

The following year his mount, Land Lark, met with a drastic accident when coming down at the Chair and in 1976 he rode Gay Kindersley's Black Tudor into tenth place in the National. On that incredible day when Red Rum totally re-wrote the record books by achieving an unprecedented third Grand National victory, Graham fell at the 12th fence with Prince Rock. He came home in 12th position on the Gordon Richards-trained Tamalin in 1978 and, making his final appearance in the race 12 months later, signed off a highly reputable career when falling at the second Becher's Brook on Lord Leverhulme's Mr Snowman.

Among his many other important successes were with Deny's Adventure in the 1973 Arkle Challenge Trophy; with Kasttrup in the Coral Golden Handicap Hurdle Final again at Cheltenham the next year; and with Master Spy in Newbury's Mandarin 'Chase in 1977. Graham won the Arkle Challenge Trophy for a second time in 1978 with a future Gold Cup winner Alverton and in his final year as a jockey scored a fine victory with Tim Forster's Casbah in the Cheltenham Grand Annual Challenge Cup Steeplechase.

Upon retiring, Graham Thorner became a trainer at Wantage in Oxfordshire and among the best horses he turned out were Get Out Of Me Way, Inish Glora and King's Parade. He is still a regular visitor to Aintree on Grand National day, where his informed and enlightened pre-race comments on all contestants are eagerly sought by the press.

Thomas Carberry

Born on 16 September 1941 at Garristown in County Dublin, Tommy Carberry became an apprentice with trainer Dan Moore at Ballysax Manor in County Kildare upon leaving school but after two years he was considered too light for a National Hunt stable. Transferring to Mr J.J. Lenehan, he rode his first winner on the flat in May 1958 and became a regular visitor to the winner's enclosure, to such an extent that he won the Apprentice Jockeys' Flat-race Championship in that same year.

More interested in steeplechasing, however, he returned to Ballysax Manor when he was heavy enough and quickly established himself as one of the leading riders over fences in Ireland. His first encounter with the Grand National came when he was booked by the Lambourn trainer and former jockey Jack Dowdeswell to ride Mr What in the 1963 Aintree showpiece. The ageing gelding had won the race five years before when he'd been sent out by Irishman Tom Taaffe and in the meantime proved himself something of a Liverpool specialist, finishing third in the National in both 1959 and 1962.

Mr What started at 66–1 at Aintree and although his starting price reflected the old hero's chances, he gave his jockey a guided tour of those huge fences until being brought down four from home. Although not required for the race the following year, Tommy Carberry made his first successful raid on an English racecourse when winning the Massey-Fergusson Gold Cup at Cheltenham later in the year and a most memorable occasion it was. With the mighty Arkle leading at the final fence that day, the 8–11 favourite was challenged by Buona Notte and the striking grey mare Flying Wild on the run to the line and, riding a superb finish reminiscent of his days on the flat, Tommy got Flying Wild up in the final yards to win by a short-head from Buona Notte, with the Pat Taaffe-ridden favourite a length away in third place.

In 1965 he rode the French-owned Vulcano for Ryan Price in the National but, once again, his race came to an end fences from home when he was forced to pull up; 12 months later he fell at the first Becher's Brook when partnering Dan Moore's Packed Home. Riding this horse again in the chaotic Aintree event of 1967, like all the others except John Buckingham, Tommy encountered an enormous amount of interference at the 23rd, yet still managed to get his mount safely round fifth place.

For many years it appeared Tommy Carberry would never gain success over the demanding Liverpool fences and though consistently riding plenty of winners his efforts at Aintree remained unrewarded. Great Lark refused at Valentine's first time round in 1968; Kilburn fell at the second Becher's the next year; and after missing the 1970 race Tommy again had a fruitless journey when falling with Cnoc Dubh at the tenth fence in the 1971 National.

He did have some great moments on this side of the Irish Sea, however, securing a successive Cheltenham Gold Cup double with L'Escargot in 1971 and 1972, and also further afield when winning the Colonial Cup on Inkslinger at Camdem in the United States of America and capturing the Embassy Premier 'Chase Final also with L'Escargot in 1970. This great staying steeplechaser, owned by the former United States Ambassador to Dublin, Mr Raymond R. Guest, was aimed at the 1972 Grand National in spite of some reservations from Tommy Carberry concerning the gelding's suitability for such a daunting affair. Sure enough, burdened with top weight of 12st,

L'Escargot appeared to completely dislike everything about Aintree and in a contrary mood from the start of the race was knocked over by another horse at the first open ditch. Undismayed, trainer Dan Moore immediately decided to try again the following year but agreed with his jockey that there was an urgent need to restore L'Escargot's interest in racing. At Listowel in September 1972, L'Escargot made his first appearance of the new campaign in the Kerry National over three miles, the main purpose being to hopefully commence an intensive preparation for a second tilt at the National. Giving nearly 3st away to the up-and-coming Culla Hill, L'Escargot performed brilliantly to get within a length and a half of this eight year old and all concerned with the dual Gold Cup winner expressed their delight. The next step was far more ambitious: a run at Aintree in the newly instituted William Hill Grand National Trial Steeplechase over two miles, seven and a half furlongs of the Grand National course.

On a bright Saturday at the end of October, Tommy discovered a new enthusiasm in the horse, with L'Escargot jumping the big fences with a flair that had been lacking when they last visited Aintree. Again giving away weight to all his ten opponents, the American-owned gelding was well in contention at the Canal Turn but when the outsider Glenkiln turned on the pressure approaching the penultimate fence, the weight difference told. Glenkiln, in receipt of 31 pounds from the Irish favourite, won by 12 lengths with the useful Gyleburn 4 lengths back in third place. Though perhaps insignificant at the time, it was a relatively new trainer named Donald McCain from nearby Southport who trained Glenkiln.

Another second placing at Punchestown followed, after which L'Escargot was sent back across the Irish Sea to run in the Sundew 'Chase at Haydock Park and after another perfect display of jumping Tommy Carberry produced another scintillating run from the last fence to beat the very good Spanish Steps by a short-head, with The Laird 30 lengths back in third place. Although beaten by a short-head back home at Punchestown in December by Lockyersleigh, L'Escargot had put up a splendid performance in this two-and-half-mile hurdle race and after finishing seventh in the Leopardstown 'Chase behind the favourite Sea Brief the hopes of all connected with the horse began to rise for his Liverpool appointment at the end of March.

Before then, though, there was the little matter of Cheltenham and a courageous attempt to win the Gold Cup for the third year in a row. For jockey Carberry, that National Hunt Festival at Prestbury Park could not have begun better, with Inkslinger – who had provided Tommy with that fabulous victory in America – winning the National Hunt Two-Mile Champion 'Chase on the opening day of the fixture. In the Gold Cup, L'Escargot jumped well throughout and, although there with a chance at the 20th, weakened towards the end to finish an honourable fourth behind The Dikler, Pendil and Charlie Potheen.

L'Escargot was Tommy's sole ride at Liverpool that spring and as the 38 runners paraded before the race there was plenty of support for the Irish pair, who finished up second in the betting at 11–1 behind the joint favourites Red Rum and the Australian champion Crisp. At joint top weight with Crisp on 12st, L'Escargot again jumped well in the packed field and was lying in 17th place at the Water Jump, while Crisp was a long way ahead of the rest. Still some way behind the runaway Australian horse at the second Canal Turn, Tommy began making ground through the 16 ahead of him and at the last ditch L'Escargot began to run on. Finishing third a good way behind the winner Red Rum and runner-up Crisp, Tommy was at last convinced that with luck they could win a Grand National. An even more intensive plan of campaign was introduced for a third assault on Aintree, with owner Mr Guest also convinced that at last he had a horse capable of winning the race he had for so long wanted to win.

It was a case of 'the best laid plans', though, when in his first race of the build-up to the National, at Listowel in September 1973, L'Escargot uncharacteristically fell. At Punchestown at the end of December, however, his jumping was back to its usual fluency when he finished third in the Morgiana Hurdle. Back over the major obstacles at Sandown Park in the Gainsborough 'Chase on the first day of February, the gelding demonstrated his well-being with a robust display, finishing in fourth place, less than six lengths behind the winner Kilvugan. After running down the course in the Leopardstown 'Chase, it was back to England for the Cathcart Challenge Cup at Cheltenham. Another excellent display of fencing kept L'Escargot well in touch throughout the race and it was only in the closing stages that the favourite Soothsayer got his measure and went on to beat him by four lengths. For Tommy Carberry, the Cheltenham meeting was not without its satisfaction, though, the jockey winning the Sun Alliance 'Chase on the Duchess of Westminster's classy youngster Ten Up.

On the first day of the Liverpool spring meeting, Tommy rode Dan Moore's Frou Frou into fifth place behind Clear Cut in the Topham Trophy 'Chase over the National fences and without any other rides at Liverpool before the big race, he was able to concentrate on the main task.

Again second favourite at 17–2 behind the Bishop Auckland-trained Scout, L'Escargot was well up with the pace for the whole of the first circuit and after jumping the Water Jump in fifth place settled well for the long run home. Tracking the leader Charles Dickens going to Becher's, they were out-jumped

119

at this obstacle by Red Rum and from there on all the survivors ran in the wake of last year's winner. In close touch at the second last, L'Escargot was beaten for speed after this, with Red Rum racing clear to win by seven lengths from Tommy Carberry and L'Escargot, with the long-time leader Charles Dickens third ahead of Spanish Steps, Rough Silk and 12 others.

A fortnight later L'Escargot had his final contest of that very busy term and again gave a magnificent account of himself in finishing second again in the Irish Distillers Grand National at Fairyhouse. Still convinced that their horse could succeed at Aintree, the whole team at Dan Moore's yard set themselves the task of preparing him for one last attempt at the supreme test.

To most racegoers, the gelding's efforts in what turned out to be his final season's racing were far from impressive and it became obvious that increasing age had blunted his speed. After finishing a remote sixth in the Molony Cup 'Chase at Thurles on his second outing, questions arose concerning the gelding's appetite for racing. When he subsequently performed lifelessly in the Leopardstown 'Chase, L'Escargot looked but a shadow of his former self.

In a situation impossible to imagine not long before, the horse was allowed to start at 20–1 for the National Hunt Two-Mile Champion 'Chase on the opening day of the reduced Cheltenham Festival fixture. Sadly, again he was well beaten into fifth place behind fellow Irish challenger Lough Inagh. For Tommy Carberry it was a low point in his career but the luck which appeared to have deserted him quickly returned later that afternoon when riding fellow countryman Jim Dreaper's Brown Lad to a comfortable victory in the Lloyds Bank Hurdle. Two days later, Tommy partnered the same trainer's Ten Up in the Cheltenham Gold Cup and, despite making a mistake two from home, recovered well to run on nicely and win by six lengths.

After such a successful spell at Cheltenham, Tommy Carberry obviously harboured thoughts of Aintree and his long-awaited appointment there with L'Escargot but he was forced to push such considerations to the back of his mind due to an engagement at Fairyhouse the Monday before the National. Teaming up again with the brave old warrior Brown Lad in the Irish Distillers Grand National, they proceeded to give the opposition a lesson in jumping and won by eight lengths.

The dreadfully heavy ground which had plagued much of racing at that time – and in fact led to much of Cheltenham's principal meeting being abandoned – was thankfully no longer a problem by the time everybody's interests became focused on Aintree. The feature race on the first afternoon at Liverpool was the Topham Trophy Steeplechase across the National fences and Tommy Carberry, again riding for Jim Dreaper, gave notice of his intentions when winning impressively on Our Greenwood.

This time carrying his lowest weight ever in his four Nationals, L'Escargot was receiving 11lb from Red Rum and with the dual winner aiming for an unprecented third victory in the race, the Southport-trained gelding went off the 7–2 favourite, with L'Escargot second-best backed at 13–2. Rough House, Money Market, Land Lark, Junior Partner and Rag Trade were the most heavily supported of the remainder. The start was delayed for some 15 minutes when Junior Partner spread a plate but when eventually despatched the 31 runners made their customary charge towards the first fence.

With Zimulator blazing an early trail, they all jumped the initial obstacle well, except for Shaneman, and at the next Junior Partner also departed from the contest. Glanford Brigg took over after Zimulator came down at the fourth and at Becher's Brook Spittin Image, Barona and April Seventh also came to grief. At the next, the seventh and smallest on the course, Tommy Carberry had a hair-raising moment when L'Escargot hit the fence very hard, almost unseating his rider. Losing his irons with the impact, Tommy finished up around his mount's ears, clinging to the gelding's neck, but with immense talent only a master horseman can demonstrate, he was soon back in the saddle and jumped the Canal Turn just behind the leading group. Back on the final circuit, Red Rum took up the running after Valentine's Brook but at the very next fence L'Escargot was racing alongside the leader and running well within himself. Both Brian Fletcher on Red Rum and Tommy astride L'Escargot watched throughout their run for home for the other to make the slightest mistake, but with two great horses such as these they could have waited forever and now was the time when true jockeyship came to the fore. Touching down as one over the final fence, the deafening roars were mainly for the favourite Red Rum, but with two stout-hearted horses and excellent jockeys riding flat-out the cheers changed very rapidly to be for both. Quickening the better before the elbow, L'Escargot asserted his authority to race away and win by 15 lengths from the very brave Red Rum, with Spanish Steps third, Money Market fourth and The Dikler fifth of the ten that finished.

The scenes of happiness in the winner's enclosure went on long and very noisily but in the finest warm-hearted manner possible the owner, Raymond Guest, announced that he was immediately retiring L'Escargot and presenting him as a gift to his trainer's wife, Joan Moore.

A season which for so long had caused anxiety and doubts had finally reached a wonderful climax beyond the dreams of those who had worked so hard to accomplish the impossible. Their greatest rewards were the memories which would live with them forever.

Now riding for both Dan Moore and Jim Dreaper, Tommy continued to ride many winners for both, as well as for other smaller trainers whenever available. At Cheltenham in 1976 Tommy rode a waiting race on Tied Cottage in the Sun Alliance 'Chase before sending his mount to the front at the last fence and running on to win most comfortably. He was without a mount for that year's Grand National but the following year he continued his Cheltenham winning ways with Town Ship in the Lloyds Bank Hurdle and the Daily Express Triumph Hurdle astride Meladon.

Partnering Jim Dreaper's War Bonnet in Aintree's big race in 1977, they parted company at the first when brought down and then, returning 12 months later aboard his former Cheltenham winner Tied Cottage, the 9–1 second favourite fell at Becher's Brook first time round when holding a clear lead.

That was Tommy Carberry's last appearance as a jockey in the National. Early in the 1980s he began training at Ballybin in County Meath. His success in this sphere was nowhere near as staggering as that which took him to the very pinnacle of greatness as a jockey. Having married Dan Moore's daughter Pamela, they raised two sons, Paul and Philip, and naturally the boys followed their father into racing, influenced greatly by tales of their dad's glory days with such horses as L'Escargot, Inkslinger, Flying Wild, The Brockshee and Anaglog's Daughter.

As time was to prove, the victory of L'Escargot was to be the last Irish-trained success in the Grand National for 24 years and when the luck of the Irish at last returned to Aintree, Tommy Carberry was there to witness it and enjoy an abundance of pride for more than one reason.

John Martin Burke

Born in County Meath in February 1953, John Burke came to England to ride as an amateur for leading trainer Fred Rimell in 1970, and while he rode his fair share of point-to-point winners he had to wait until February 1973 before gaining his first success under rules at Ludlow.

The occasion was the Ludlow Hunters' Steeplechase and the young Irishman put up a fine performance here to win on the locally trained newcomer Some Man. With stable jockey Ken White sidelined through injury, John Burke was given the opportunity to take over the further education of Rough House, a promising young 'chaser of Fred Rimell's. Their opening public contest together was the Overbury Amateur Riders' 'Chase at Cheltenham, when they finished a decent fifth. The following December, Rough House and John won the Stoneleigh Handicap 'Chase at Warwick.

At Sandown in January 1974, they romped home in a three-mile amateur riders' 'chase and after running on well in the closing stages to finish third in the Kim Muir Memorial Challenge Cup at the Cheltenham Festival, Rough House became a popular choice for the forthcoming Grand National.

Fourth in the betting at 14–1, Mr John Burke took the mount on Rough House at Aintree, a rapid rise for an amateur who was still young. They were among the leading division until falling at the first Canal Turn.

At the start of the next season John turned professional and was soon winning races for Fred Rimell on a regular basis. With Rough House winning the Charisma Records Handicap 'Chase at Kempton on his second outing, John looked forward to another Grand National with the gelding. He scored a hat-trick of victories with Sir Edward Hanmer's brilliant young novice Royal Frolic, won the four-mile Bass Handicap 'Chase at Cheltenham on Junior Partner and his third win of the season on Rough House in the valuable Great Yorkshire 'Chase at Doncaster.

Even more strongly fancied than last year, Rough House started third in the betting at 12–1 behind Red Rum and L'Escargot at Aintree on 5 April 1975 and, riding as a professional in the National for the first time, John Burke was hopeful that he would at least have a clear round. Alas, it was not to be. Rough House fell at the fence before Becher's first time round. That National was won, as previously described, by L'Escargot at his fourth attempt in the race. The horse which finished behind him in tenth and last place was the chestnut gelding Rag Trade, trained in Epsom by Arthur Pitt.

John Burke succeeded Ken White as Fred Rimell's stable jockey when the latter was forced into retirement through injury in 1976; his speedy advancement since turning professional was due solely to the jockey's talent and determination.

In what was to be a season to beat all seasons, Fred Rimell carried all before him in terms of prize-money won and the majority of those rewards were due in part to the dexterity of John Burke. Rough House again came good; Comedy of Errors improved in leaps and bounds; Royal Frolic impressed with every race; but the newcomer to Kinnersley, Rag Trade, initially flattered to deceive. At Ascot in January a recent import from Ireland, The Pilgarlic, carried John to victory in the Thunder and Lightning 'Chase and, brought along superbly by Fred Rimell, Rag Trade scored a fine victory in Chepstow's Welsh Grand National.

Royal Frolic won his third race of the campaign at Wolverhampton in workmanlike fashion and, at Haydock Park at the beginning of March, followed it up with a comfortable victory in the Greenall Whitley Breweries 'Chase. At the Cheltenham National Hunt Festival John Burke's mount was thought to be out of his depth against horses such as Bula, Brown Lad and Colebridge in the Cheltenham Gold Cup but, after giving a fine display of fencing, he stayed on really well for a five-length victory over Brown Lad, Colebridge and Money Market.

For many, the highlight of any jumping season is Liverpool and the Grand National, whether it be because of the unique unpredictability of the contest, the amount of money wagered on it, or the dramatic spectacle the race produces. The event is discussed far and wide for weeks beforehand.

John Burke came third on the first day at Aintree on the favourite The Pilgarlic in the Topham Trophy 'Chase over the National fences, second the next day with the outsider Keilder Forest in the George Novices Hurdle and, like all 31 of his rival jockeys in the big race 24 hours later, hoped for the best while fearing the worst.

On the basis of his victory in the Welsh Grand National, plus the present form of trainer Fred Rimell, Rag Trade figured prominently in the National betting, starting at 14–1 behind the favourite Barona and such notables as Red Rum, Jolly's Clump, Tregarron, Money Market and Prolan.

Away to a good start after only a three-minute delay, Highway View made the early running from Spittin Image, Money Market, Perpol and Nereo, with the remainder closely bunched behind. At Becher's, Tregarron, Tudor View and Glanford Brigg fell, while Spittin Image now showed the way to a group including The Dikler, Money Market, Golden Rapper and Prolan. Jumping the Water at the halfway stage, Spittin Image led from Spanish Steps, Golden Rapper, Money Market and The Dikler, with Eyecatcher and Rag Trade moving into prominent positions. With the survivors well strung-out by the time they reached the second Becher's, Churchtown Boy took over as Spanish Steps began to weaken, and Barona, Ceol-na-Mara and Sandwilan moved into challenging positions. Between the last two fences Red Rum and the Brian Fletcher-ridden mare Eyecatcher appeared to have the race to themselves, with the latter slightly having the edge over the famous dual winner. Landing on the flat, however, after the final fence, Rag Trade suddenly ranged up alongside the leading pair and, moving across to the stands side of the run-in, began gaining rapidly on them both. Striking the front some 200 yards from the line, Rag Trade withheld the powerful renewed challenge of Red Rum to win by two lengths, with Eyecatcher eight lengths further back in third place and Barona, Ceol-na-Mara and The Dikler ahead of the ten remaining survivors.

There were the customary ecstatic scenes in the unsaddling ring, with Fred Rimell jubilant at having welcomed back the fourth horse he had trained to win the world's greatest race. John Burke looked somewhat surprised at the extent of the congratulations heaped upon him. It was hard to believe he had ridden his very first winner barely three years before.

After only two visits to a racecourse, Haydock and Newbury, in the early part of the new season – both unsuccessful – Rag Trade appeared to have broken down and the delicate task of restoring him to full fitness began at the

Kinnersley stable. It was a worrying time for Fred Rimell and his team, with most of his former stars either injured or completely off-form and it was a period which ended with the trainer uncharacteristically failing to appear among his leading rivals in the top bracket.

It was a young bay gelding recently purchased in Ireland called Andy Pandy who became the main hope of the yard when he gave a prominent showing for John Burke in their opening contest together at Chepstow. Beaten a length into second place by Dawn Breaker in the Mercedes Benz 'Chase over three miles at the Welsh track, the jockey expressed the opinion that the horse needed a longer distance. His judgement was soon proved to be correct.

A fortnight after the Chepstow race, Andy Pandy won the three-and-a-half-mile Charisma Records 'Chase at Kempton Park very comfortably, despite making a number of mistakes which his connections knew could be ironed out in due course. Sure enough, just over a month later, John Burke enjoyed a fabulous display of jumping from the gelding when taking the Watney's Special Handicap 'Chase over a similar distance at Warwick. A disappointing run in Newbury's Hennessy Cognac Gold Cup was followed by a much improved effort when Andy Pandy finished fourth in a well-contested Anthony Mildmay, Peter Cazalet Memorial 'Chase at Sandown Park in January.

All at Kinnersley were now convinced they had a potential Grand National contender in their midst. These views were shared by many racegoers after Haydock Park's Malcolm Fudge National Trial 'Chase in February in which Andy Pandy gave a flawless exhibition of jumping and determination in holding off the late challenge of Sir Garnett to win somewhat comfortably by half a length. A long way behind, Red Rum finished last of the six runners.

Installed as the 15–2 clear favourite for the Grand National, Andy Pandy looked the picture of health during his final wind-up gallops at home and travelled to Liverpool with every likelihood of providing Fred Rimell with an unprecedented fifth success in the race. Just 24 hours before the big race, this eventuality seemed even more possible when John Burke rode the Rimell-trained Samuel Pepys to a shock victory in Aintree's Maghull Novices Hurdle.

Eventually away to a good start, the Grand National field made their usual powerful dash to the first fence. Not for the first time this obstacle took its toll, with Huperade, Spittin Image, Willy What, Duffle Coat, War Bonnet, Pengrail and High Ken all making a premature exit. When Winter Rain, Sebastian V and Castleruddery fell at Becher's, the outsider Boom Docker took up the running and quickly opened a clear advantage which, by the time they approached the end of the first circuit, had stretched to some 25 lengths. Still well clear over the Water Jump, Boom Docker turned back out into the country with Andy Pandy, Hidden Value, What A Buck, Brown Admiral, Roman Bar and Red Rum all now chasing the runaway in earnest. Without any warning at all, Boom Docker suddenly pulled himself up at the 17th, leaving Andy Pandy at the head of the remainder. Jumping with a fluency which was a delight to watch, John Burke's mount increased his lead at every fence on the run down to Becher's Brook for the second time. Here, Andy Pandy took off beautifully but the big drop on the landing side caught him out and he crumpled on landing. Seconds later Red Rum cleared the Brook perfectly, well on his way to re-writing the record books. John Burke was joined on the ground by Sam Morshead, who had fallen with another Rimell hopeful, Brown Admiral.

Some weeks later at Sandown Park Andy Pandy redeemed himself when carrying John to a stylish win in the Whitbread Gold Cup and the Irishman finished the season 11th in the jockeys' table with a total of 33 winners.

In 1978 he rode Brown Admiral into tenth place behind Lucius in the National a few weeks after partnering Connaught Ranger to victory in the Daily Express Triumph Hurdle at Cheltenham. The following year he came sixth on his former Gold Cup winner Royal Frolic in Aintree's premier event. He was less fortunate with his old Cheltenham hero in the 1980 renewal at Liverpool when Royal Frolic refused four from home.

Riding County Cork trainer John Walsh's Senator Maclacury in the 1981 National, John got the gelding round into fifth place behind the fairytale winner Aldaniti and, after missing the 1982 race, rode the 100–1 chance Hot Tomato in 1983. They were well tailed-off when falling at the last fence.

Shortly after that race (won by Corbiere), John took part in the making of the film *Champions*, the heart-warming story of Bob Champion and Aldaniti's struggles against adversity. Actor John Hurt played the part of Bob Champion and for the jumping sequences John Burke doubled for him by riding Aldaniti's double in the film, Flitgrove.

Aboard the strongly fancied Toby Balding-trained Lucky Vane in 1984, John rode a fabulous race on the nine year old to finish fourth, some eight lengths behind the winner Hallo Dandy but the following year he was less lucky, when he was forced to pull up after Valentine's Brook first time round when Lucky Vane became lame.

John Burke hung up his boots in 1985. While working for trainer Simon Christian at his Severn Stoke stables, he suffered a heart attack from which he died in February 1995. It was a sad end for a man who was a friend to everyone he met and who was a horseman of exceptional ability.

SIX

Thomas Brendan Stack

Racing records show quite clearly that many Irishmen have become champion National Hunt jockeys, mainly from a racing, point-to-point or hunting background. Tommy Stack, however, though most certainly a product of the Emerald Isle, differs greatly in this respect, for there was no hint in his pedigree which in any way indicated a future on the turf.

Born in County Kerry on 15 November 1945, Tommy was educated at a Jesuit College and upon leaving became an insurance clerk; a rather inauspicious beginning for someone whose future activities were to make him a household name. His eventual involvement in the unpredictable and often hazardous world of steeplechasing came about through two former schoolmates, Robert Barry and Barry Brogan. The latter frequently invited Tommy Stack to spend weekends at his home, which, as it turned out, was a racehorse training establishment run by Barry's father, the former jump jockey Jimmy Brogan. Soon captivated by everything to do with horses, Tommy began taking a more active part in the affairs of the stable, particularly after the sudden death of Jimmy Brogan.

With his friend Barry now in charge, Tommy readily assisted in any way he could and before long decided to attempt to make a future for himself in racing. Frustratingly, his letters seeking employment to ten of the leading trainers in England proved fruitless and it was only through a casual introduction to the famous Yorkshire trainer, veteran Bobby Renton, that the opportunity he craved came about.

Arriving at Renton's Ripon stables while still only 19 years of age, the would-be jockey Stack welcomed his involvement in the day-to-day chores of a racing stable. But more important to him was the chance to ride, if only on the gallops, on a regular basis. His first racecourse success came some two months later as an amateur, a capacity he continued in until turning professional two years later.

By the end of the 1970–71 season Tommy Stack had acquired for himself a reputation as a stylish and highly effective jockey, which was evidenced by his appearing for the first time in the top jockeys' table in eighth place with 50 winners to his credit. Still at Oxclose – the Ripon training quarters of Robert Renton – the 83-year-old trainer informed him that he intended retiring and Tommy was asked to take over the yard. Agreeing to attempt the dual role of trainer/jockey on a temporary basis at least, he rode the last winner saddled by Renton at Ayr on 5 February 1971 in the Girvan Handicap 'Chase over two-and-a-half miles. That winner, a six-year-old Irish-bred bay gelding, was named Red Rum.

Despite all his efforts and although gaining some victories as both a trainer and jockey, Tommy found the arrangement unsatisfactory. Before long he handed over responsibility for the stables to Tony Gillam. Straightaway his action in the saddle returned to its former rhythm and, always hungry for rides, Tommy eventually caught the attention of Bishop Auckland trainer William Arthur Stephenson.

Becoming first jockey to Stephenson was a major turning point in Tommy Stack's future career, for with an abundance of equine steeplechasing talent available to him he went from strength to strength. Among the important races he had already won were the Mildmay 'Chase at Aintree with Larry Shedden's Explicit; Haydock Park's Greenall Whitley 'Chase on the Ken Oliver-trained Young Ash Leaf; the Rowland Meyrick Steeplechase twice, with Jomon, and the Cheltenham Grand Annual Challenge Cup with Well Packed.

In his first encounter with the greatest 'chase of all, Tommy rode the 50–1 shot from Newcastle-Upon-Tyne, Final Move, into 11th place in the 1971 Grand National. The following year at Aintree he only got as far as the first fence where he fell with Saggart's Choice and after missing the event in 1973 he partnered Arthur Stephenson's 7–1 favourite Scout safely home, 11th of the 17 finishers, in 1974.

After he fell at the second fence with Clear Cut in the 1975 National, the usual cynical sections of the media dared to suggest that Aintree's supreme test was possibly 'one leap too far' for Tommy Stack. The fact that he became, at the end of that season, champion National Hunt jockey with 82 winners either escaped their knowledge or – more likely – proved an even more perverse excuse for criticising him. With the break-up of the Donald McCain and Brian Fletcher partnership, so long an integral part of the incredible Red Rum success story, Tommy Stack suddenly found himself the centre of attention as far as the press were concerned.

The 1976 Grand National produced probably more concerted and diverse interest than any before, with the incredible locally trained hero Red Rum attempting to achieve the impossible – an unbelievable third victory in a race so many great horses had failed to win even once.

Nobody realised the responsibility, sense of occasion or potential record-breaking task which lay ahead more than Tommy Stack himself on that first Saturday in April 1976. The single consolation was that at least he and his mount were not the most heavily backed of the 32 runners.

Producing his customary superb performance over those mightiest of all steeplechasing's obstacles, Red Rum gave a sublime display of perfection which uplifted his rider to a level of exuberance he had never before experienced. The majestic leap at every fence, the astute avoidance of interference and, most of all, the obvious delight that the horse displayed in being a part of this very special test which epitomises the eternal struggle of life itself, were all clear to see.

In failing to win that third Grand National Red Rum lost nothing in defeat, nor did his jockey Tommy Stack. What they gained far outweighed the loss, for Red Rum and his rider displayed, in a manner rarely seen, the dignity of grandeur hitherto only ever imagined.

In the jockey's own words:

> To partner such a being as Red Rum was more than a mere privilege.
> It was a gift from on high, a so rare opportunity to briefly taste the
> exhilaration of being a part of something unknown to but a select few.

Tommy Stack won his second jockeys' championship after a fabulous term of brilliance at the end of the 1976–77 season, which included a hard-fought victory on True Lad in the Schweppes Gold Trophy Handicap Hurdle at Newbury and a Cheltenham Festival success with the Ken Oliver-trained Tom Morgan in the Grand Annual Challenge Cup. But by far the most memorable moment of that year was, and would forever remain, that afternoon in April 1977, when Red Rum defied all the odds to win his third Grand National. There can be little said to describe the majesty, bravery and absolute perfection of an occasion which will forever be revered in the annals of sport the world over. What can be said is that on that day, still bright in the memories of all privileged to have witnessed it, a combination of horse and man found a common purpose which in its coalescence defied and conquered the bounds of expectation.

Sadly, later that year Tommy suffered a dreadful injury when, in the paddock at Hexham, his mount reared up and fell backwards onto him, resulting in Tommy shattering his pelvis. After many months in traction he returned to the saddle in early March, determined to ride Red Rum in the forthcoming Grand

National. Unfortunately, Rummy bruised a foot just days before the race and was withdrawn at the last minute. The Barnsley trainer Steve Norton provided Tommy with a late ride in the race aboard his ten-year-old Hidden Value but their involvement in the contest was short-lived for they fell at the second fence. His last big triumph of that championship year came at Sandown Park in the Whitbread Gold Cup when, making almost all the running on Strombolus, he resisted the strong, late challenge of Spartan Missile to win by a length.

Just a few weeks after this triumph Tommy Stack announced his retirement and subsequently joined the company responsible for the administration of the Coolmore Castle Hyde and Associated Studs in Ireland. He was based at the Longfield Stud in County Tipperary until taking out a full trainer's licence in 1988 and, still involved in thoroughbred breeding, has turned out his share of winners in his homeland.

Among the best-known horses he has trained are Kings Mill, Las Meninas, Title Roll, Kostroma and Runyon, and the major events he has won in his capacity as a trainer include the Goffs Cartier Million, Derrinstown Derby Trial, the Anglesey Stakes and the Irish Champion Hurdle.

It is always a delight and pleasure to encounter Tommy Stack at Aintree each Grand National day, when he is always ready with a stream of anecdotes concerning horses, jockeys and races gathered from the days when he was such a vital and valuable member of the English jumping scene.

Bertram Robert Davies

Born into a farming family at Frodesley near Shrewsbury in May 1946, Bob Davies was tutored by his father Eric and learned to ride almost as soon as he could walk. A fine horseman himself, Eric Davies had been a sergeant-instructor at the Weedon Cavalry school when serving with the Shropshire Yeomanry during the Second World War and was proud and delighted with the splendid progress his son quickly made in the saddle.

Young Bob was soon competing in all the local pony club activities and while still only eight years old was hunting with the South Shropshire hounds. Six years later he won his first point-to-point at Wheatland on one of his father's horses.

Gaining a Batchelor of Science degree in Agriculture caused little if any interruption in his riding pursuits and as an amateur he won his first race under rules at Newton Abbot's Easter meeting in 1966. Partnering an ageing Cornish-trained gelding named Ellen's Pleasure in the Dartmoor Handicap 'Chase, they won comfortably by four lengths and among the riders behind him were Josh Gifford and Sir Mark Prescott, who were both to make their names as leading trainers in the future.

Bob's total number of winners for that season numbered six, and twelve months later, still as an amateur but now riding regularly for trainer Les Kennard, that figure had more than trebled to take him into fourth position amongst the leading non-paid riders with 19 victories to his credit. With Chris Collins, Nick Gaselee and Brough Scott ahead of him in the table, Bob could feel well pleased, for those behind included John Lawrence and Tommy Stack. It was also during that purple patch that Bob tasted the excitement of the Aintree Grand National meeting, though not as a competitor in the showpiece event. Riding his father's horse Manicure in the Coronation Hurdle, they fell at the third flight from home but his enthusiasm remained undampened.

Turning professional at the beginning of the 1967–68 season, Bob Davies rose to prominence at a rapid rate and in the space of three weeks between 9 and 21 August he rode his first winner, Princely Act, at Devon and Exeter and then a treble at the same venue on Rich Flavour, Roddie B and Bigamist. With these quick successes he lost his right to claim the three-pound allowance but this in no way impaired Bob's ferocious appetite for winners.

Among his many other winners for trainer Les Kennard were Jack Valentine, Pennyless, Clarion Call and Aria Royal and the jockey's obvious ability soon attracted the attention of the Kingsbridge handler David Barons.

It was in that first term among the paid ranks of riders that Bob made a return trip to Aintree and this time he was among the 45 riders weighing-out for the Grand National. His mount was the Barons-prepared nine-year-old Beecham and although they made an early departure from the race when falling at the first open ditch he finished the season with 40 winners and in eighth position among the leading jockeys.

His strike rate increased during the next period of National Hunt racing and it was during this spell that another trainer secured second claim on the services of Bob Davies – Colin Davies of Chepstow. Among the 12 winners he chalked up in next to no time for this new retainer were Lucky Streak and Colditz Story, both at Haydock in January 1969. It was also during this session of jumping that Bob won his first race at the Cheltenham Festival, winning the Mildmay of Flete Challenge Cup comfortably on Specify.

Booked to ride The Inventor for Eric Cousins in the National, Davies took a nasty fall when Ashiq bungled the last flight at Wincanton just two days before the big race, leaving Bob with two broken vertebrae and out of action for a month. When fit again an exciting tussle for the championship with his future brother-in-law, Terry Biddlecombe, developed, ending with them eventually sharing the honours by each riding 77 winners.

Early victories in the next campaign – with, amongst others, Rock Sound at Ludlow and Cheltenham; Woodleighs and Prince Hilbre, both at Stratford;

Sixer, again at Cheltenham; Indian Yeldah at Kempton; Irish Laurel at Taunton; and a runaway win in the Grimley Novices 'Chase at Worcester on Steves Pigeon – set Bob well on the way to another excellent tally for the season. At Ascot in late November he won the feature event, the 'Black and White' Gold Cup 'Chase on the Wirral-trained Cool Alibi and at Sandown's Grand Military Meeting in the spring he rode a brilliant finish in driving Solomon II to victory in the Imperial Cup, beating the Josh Gifford-ridden favourite Potentate by a neck.

With most of his colleagues at Liverpool for the Grand National fixture, Bob Davies, without a mount there, competed at Devon and Exeter, where he won three events with His Lordship, Sea Dart and Kelanne. Although he was sorry to have missed two Nationals on the run, he finished up as champion jockey with 91 wins to his credit.

In what, by his standards, was something of a disappointing year the next time round, Bob Davies finished eighth among the leading riders with 57 victories, but he was back with a vengeance the following term to regain the championship with 89 winners under his belt.

In retrospect it seems unusual that a horseman with such outstanding ability, who, through a five-year spell, had won the jockey's championship twice and shared it on another occasion, should in that period not have ridden in the Grand National. This situation was remedied, though, in 1973, when Bob partnered Prophecy for the Barons' stable in the Aintree spectacular. Even having to put up two pounds overweight was considered no drawback for the chestnut he had already twice ridden to victory that year. Jumping well throughout a very fast-run race, Prophecy took the Water Jump in 18th position. With the main bunch still some way behind the runaway, Crisp, Bob Davies moved his mount nearer to the front at the second Canal Turn. Clearing Valentine's in 12th place, Prophecy was putting in his best work towards the end but was no match for Red Rum, Crisp and L'Escargot, yet he finished a respectable eighth of the 17 to complete the course.

It was to be another long spell before Bob again competed in the National, during which time he became first jockey to David Morley at Bury St Edmunds. It was this trainer who in 1977 provided him with his next chance at National glory. Riding Geoff Hubbard's Duffle Coat in that race which was to place Red Rum among racing's immortals, Bob got no further than the first fence where Duffle Coat fell.

For too many critics within horse racing, Bob Davies was no longer a force to be reckoned with over the sticks; he had lost his place in the annual championship table. As had happened so many times before, it took that greatest of all proving grounds, Aintree's Grand National, to force words to be swallowed and faces to redden.

In 1978, facing yet another Grand National as a mere spectator, Bob Davies received a phone call from the Penrith trainer Gordon W. Richards requesting him to ride Lucius in the big race at Aintree in just four days' time. The stable jockey David Goulding had aggravated an old back injury just two days before at Wetherby and it was a compliment to Bob that he was the first person Richards thought of as a substitute. Bob, of course, was delighted to accept the offer and although unable to meet his mount until National day, he was already impressed by the current form of the horse. A winner three times and only once lower than the first two in his other five races, the nine-year-old bay gelding Lucius had proved to be a tough and hard-working character. The only question mark about him was whether he would cope with the peculiarities of the Liverpool fences. But then that uncertainty applied to almost all the runners in the race.

To the relief of most of the competitors, the triple winner Red Rum was withdrawn at the eleventh hour but, that consideration apart, the Grand National was still four and a half miles of the toughest country anywhere in the world and as unforgiving and treacherous as it had been since Lottery first won in 1839.

The previous winner, Rag Trade, started favourite at 8–1, with Tied Cottage at 9, the locally owned Master H on the 10–1 mark and So, Churchtown Boy and Lucius also strongly supported at 14–1. From a good start the 37 runners raced away and after Teddy Bear II, Otter Way and Cornish Princess fell at the first, the usual strategy of most jockeys to settle into a trouble-free rhythm and avoid as much interference as possible was adopted. With the Irish challenger Tied Cottage proving a headstrong handful for his jockey, he charged over the first obstacles well ahead of the rest until at Becher's Brook he took one liberty too many. Lucius was left briefly in front until the Chair where he was passed by Sebastian V, Drumroan, Harban and Roman Bar. Back in the country for the final circuit Ridley Lamb was enjoying a wonderful ride on Sebastian V at the head of affairs. Over Becher's and beyond, the leader jumped perfectly while close behind Bob Davies held Lucius in check in the belief that something needed to be kept in reserve for the final run to the line. Roman Bar, Coolishall, The Pilgarlic, Lord Browndodd and the strongly ridden Drumroan all raced into contention coming to the 28th and it was here that Lucius made his only mistake, blundering on landing. Astutely allowing his mount time to recover, Bob brought Lucius right back into the fray at the last fence, alongside Sebastian V, Lord Browndodd, Coolishall, Mickley Seabright and The Pigarlic. Producing a well-timed run after landing safely, Bob took Lucius smoothly to the front where he was now strongly pressed by running-on Sebastian V and, in the final 100 yards, an extraordinary late challenge from the Irish outsider

Drumroan. In one of the closest finishes seen in the race for many years, Lucius held on to win by half a length from Sebastian V, with Drumroan a neck behind in third place and Coolishall, The Pigarlic, Mickley Seabright and Lord Browndodd finishing as close to the principles as one would see in a five-furlong flat race. Less than three lengths covered the first five past the post but for winning owner Mrs Whitaker, trainer Gordon Richards and certainly jockey Bob Davies, those seconds when Lucius held on for victory were moments to savour and remember forever.

The following year, incredibly, Bob found himself in a similar situation regarding the National, when through the injury of another jockey he was substituted on the morning of the race to partner Nicky Henderson's Zongalero. A 20–1 chance, the gelding was left in front early after the fall of Purdo at the first Becher's. Striding out well, Zongalero led the field back onto the racecourse at the end of the first round. Only just avoiding a massive pile-up at the Chair caused by two loose horses, Bob was still up front going back to Becher's Brook. It was here that the challenging Alverton fell and from then on the contest developed into a battle of tactics between the riders of Rough And Tumble, Zongalero, Rubstic, Wagner and The Pilgarlic. At the last fence there were three in line abreast – the Scottish-trained Rubstic nearest the stands, Zongalero in the centre and that immaculate jockey John Francome on Rough And Tumble on the inner. Staying out the trip best, Rubstic held off the persistent challenge of Zongalero to win by a length and a half from Zongalero, with Rough And Tumble five lengths away in third place. Once again Bob Davies had proved his tremendous talent in coming so close to a dual victory in the race which will always remain the most demanding for any jockey.

After incessant rain, the going on Grand National day in 1980 was atrociously heavy and resulted in only four of the original 30 runners completing the course – unfortunately Bob Davies was not one of them. Riding Mick Naughton's The Vintner, Bob was badly hampered at the Chair and eventually pulled his mount up after jumping the first fence on the second circuit.

Missing the race again in 1981, Bob partnered Stan Mellor's third-placed from that year, Royal Mail, in the 1982 renewal at Aintree but, when up with the leading group, they fell at Becher's Brook first time round.

Within weeks of his last involvement with the Grand National, Bob Davies announced his retirement. The jumping scene was the poorer for this decision. He became employed by the Jockey Club and has since carried out his duties as Clerk of the Course at both Bangor-on-Dee and Ludlow with the same commitment and sense of responsibility he showed when he was in the saddle.

Maurice Allen Barnes

The son of former jockey Tommy Barnes, who finished second on Wyndburgh in the 1962 Grand National, Maurice Barnes was born in Cumbria on 18 February 1951. As one would expect from such a pedigree, upon leaving school he became an apprentice jockey to his father.

His career was conducted mainly in the north of England on such tracks as Hexham, Carlisle, Perth and Ayr and appropriately he scored his first racecourse success with Proud King, a horse trained by his father, at Hexham in September 1969. Before the end of that season he had ridden the horse to a further three victories. During the following term, Maurice rode the winners of 15 races on such horses as Ocean Legend, Tipperwood, Skiddaw View, Fair Vulgan and Kilmogany Five.

Becoming attached to the stable of Charlie Bell at Hawick in Roxburghshire provided the youngster with the opportunity of riding a greater variety of horses and, without the benefit of a weight allowance due to the amount of winners ridden, Maurice continued to maintain a good average.

Among his early victories in the new season were two trained by his father Tommy – Grey Coat at Kelso and Proud King in the Huntsman's Handicap 'Chase at Teeside Park. Another of the jockey's favourites, Kilmogany Five, provided him with a hard-fought triumph when winning by a head, and then the same again from Chandigar and Off The Cuff in the Belston Handicap 'Chase.

At Newcastle at the end of January, Maurice Barnes was involved in another close finish in the four-mile-and-one-furlong Eider 'Chase, when after being overtaken on the run-in he rallied his mount Fair Vulgan to regain the lead and win by a neck from Sir Roger and The Spaniard. It was the jockey's most important victory so far and at the beginning of April he made his first acquaintance with Aintree.

Taking the leg-up on Kilmogany Five in the important Topham Trophy 'Chase over one circuit of the Grand National course, they made a mistake at the Water Jump and from there on trailed the leaders until being brought down at the second open ditch.

A little over a week later at Ayr, Maurice gave one of the most brilliant displays of horsemanship ever seen at the end of an important steeplechase. Riding the seven-year-old Quick Reply for Charlie Bell in the Scottish Grand National, he began making steady progress from the eighth fence to take up the running at the third-last but two fences later, the gelding made a complete hash of the final obstacle and although Maurice Barnes made a fine recovery he lost his irons in the process. Strongly challenged on the run for home by both Slaves Dream and Esban, Maurice responded resolutely by riding out a finish more appropriate to a five-furlong sprint to win by two lengths and a head.

During the following season, Maurice struck up a successful partnership with a horse named London Express, which carried him to 4 of the 21 victories he recorded that term and over the next four years. Although his career was almost completely confined to the northern circuits, he maintained an average of 24 wins for each period of activity.

It was in March 1977 that Maurice was engaged to ride a horse at Wetherby which would eventually bring his name to the fore of steeplechasing renown. The eight-year-old Rubstic had only recently come under the care of trainer John Leadbetter at Denholm in Roxburghshire, after proving a little disappointing for Penrith handler Gordon W. Richards. The rendezvous for the first meeting of horse and jockey was Wetherby in Yorkshire; their undertaking, the Micklethwaite Handicap Hurdle over three miles. Keeping his mount well to the fore during the course of the contest, the gelding jumped splendidly all the way and, though outpaced in the closing stages by the winner Sun Lion and runner-up Midao, he put his best work in at the finish to secure a respectable third. Ten days later at Ayr they finished third again, this time over the major obstacles in the Arthur Challenge Cup 'Chase and the fact that both horses in front of them were seasoned 'chasers gave rise to optimism for the future.

During the 1977–78 season Rubstic had three different jockeys before being re-united with Maurice Barnes and, from there, the partnership went from strength to strength. Third in a three-mile-and-three-furlong 'chase at Ayr, an all-the-way victory in the St Helens Handicap 'Chase over three and a half miles at Haydock, and a very creditable second over the same distance in the Stan Mellor Cup at Nottingham brought the opening part of that term to a most satisfactory conclusion. With the New Year came the most severe test – the four-mile Bass Handicap 'Chase at Cheltenham. Once again Rubstic and Maurice Barnes gave an extremely good account of themselves. Always prominent, the gelding's jumping was faultless and if they were little outpaced in the closing stages they still finished a highly commendable fourth behind some very good staying 'chasers.

At Kelso in March they were again fourth behind King Con after making a series of mistakes, but a week later at Sedgefield Rubstic simply toyed with the opposition in the Durham National to win by ten lengths from Cartwright and Little Swift. A most ambitious, yet necessary, task awaited Barnes and Rubstic in their next engagement, the William Hill Scottish National over an extended four miles at Ayr. Up against such seasoned performers as Peter Scot, Coolishall, Sebastian V, Current Gold and Sand Pit, John Leadbetter's representative was allowed to start at 11–1. Yet again, keeping pace throughout with the leaders, Rubstic fenced fluently with speed the whole way and, running on well in the closing stages, finished a good second, seven lengths behind the winner King Con, who was in receipt of 15 pounds from the runner-up. Back at Haydock Park on May Day in 1978, Rubstic and Maurice finished fifth, just over seven lengths behind the winner Cancello, over a distance now obviously too short for the Scottish-trained gelding.

A carefully planned programme for Rubtsic was now initiated for 1979, with the Grand National the main aim. Everyone connected with the project was excited, hopeful, but above all dedicated to the purpose of the exercise.

Extraordinarily, Maurice Barnes found himself facing a Grand National for the first time with a horse also new to Aintree who had been trained by a man in Scotland who very few within racing had even heard of. As always, the opposition on the big day was daunting, quite apart from the awesome severity of the course itself. With the Cheltenham Gold Cup winner Alverton and his partner Jonjo O'Neill heading the market at 13–2, the unknown team from north of the border drew little attention and held little appeal. Mr Snowman, American-ridden Ben Nevis, Coolishall, Rough And Tumble, Rambling Artist and The Pilgarlic all attracted their share of support, but among the 34 contestants some late money for Rubstic lowered his odds to 25–1 by the time of 'the off'.

Right from the start, Bob Champion took Purdo to the front in an attempt to avoid early interference and at the first fence they were clear of the fallers Vindicate, Sandwilan and Wayward Scot. Purdo came down at the first Becher's, whereupon Bob Davies found himself at the head of affairs with Zongalero. He was still there when approaching the Chair, at which point Alverton suddenly came into contention. Two riderless horses had ranged up alongside the leaders over the previous two fences but at the biggest and widest obstacle on the course they suddenly decided to wreak their havoc. Cutting right across the front of the oncoming runners, the delinquent pilotless horses brought no less than nine runners to the end of their quest. Alverton, Rough And Tumble and Zongalero now commanded the procession back into the country but at Becher's, for the last time, Alverton misjudged his leap and fell, fatally injured. With Maurice Barnes carefully steering Rubstic through the chaos, they joined contention with the front-runners crossing the Melling Road for the final time. At the last fence they breasted the obstacle together with Rough And Tumble and Zongalero. Staying on by far the better on that long run to the winning post, Rubstic ran out his race in the bravest possible manner to win by a length and a half from Zongalero, with Rough And Tumble five lengths further back in third place and the remaining survivors, The Pilgarlic, Wagner, Royal

Frolic and Prime Justice, bravely seeing out the journey in the gamest fashion.

For the very first time in the history of this tremendous event, a horse trained in Scotland had at last captured steeplechasing's greatest prize. Even more significant was the fact that those so often forgotten – though vitally valuable – participants of this 'pastime of the Gods' had achieved that which so few can even dare hope to accomplish.

Attempting a repeat victory the following year, Rubstic, the 8–1 favourite, this time found the Chair one leap too far, tumbling out of the contest at the halfway stage to the dismay of all. As a veteran performer in that emotional National of 1981, Rubstic as always gave his all and jumped brilliantly to finish seventh behind Aldaniti and Bob Champion. It was a most fitting swansong for both Rubstic and Maurice Barnes, partners for one splendid moment in time, a moment of glory which evades countless thousands and which only the blessed can appreciate to the full.

Like his father before him, Maurice Barnes became a trainer when he finally called it a day as a jump jockey and, most fittingly, returned as a guest of the executive of Aintree in April 1995 to take part a special fund-raising enterprise in aid of the Bob Champion Cancer Research Trust. The opening event on Grand National day 1995 was the Martell Bob Champion Cancer Trust Handicap Stakes over six furlongs on the flat and comprising ten past winning Grand National jockeys. Totally removed from the experience which they all encountered during their illustrious gallop to glory, their sprint that afternoon allowed no time for tactics or strategy but, in a momentary glimpse of days long gone, Maurice Barnes brought the Preston-trained seven-year-old Chinour home a clear length-and-a-half winner from Bob Champion on Invocation, with Tommy Stack third on Sharp Conquest and Tommy Carberry fourth on Great Hall.

Still a regular visitor to Aintree in his capacity as a trainer, Maurice Barnes is always a jovial, interesting and voluble companion to all who venture to engage him in conversation. But most of all he remains that jockey 'from the sticks' who showed them all the way home on the day it mattered most.

Charles Fenwick

If, as many say, it takes all types to make a world, then Charlie Fenwick must surely number among those types. A person of intense determination, he set himself at a very early age an assignment which few but the very wealthy or those possessed of the most vibrant imagination could ever dream of accomplishing.

A merchant banker from Baltimore in the United States of America with unlimited financial resources at his disposal, Fenwick was a highly talented horseman in his own country who had already won the famous Maryland Hunt Cup over timber three times. Yet still his burning desire was to ride the winner of the Aintree Grand National, a race about which as a young boy he had heard a great deal from his grandfather, Mr Howard Bruce. It was this gentleman who had, in 1928, watched with excitement as his own Maryland Hunt Cup winner, Billy Barton, came to the final fence in the Grand National alongside the only other survivor of a most calamitous race, the 100–1 outsider Tipperary Tim. The drama of Billy Barton's last fence fall, resulting in the first 100–1 winner of the great race, has long passed into Aintree folklore but for the grandson of Howard Bruce that dream of success so cruelly snatched from his ancestor became the focus of his future pursuit.

It was while on a shooting holiday a long way from his native Maryland that Charlie Fenwick's father-in-law, Raymond C. Stewart junior, discussed over dinner with his Yorkshire guests the possible purchase of a six-year-old chestnut named Ben Nevis. Naturally unaware of the gelding's lamentable past form in point-to-points, he inspected the animal in a field the following day and bought him, untried, on the spot. Upon arriving in America, Ben Nevis was given much closer scrutiny by Charles Fenwick, who secretly suspected his father-in-law must have been enjoying some fine liquid refreshment at the time he purchased such a creature. Not only was the horse small and weedy-looking but, within minutes of encountering the newcomer, Charlie detected an excitability and hot temper which, to say the least, was disconcerting.

Put into training, though, the horse showed an unusual interest in all aspects of his preparation and his new surroundings. Even more importantly, he adapted incredibly well to the new type of timber obstacles he was faced with. To everyone's surprise and extreme delight, Ben Nevis ran up a sequence of 12 wins in his adoptive country, including the Maryland Hunt Cup in both 1977 and 1978 and on the latter occasion he set up a new time record for the race. In all his races he was ridden by Charlie Fenwick and after that second memorable victory in Maryland's most famous steeplechase the rider decided to discover if the horse could possibly be suitable for Aintree. There was only one place to ascertain this and that was back in England, with a trainer who knew his trade fully, including the requirements for a likely Grand National contestant.

The man chosen was Captain Tim Forster of Wantage in Oxfordshire, who had already trained Well To Do to win the Aintree classic and had an impressive record at every level of the sport. For their attempt in the Grand National, Charlie took a four-and-a-half-month break from his career as a banker and moved his wife Ann, together with their two daughters, son and nanny, to

England where he himself also needed to prepare for the British 'way of 'chasing'.

After 12 wonderful victories in the States, Ben Nevis and Charlie suffered seven ignominious failures in their first term on this side of the Atlantic, yet the gelding's reputation over timber and the rider's obvious dedication inspired the British public sufficiently for them to start joint fourth favourite in the 1979 National betting at 14–1.

On the good ground which he acted best on, Ben Nevis jumped superbly and kept well in touch with the leaders out in the country and back onto the racecourse near the end of the first circuit. With a cluster of loose horses preceding them, the leading group suddenly faced that dilemma which all jockeys most detest. With a riderless horse careering to and fro in front of the gaping ditch which forms only the first part of the fearsome obstacle the Chair, Ben Nevis collided with the confused animal while jumping. Charlie Fenwick was not the only rider whose National hopes ended at the 15th jump; eight others also were brought down or fell amid the chaos.

Determined to keep the dream alive, Charlie returned to America leaving Ben Nevis behind with Tim Forster to be trained again for a second appointment with Liverpool's famous test of spirit, commitment and skill. This time round, Charlie was unable to take an extended leave of absence to ready himself for the fray ahead and on five occasions before the Grand National of 1980, he took weekend flights to and from the United Kingdom to ride Ben Nevis in the events chosen by the trainer as a build-up for the greatest race of all. Coming second at Lingfield and Warwick in November proved to be promising performances for what lay ahead but it had to be admitted that the gelding's form was less appealing than that shown the previous season.

Still without a win after 12 races in this country, Ben Nevis was this time totally ignored in the Grand National betting at 40–1, albeit more because of the dreadfully heavy going he hated than his disappointing lack of form. Last year's winner Rubstic was 8–1 favourite, with Jer, Zongalero, Rough And Tumble and Another Dolly also well supported. As they lined up at the start, Ben Nevis's connections were most concerned to see that the gelding was sweating up badly.

Once on their way, the awful rain-soaked ground began to take its toll, with Jer, Mannyboy, Salkeld and Churchtown Boy falling victims at the third and Another Dolly coming down with So And So at Becher's Brook. For the remainder of the first circuit, there were few other fallers but all could see when the runners approached the stands that they were finding the conditions very gruelling. Lying among the first four at this stage, Ben Nevis was obviously far from comfortable in the very heavy going but he bravely retained his position nearing the halfway stage. Delmoss jumped the Chair fully ten lengths clear of the rest and raced on, leaving Rubstic a faller here. Ben Nevis brushed through the top of the obstacle which had eliminated him from the previous year's contest – his only semblance of a mistake this time. Back out in the country, he moved into second place behind Delmoss. Another seven fell by the wayside at the 19th and with many now visibly labouring it became apparent that there were only going to be a handful of finishers. Surprisingly still bowling along on the going that was completely against him, Ben Nevis made a forward move going into Becher's for the last time and jumped it perfectly alongside Delmoss, who, now exhausted, fell on landing. Three To One and Jimmy Miff also came down here and with Ben Nevis out on his own over the Canal Turn and Valentine's his nearest rivals were Rough And Tumble and The Pilgarlic. With only three fences left, Ben Nevis held a clear advantage over just three solitary rivals. Although the nearest of these, John Francome on Rough And Tumble, reduced his lead to seven lengths coming to the last, Charlie Fenwick simply concentrated his efforts in safely clearing it. Landing well, Ben Nevis galloped courageously away to win, passing the winning post 20 lengths clear of Rough And Tumble, with The Pilgarlic ten lengths further back in third place and the only other to complete the course, Philip Blacker on Royal Stuart, a remote fourth.

Dazed disbelief, numbness and consummate pride formed an interesting combination on the face of 32-year-old Charlie Fenwick as he was interviewed by David Coleman for BBC Television. Among those he paid the greatest tributes to were the gallant Ben Nevis, the owner Redmond Stewart and a man named Howard Bruce, his grandfather who, 52 years earlier, had suffered the sadness of defeat in a race with a far less rewarding conclusion. Charlie Fenwick was the first amateur rider to win the National since 'Tommy' Smith 15 years before. He too was an American.

Robert Champion MBE

In every sphere of human endeavour, there are rare moments of sublime achievement when the spirit is lifted with admiration and the heart filled with a pride inexplicable, overwhelming and heart-warming. The mastery of Don Bradman knocking spots off English bowlers; the grace and humility of Jesse Owens overcoming prejudice at its most vile in the Berlin Olympics; Edmund Hilary and Sherpa Tensing risking all in their singular battle against the elements; and that dignified footballer Bobby Moore raising the Jules Rimet World Cup to an adoring nation at Wembley in 1966 – all moments to enjoy, to cherish and, most of all, to remember when our own lives reach a stage when we question its purpose. In the last 25 years of the twentieth century, another person emerged, from the unlikely surroundings of the world of steeplechasing, to lay claim for the right of inclusion into such a place in history.

Not that Bob Champion ever set out with such high intentions, or indeed that he expected to do anything other than earn a living doing something which gave him his greatest pleasure: riding horses over obstacles in races.

Born on 4 June 1948 into a family in the north-east of England which could claim to have seven generations of professional huntsmen in their lineage, it would no doubt have been considered sheer heresy for the latest male addition to the Champion clan to think of any other livelihood than one associated with horses. As a small boy, however, Bob initially developed a dislike of horses as a result of falling from his pony into a patch of stinging nettles. For some time his main interests consisted of pottering about on a local farm and, above all, driving the tractors there.

At the age of ten, young Bob at last began to overcome his fear of horses and was soon spending all his spare time with them, either grooming them, exercising them or, best of all, riding them over any obstacles he could find. When he was 15 Bob was sent to live with an aunt and uncle who had a farm in Wiltshire and although this involved him having to attend a nearby technical college he was delighted to discover that his new guardians invariably had a couple of point-to-point horses in training. He was soon a regular competitor at many point-to-points and rode his first winner, Holmcourt, in the Tedworth Adjacent Hunts race at Larkhill.

By now determined to become a jockey, by the age of 19 he was an accomplished enough horseman to be taken on by trainer Toby Balding at Fyfield near Andover in Hampshire, as one of a number of amateurs employed there. To secure his amateur status Bob doubled as a temporary farm manager at the training establishment but within a few days he broke several bones in his foot when a horse he was riding rolled over with him. Prior to being allowed back in the saddle, Bob had to work in Mr Balding's office, but before long and to his great delight he was given the chance to ride in his first race under rules on the novice Swiss Knight over fences at Worcester. Pulling his mount up on that occasion, Bob scored his first success at Plumpton on the 20–1 outsider Altercation, much to the surprise of everyone at the yard.

Towards the end of April 1968 he had ridden a total of eight winners as the amateur Mr Champion but after some misunderstanding with the stewards of the Jockey Club Bob was requested to take out a professional jockey's licence, which was duly issued on 6 May. One week later, at Wye, he won his first race as a 'rider for hire' on the Toby Balding-trained Sailor's Collar.

142

In February 1969, with both his main jockeys unavailable to ride the veteran Highland Wedding in the four-mile Eider Steeplechase at Newcastle, trainer Balding took a chance with the enthusiastic young Bob Champion. On very soft ground, which was in his mount's favour, Bob rode a copybook race all the way, survived a last-fence error by his horse and still won fairly comfortably. At the end of March, Highland Wedding won the Grand National with Eddie Harty back on board.

By the end of that season Bob had a total of 15 winners to his credit but over the next few years, having lost his claiming allowance, he entered that lean period all jockeys in such a position encounter. Rides came few and far between and he began to seriously have doubts about his future in the sport he so enjoyed. To cap it all, Bob suffered a broken left ankle while preparing to take a horse on the gallops. It was not until 12 January 1971 that he once again enjoyed the thrill of riding into the winner's enclosure, this time at Nottingham after winning with You're Lucky. A few weeks later, at Taunton, he won on a little mare called Country Wedding and was over the moon when Toby Balding informed him he would be riding her again in the Grand National at Aintree.

It was a dream come true for Bob, who, like all jump jockeys, hoped against hope that one day he would discover the thrill of riding in that most famous of all steeplechases. The elation was too quickly extinguished this time, though, with Country Wedding being brought down at the very first fence when last year's winner Gay Trip fell directly in front of them. It was a similar story the following year at Aintree, when Country Wedding fell at Valentine's Brook first time round. Once more, with only ten winners for the period, Bob was in the doldrums.

After five years with Toby Balding, Bob left his employ, feeling that he was getting nowhere fast, and decided to give freelancing a try. Almost at once he was offered a retainer by a new trainer just setting up at Lucknam Park near Chippenham in Wiltshire. Monty Stevens was the man's name and on his third ride for him at the beginning of the 1972–73 season Bob rode Winden to a 12-length victory at Devon and Exeter. His new surroundings and racing commitments brought a welcome turn of luck for Bob Champion, with visits to the winner's enclosure becoming much more frequent. Equally encouraging were the offers of rides from other trainers.

His third attempt in the Grand National came in 1973, the year Red Rum made up an impossible amount of ground after the last fence to win in the closing strides of the race. Bob's mount, Hurricane Rock, was one of those 100–1 no-hopers who over the last couple of years had completely lost his form, his interest and most of all any ability he formerly had. To everyone's surprise, none more so than his jockey, Hurricane Rock ran a fabulous race and incredibly, moved into third place behind Crisp and Red Rum approaching the third-last. Still in that position after landing over the final obstacle, Hurricane Rock had by then given his all and slowed almost to a walk by the time the winning post was reached. They finished a highly commendable sixth of the 17 which finished.

The tragic, darker side of racing came starkly, swiftly and so cruelly to the fore barely a month later at Newcastle in the Whitbread Gold Cup, when Josh Gifford's stable jockey, Doug Barrott, was killed when falling at the fifth fence with his mount French Colonist. It is the moment all involved in steeplechasing fear and yet live with on a daily basis, and in itself it is a testament to the courage, comradeship and quiet dignity of all who ride 'over the sticks'.

Bob Champion ended that season with 29 winners. Early in the next term he totted up a fair number of successes in a matter of weeks, which brought him the attention of Findon trainer Josh Gifford, a former champion jockey who finished second in the 1967 Grand National aboard Honey End. It proved a highly successful partnership, with Bob now starting to appear in the top jockeys' table. In 1975, he again steered a clear round in the National to finish sixth on Josh Gifford's Manicou Bay.

At Huntingdon on 25 October 1975, Bob won on each of his four successive rides – Man On The Moon, Blue Bidder, Captain George and Clare Dawn – all saddled by Josh Gifford. With Josh without a runner in the next National, Bob Champion partnered Lord Chelsea's well fancied Money Market and once again brought his mount safely home in 14th place behind the winner Rag Trade.

By now, though, Bob was beginning to have weight problems, often finding it difficult to make 10st 7lb and in the 1977 Grand National he actually rode Michael Scudamore's Spittin Image carrying 5lb overweight. They came down at the first fence.

Aboard the strongly fancied Shifting Gold at Aintree the following year, he had no need to concern himself, for his mount carried top weight of 11st 6lb but once again he failed to get round, this time falling at the tenth fence.

At Josh Gifford's Findon stables Bob had formed a strong attachment to a white-faced chestnut named Aldaniti, with whom he had finished a respectable third in the 1977 Hennessy Gold Cup at Newbury. There was an element of pity associated with Bob's affection towards the horse simply because, like himself, Aldaniti had suffered an ongoing series of setbacks through leg injuries. These considerations aside, the gelding had proved to be a dour battler and a stayer of some merit, just a little short of Gold Cup class. The horse did, in fact, finish a distant third to the ill-fated Alverton in the 1979 Cheltenham Gold Cup.

After a brief but interesting break in the United States, where he rode a number of winners, Bob returned to Britain in time for the start of a new campaign which quickly brought him his biggest win so far, a victory on Approaching in the Hennessy Cognac Gold Cup. On the last day of March 1979, Bob Champion went out on Purdo to compete in the Grand National for trainer Nick Gaselee and, after making the early running on the inside over the first five fences, they fell at the first Becher's Brook.

At Stratford in May 1979 Bob received a kick in the testicles when attempting to remount Fury Boy, who he had fallen with him at the final fence. In tremendous pain, Bob did manage to regain his place in the saddle and without irons went on to win the Brailes Novices 'Chase from the only other survivor. It was Bob's final win of the season and his 355th of his career. It came dangerously close to being his last-ever triumph.

Within weeks Bob Champion's life literally fell apart when, after receiving attention and examinations from specialists, it was confirmed that he had cancer. As was the case for so many unfortunate souls before and since, that word sounded like a death sentence. Over many torturous months he suffered dreadfully from the agonies and indignities of chemotherapy treatment. To face what Bob Champion – and so very sadly, a multitude of others – faced takes a certain type of courage for which no medals are awarded. Yet such is the miraculous depth of the human spirit that any horror is mentally sustainable. Throughout this, the most difficult and anxious period of his life, Bob retained his sanity with thoughts of a white-faced gelding carrying him safely and triumphantly in the Grand National at Aintree.

Bob was regularly visited by Josh Gifford and Nick Embiricos, the owner of Aldaniti, both of whom were aware of his fantasies concerning their horse and considerately refrained from informing him of the latest breakdown of the gelding.

The long road back from that harrowing encounter with the unknown was an ordeal in itself, with his muscles wasted, his vitality non-existent and a body so washed out that he couldn't recognise it as his own. Slowly but surely, and so very gratefully, Bob began to make progress, though, and he even ventured back across the Atlantic to visit his friend Burly Cocks in America. A major turning point occurred while he was there; he rode a flat-race winner, which was an enormous boost not just to his confidence but also to his resolution.

Once back in England, Bob found his old job at Findon had been kept open for him by the caring and generous Josh Gifford. Although his early rides proved less easy and natural than before, the patience granted to him by everyone at the stables started to bear fruit.

Gently nursed backed to fitness by that devoted groom Beryl Millam,

Aldaniti also slowly began showing signs of interest and energy in his work. When joined on the gallops by Bob Champion, that old buzz they generated in each other returned and it was as if the two old crocks each realised they had been given a second chance to justify their right to be.

Grand National day dawned bright and clear on that first Saturday in April 1981 and with 39 runners the customary annual frantic search by the public to find the winner once again produced the greatest volume of money the bookmakers would take in a single day. That brilliant hunter-chaser Spartan Missile was 8–1 favourite, with Aldaniti the next-best supported at 10–1 – due more to sentiment than assessment of form. Other tried and trusted friends attracting plenty of financial interest included Rubstic, Zongalero, Royal Mail, Royal Exile and Royal Stuart.

The rank outsider Kininvie went into an early lead and cleared the first well but, just to his rear, Aldaniti brought a gasp of alarm when he was almost caught out by the drop and landed nearly on his nose. Coping brilliantly with the lapse, Bob allowed his mount plenty of time to recover and continued towards the rear of the field. With Kininvie still making the running, he cleared Becher's in front of Choral Festival, Carrow Boy, Zongalero, Pacify and Tenecoon. Going well in 12th place was the favourite Spartan Missile and much further back on the wide outside came Aldaniti, by now accustomed to the peculiarities of the fences he was facing for the first time. After rounding the Canal Turn, Aldaniti surprised everybody by making a forward move and when Tenecoon fell at the big ditch after Valentine's Bob Champion suddenly found himself in front. Striding out beautifully on the run back to the racecourse, Aldaniti held a narrow lead over the Chair from Sebastian V, Royal Stuart and Zongalero. After clearing the Water Jump in this order, they swung round to the left and began the final circuit. Just when Spartan Missile was beginning to make ground from the rear, he made a costly error at the 18th and any chance of the favourite being involved in the finish seemed to have disappeared. A brilliant leap at Becher's Brook maintained Aldaniti's advantage and, still clear and running well within himself at the Canal Turn, his nearest challengers were the previous winner Rubstic and Phil Blacker on Royal Mail. The cheers began ringing out for the gallant leaders a long way before the finish, with virtually everyone present and countless millions of television viewers willing the resurrected horse and jockey home. At the third from home Aldaniti made a slight mistake and lost some of his momentum, allowing Royal Mail to move into a challenging position, but Rubstic was by now a spent force. At the penultimate fence Royal Mail struck it hard while the leader jumped clean and true and as Bob lined up the chestnut for the last jump they looked certain to win by a long margin. Landing safely on the flat, Bob sat down to ride out his partner – when suddenly, seemingly from nowhere, those tell-tale drumming hoof-beats brought the warning that Spartan Missile was gaining on them with every yard. From the elbow down that wickedly long final run to the post, Bob Champion forced every remaining ounce of energy in his battered body into one last supreme effort to turn that dream which had sustained him in his darkest hours into glorious reality. Responding excellently to his rider's urging, Aldaniti held on to win by four lengths from Spartan Missile, with Royal Mail two lengths further back in third place, followed by Three To One, Senator Maclacury, Royal Exile and Rubstic.

At a racecourse which so regularly produces results which stretch the imaginations of people the world over to the extreme, Aldaniti and Bob Champion, on that most wonderful day, surpassed all that had gone before, at least in terms of presenting the most emotional scenes of joy and well-being ever witnessed at any sporting venue.

An attempt to repeat that once in a lifetime experience in 1982 failed when Bob and Aldaniti fell at the first fence and for both horse and jockey it was their final appearance in competitive racing. When he retired Bob became strenuously involved with the Bob Champion Cancer Trust and through all the years since that most memorable day many millions of pounds have been raised through his efforts. A regular annual feature of the enterprise was the nationwide walk with Aldaniti to Aintree over a six-week period leading up to each year's National. The sad demise of that great old white-faced chestnut several years ago brought an end to that most appreciated effort but Bob still works tirelessly raising funds for the Trust he put his name to.

Taking out a trainer's licence in July 1982, he trained for a brief period at Newmarket. The best horse he turned out was Pats Minstrel, and the most important race he saddled the winner of was the Royal Artillery Gold Cup.

In the autumn of the year 2000, Bob suffered a heart attack from which thankfully he has now recovered, although it did prevent him being at Aintree for the 2001 Grand National. He did, however, host a gathering at the Royal Liverpool Philharmonic Hall just five days before that race in aid of charity and he received a standing ovation from the mainly Liverpudlian audience.

His and Aldaniti's story proves that dreams really can come true and they can, thank God, very often provide a new lease of life.

SEVEN

Mr Charles Richard Saunders

Born a farmer's son in 1933 in Northamptonshire, Dick Saunders could well be said to be a throwback to an earlier, saner and far more pleasant period of British history – to a time when standards still stood for something, good manners at every level of society were established from the earliest age and possessing a sense of purpose was recognised and admired.

He may well have inherited privileges denied many others but, far from taking them for granted, Dick Saunders involved himself from his youth in every level of farm work and in developing an energy and efficiency in all his endeavours. As a farmer's son, his concern for the countryside, all its inhabitants and their future came quite naturally to Dick, as did his attraction to the horse and everything equestrian.

A very competent rider from childhood, Dick's every spare moment was spent astride a pony with the pony club and later on the more robust of the species hunting and point-to-pointing. He began making a habit of winning the Pytchley Hunt members' race during his late teens but when his father gave him ten acres of land with instructions to 'get on with it', he more or less semi-retired from his riding activities to do just that. He set himself a ten-year target in which to expand 'his' farm to 1,000 acres, so his time in the saddle was severely curtailed while he proceeded to make a success of his career. Through sheer hard work and application, his land stretched to some 3,000 acres by the time that ten-year deadline was reached.

By the early 1960s Dick Saunders was competing in the point-to-point field again and it was soon clear that those years of lost competition had not impaired his judgement, determination or talent as a horseman. He began riding under rules in hunter 'chases, achieving his first success in 1966 and gaining over 100 further victories in this category of National Hunt racing, along with a similar number in point-to-points, before hanging up his boots.

In 1969 Dick was engaged to ride the outsider Steel Bridge in the Grand National after having won with him at Punchestown, but after having to put up 8lb overweight on the horse at Wye, where they finished unplaced, he was 'jocked off' for a jockey able to make the allocated 10lb. That rider was Richard Pitman and he finished second with Steel Bridge at Aintree behind Highland Wedding.

Dick did, however, often ride in the Liverpool Foxhunters' 'Chase over Aintree's big fences and in 1970 was aboard Lady Kin in the race when she fell at Becher's. Quickly remounting, he fell again at the 14th and once again clambered back into the saddle. His never-say-die attitude eventually earned him second place in the race behind the only non-faller Lismateige, ridden by Andrew Wates.

Seven years later he partnered the Stan Mellor-trained Alpenstock in the National Hunt 'Chase Challenge Cup, a race over four miles confined to amateur riders, at the famous Cheltenham National Hunt Festival. Moving steadily through the field in the final mile, Dick brought Alpenstock with a determined challenge at the second-last and drove his mount out for a comfortable 15-length victory from Kings Or Better and Dark Spectre.

Having ridden many of Frank Gilman's point-to-pointers for about 15 years, Dick and the Leicestershire farmer got on famously, which had more to do with their friendly, down-to-earth personalities than the fact that they were both farmers. Gilman bred and trained his own horses and after his stable jockey Terry Casey ceased riding to become a trainer his obvious replacement, so far as Frank Gilman was concerned, was Dick Saunders.

Gilman's pride and joy was a compact bay gelding he had bred himself called Grittar, the name being a combination of sire and dam's names, Grisaille and Tamara. Already having proved himself a fair hurdler under rules, Grittar was consigned to a spell of point-to-pointing to sharpen up his talents over the more exacting obstacles. In 1979 Dick Saunders rode him to an impressive win at one of the best organised point-to-point venues around, Newton Bromswold. The partnership was temporarily suspended when Dick received an injury and in his absence his 20-year-old daughter Caroline proved a worthy substitute, winning several point-to-points and hunter-chases over the next two seasons.

In February 1981 Grittar was reunited with his former partner Dick Saunders in the Foxhunters' 'Chase at Wetherby. Although always prominent in the contest, the gelding appeared a little one-paced over the final three fences, finishing fifth behind the Peter Greenhall-ridden Cheekio Ora. At Leicester on the second day of March, Grittar produced a sparkling display of positive jumping and stayed on most impressively to win by six lengths from

Oliver Sherwood on the very good Shannon Bridge in a field of 13. To many seasoned racegoers, the next step in the Gilman–Saunders plan of campaign for Grittar was bold, extremely ambitious, but also, many thought, woefully ill-advised.

The Christie Foxhunter 'Chase Challenge Cup over the exact Gold Cup course and distance of three and a quarter miles at the Cheltenham Festival as always attracted the finest hunter-chasers in the land and from across the Irish Sea. Such outstanding performers as Shannon Bridge, Persian Scimitar, Honourable Man and Queensberry Lad were in the line-up and with such formidable opposition Grittar was allowed to start at 12–1. Making a total nonsense of his market price, Grittar, superbly ridden by the ageing Dick Saunders, took up the running at the 16th and from there on made a virtual procession of the proceedings to win by an unextended 12 lengths.

So revealing was Grittar's performance at Cheltenham that when he appeared at Aintree some two weeks later the gelding started a hot favourite at 7–4 for the Haig Fox Hunters' Steeplechase over two miles and six furlongs of the notorious National fences. Coping brilliantly over those enormous obstacles, Grittar won even more emphatically than on his last outing at Cheltenham, keeping well to the fore all the way and, after going to the front at the fourth-last, streaking away to win effortlessly by 20 lengths from Sydney Quin, Flexibility and the veteran The Pilgarlic.

Rounding off the season with another all-the-way success by 20 lengths in Southwell's James Seely Memorial Hunters' 'Chase, the connections of Grittar now faced the problem of whether to risk their hero in next year's Grand National. That Southwell race had been run on firm ground and even the most cursory inspection of the horse could detect an alarming deterioration in the gelding's tendons, which almost completely ruled him out of even competing the following season.

Gradually restored to full fitness through the close season, however, a positive decision was taken. Grittar would be aimed at the 1982 Grand National. All his races leading up to it were carefully planned to have the gelding cherry-ripe on the day. Only one other man rode the horse competitively on that build-up, John Francome in the Whitbread Trial Handicap 'Chase at Ascot in February – and then only because Dick Saunders could not make the weight. After finishing second in that race, behind the Robert Earnshaw-ridden Cavity Hunter, Dick Saunders was back aboard when Grittar won his next race and on 18 March they had their final outing before Aintree. The event was Cheltenham's premier contest, the Gold Cup, comprising a first-class assembly of the finest jumpers in the land. Grittar performed splendidly to finish a respectable sixth behind Silver Buck.

Next it was on to Aintree, and the moment of truth for 39 horses and their riders. As always the betting was brisk, with Grittar maintaining his position at the top of the market at 7–1 from Royal Mail, the double-seeking Aldaniti, Three To One and Tragus. Away to a good start, Dick elected to take the inside route with Grittar and after jumping the first fence in touch with the leader Delmoss, he tucked his mount in behind the pacemaker. Ten horses failed to survive that first obstacle, including Aldaniti, and another four departed the contest two jumps further on at the first open ditch. The strongly fancied top-weight Royal Mail fell at Becher's Brook, while Choral Festival unshipped his rider there. With Delmoss still dictating the pace, he rounded the Canal Turn in front of Carrow Boy, Saint Fillans and Grittar, still hugging the inside rail. Well strung out as they crossed the Melling Road back onto the racecourse proper, Delmoss was still well ahead but a loose horse caused him problems as they jumped the 13th. There were only 17 left in the race as they jumped the Chair, with Delmoss still at the head of affairs, followed by Carrow Boy, Saint Fillans, Grittar, Tiepolino and the grey Loving Words, with the remaining survivors stretched out a long way behind. At the second fence back in the country the leader began to run out of steam and was easily passed by Carrow Boy, Saint Fillans and Tragus, with Grittar still moving smoothly up on the rails. Striking the front jumping Becher's again, Grittar amazingly was still so full of running that his rider chose not to restrain him and although losing a bit of ground landing over the Canal Turn, they still led comfortably at Valentine's Brook. From there on it was all over barring accidents and with such a superb horseman as Dick Saunders that probability was unlikely. At the fourth from home Saint Fillans and Carrow Boy fell, interfering so badly with Loving Words that the grey's jockey, Richard Hoare, was unseated. With a commanding lead at the final fence, Grittar made his only mistake of the entire race when jumping a little flat but, wisely left to correct himself by his rider, he landed safely. Although Hard Outlook bravely attempted a late challenge, Grittar swept clear up the long run-in to win by 15 lengths and a distance from Hard Outlook and the remounted Loving Words. In fourth place came the long-time leader Delmoss ahead of Current Gold, Tragus, Three Of Diamonds and the only other to complete the course, Cheers, ridden by Mrs Geraldine Rees.

The first to congratulate the winning rider after he had pulled up was Bob Champion, soon followed by a veritable tribe of people, including the trainer of the second horse home Hard Outlook, Andrew Wates, who 12 years earlier finished one place ahead of Dick in the Liverpool Foxhunters' 'Chase. Such are the strange twists of coincidence so often created by the greatest steeplechase on earth.

At 48 years of age, Dick Saunders was the oldest rider ever to win the Grand National as well as being the only member of the Jockey Club to triumph in the race. Immediately after weighing-in, Dick announced his retirement from the saddle and this decision means that he is one of only two men to ride in the great race only once and win it. Exactly 100 years before, in 1882, Lord Manners made his solitary ride in the event a winning one when riding his own horse Seaman to victory.

Dick Saunders is at present the senior steward at Aintree and, as ever, always finds time to chat to everyone he meets, with that friendly grin and that well-known winsome gleam in his eyes.

Benjamin De Haan

Ben De Haan was born on 9 July 1959. His mother was the housekeeper to Charlie Smith, a racehorse trainer whose brother was the famous flat-race jockey Doug Smith. On the suggestion of Charlie, the master of Uplands, Fred Winter, took Ben on as a stable boy shortly before the lad's 16th birthday and although Ben was as keen as mustard it was to be four years before he even rode in a race.

When he did, during the 1979–80 season, Ben displayed a competent ability and won his first race with Arctic Princess at Chepstow towards the end of January 1980. Eleven other winners followed at regular intervals, one being on his very first visit as a jockey to the Cheltenham Festival. Partnering Fred Winter's Stopped in the valuable Grand Annual 'Chase, Ben gave his mount a splendid ride to win most impressively from high-class opposition.

In 1981 he took part in his first Grand National on Royal Exile, finishing in sixth place behind Aldaniti and 12 months later lined up again for the race, this time on the Jenny Pitman-trained Monty Python. Going into Becher's Brook on the final circuit, Monty Python refused. By the end of that term, Ben De Haan had more than doubled his previous total to 25 wins and was starting to get noticed by other trainers, among them Mrs Jenny Pitman. With champion jockey John Francome as Fred Winter's stable's number-one pilot, Ben gladly accepted the offer of a retainer from the lady trainer, who was also beginning to make a name for herself.

It was a slow beginning for Ben at his new yard the next season and the jockey's first important success was saddled by his old guv'nor Fred Winter at Newbury in October 1982. The occasion was the Hermitage Steeplechase over two and a half miles. Astride the young black gelding Observe, Ben rode a perfectly judged waiting race before pouncing approaching the final fence and staying on well to win by two lengths from the favourite Straight Jocelyn, Dramatist and six other very useful 'chasers. There was, however, a horse in

Mrs Pitman's yard who was destined to raise the profile of both his trainer and jockey in next to no time. The chestnut Corbiere had lost a full 12 months, racing through tendon trouble but once back in action he showed signs of being revitalised in the Hennessy Cognac Gold Cup at Newbury in November, when finishing a decent fifth behind the subsequent Gold Cup-winner Bregawn. Exactly one month later, at Chepstow, Ben rode Corbiere to a highly revealing victory in the Coral Welsh National, the horse displaying outstanding courage through the final part of the three-and-three-quarter-mile trip to win by a head from Pilot Officer in a very competitive contest.

Jenny Pitman was by now convinced she had a very live contender for the Grand National in 'Corky' (Corbiere), and the betting public also felt the gelding was something special when making him 7–1 second-favourite in his next race, the Ritz Club National Hunt Handicap 'Chase at the Cheltenham Festival in mid-March. His jumping that day was faultless as always, yet despite putting in his best work towards the end Corbiere was beaten into second place by Scot Lane. Both trainer and jockey agreed the three-mile, one-furlong distance of the Cheltenham race was too short for Corbiere and accepted the fact that he needed an extreme test of stamina to be seen at his best. There remained only one place and one race where that could be guaranteed: Aintree and the Grand National.

With 41 runners set to start, the National was as big a gamble as ever. Last year's winner Grittar received most attention from the punters as the 6–1 favourite. Bonum Omen, Spartan Missile and Peaty Sandy appeared next in the market in terms of money wagered and Corbiere also came in for much support at 13–1, one point ahead of the promising Irish challenger Greasepaint. Two of the runners besides Corbiere represented trainer Jenny Pitman – Monty Python and Artistic Prince – but as stable jockey, Ben De Haan naturally selected Corbiere.

Quickly away from a good start, Ben was well to the fore alongside Delmoss at the first fence, where Tower Moss, Midday Welcome and the fancied Mid Day Gun came to grief. Over the first ditch Delmoss was applying his usual front-running habits followed by Corbiere, Royal Mail, King Spruce and Williamson, with the remainder close up. Coping superbly with the big fences, Corbiere was giving Ben an exciting ride and when King Spruce, Beech King and Three To One fell at Becher's Brook Ben had his mount well away from trouble on the inside of the course. Delmoss was still at the head of affairs over the Water Jump, closely followed by the Penrith-trained Hallo Dandy, Corbiere, Colonel Christy and Grittar, and of the remainder, Venture To Cognac and Greaspaint appeared to be still going strong. With Delmoss beginning to feel the strain, Hallo Dandy took over early on the second circuit and led over Becher's for the final time. Joined by Corbiere at the Canal Turn, these two provided a magnificent display of jumping over Valentine's Brook and the next three fences. Greasepaint was still going very well, just behind the leaders on the run back towards the penultimate fence and another Irish horse, the rank outsider Yer Man, had suddenly come into the picture, but having brought his mount safely this far, Ben De Haan was determined to hold his position. Two lengths ahead of the rest at the last fence, Corbiere doubled that distance with a faultless leap and, setting sail for home, appeared to be on his way to a decisive victory. Still clear at the elbow, Corbiere suddenly found himself with a real fight on his hands, as the strongly ridden Greasepaint came up with a most determined challenge in the final 200 yards. Whittling away the leader's advantage with every stride, Greasepaint drew ever closer over those last punishing yards but, hanging on gamely, Ben produced a spirited last-minute response. Corbiere held to win by three-quarters of a length from Greasepaint, with Yer Man 20 lengths back in third place, just ahead of Hallo Dandy.

The first woman to train a Grand National winner, Jenny Pitman could barely contain her emotions at the post-race television interview but she was noticeably lavish in her praise of Ben De Haan's jockeyship throughout the entire race.

In 1984 Corbiere carried top weight of 12st into third place in the National behind Hallo Dandy and the runner-up, again Greasepaint. They were just five and a half lengths behind the winner, after once more being given a splendid ride round by Ben De Haan. The jockey missed the race through injury in 1985, when Peter Scudamore deputised for Ben. Corbiere was foot-perfect and finished third, to the rear of Last Suspect and Mr Snugfit. This time he was just four and a half lengths behind the winner.

Re-united with 'Corky' the next year, Ben suffered the unusual experience of falling with Corbiere at the fourth fence. In 1987 he rode his old comrade in the race for the final time. Now 12 years old, Corbiere could still show his rivals how to jump those mighty obstacles but there were now younger and speedier competitors. He and Ben could only finish an honourable 12th.

Getting the leg-up from his first boss Fred Winter in 1988, Ben partnered Insure round Aintree safely for the first circuit but second time round was unseated at the 20th fence. Missing the 1989 National, he was back in the employ of Jenny Pitman in 1990 when he rode her Team Challenge into 11th place. Although the same horse refused with him in the race 12 months later, Ben steered Team Challenge round in 1992 to finish 21st behind the winner Party Politics.

Rather sadly, Ben De Hann's Aintree swansong came in the void race of

1993 when he fell at the tenth fence in the 'race that never was', aboard Jenny Pitman's Royal Athlete. Ironically, two years later, Royal Athlete won the National and provided Mrs Pitman with her second success in the race.

Ben De Haan now trains jumpers at Lambourn in Berkshire, providing a steady flow of winners each year, but can still be seen at Aintree whenever he has a runner there. It is appealing to look forward to the day when Ben will saddle his first National winner.

David Neale Doughty

The son of a Welsh steel worker, Neale Doughty was born in Kenfig Hill near Bridgend on 20 October 1957 and from his earliest years was besotted with horses. With the daring and exuberance only freely displayed by the young, Neale soon made a practice of slipping into the fields on his way home from school to ride any of the pit-ponies friendly enough to allow him to climb aboard.

His mum and dad, concerned that at the very least their son was trespassing, scrimped and saved to buy Neale a pony and from that day on his destiny was assured – although no one could have imagined to what degree.

The lure of the turf proved too enticing for Neale during his teenage years, prompting a premature departure from his studies and then employment in the racing stable of Fulke Walwyn at Lambourn and from there to the distant establishment of trainer Wilf Crawford at Haddington in East Lothian. It was while riding for this handler that Neale gained his first success, riding the outsider Gorgeous Gertie to win the Scone Novices Hurdle at Perth in September 1977. Among those behind him that day were such notable riders as Jonjo O'Neill, David Goulding and Ron Barry.

It was as a prospective replacement for the latter that Neale Doughty subsequently became employed by the Penrith trainer Gordon W. Richards and from that appointment the young Welshman's career took off.

Twelve winners during his second term were followed by 15 the following year and then, during the 1980–81 season, Neale really set the jumping scene alight, with a brilliant double success at the Cheltenham National Hunt Festival. Racing on heavy ground, he gave Current Gold a superb ride to win the Ritz Club National Hunt Handicap 'Chase by an impressive 15 lengths and later in the day was equally efficient when bringing home Lord Greystoke the comfortable winner of the Cathcart Challenge Cup. His total score at the end of that term amounted to his best so far – 21 victories. This was followed the next year with 33 winners by the end of the campaign, which included a good win on a newcomer to hurdling, Rushmoor, at Doncaster in January 1982. More importantly, Neale became acquainted with a recent addition to Gordon

Richards' string of jumpers, a cast-off from Donald McCain's Southport yard by the name of Hallo Dandy.

Something of a reformed character since moving up the north-west coast to the Lake District, Hallo Dandy had already displayed an aptitude for jumping the major obstacles with two good wins at Carlisle and Catterick before being aimed at a 'chase over Aintree's Mildmay fences on the day before the Grand National. Jumping well and running on at the finish, Neale gained third place in that well-contested event behind Peter Scudamore on Silent Valley. Some 20 lengths to the rear of Hallo Dandy, in seventh place, was the up-and-coming Irish horse Greasepaint. Their paths were destined to cross again at the same venue.

Twenty-four hours later Neale Doughty encountered for the first time the anxiety, thrills and sheer ecstasy of competing in the Grand National on his Cheltenham winner Current Gold. Despite the fact that the ground was unsuitable for his partner, Neale kept the horse clear of trouble through the first round before moving up into a challenging position at the second Canal Turn. Having jumped a bit low at one of the early fences, Current Gold raced on with a large branch of spruce attached to his girth strap. Not quite staying out the extreme distance, Current Gold finished a decent fifth behind the winning favourite Grittar.

On the second Saturday in April 1983, Neale Doughty weighed out for the Grand National to partner Hallo Dandy, a 60–1 outsider which had been carefully brought along by trainer Richards with but this one race in mind. Steering a course down the outside of the track, Neale patiently kept his mount clear of all likely interference throughout the first circuit but moved up to the leaders soon after passing the halfway stage. The nine year old jumped beautifully throughout the entire trip and, until running a little out of steam after the second-last fence, looked a threat to all the main contenders. Hallo Dandy finished fourth behind Corbiere, Greasepaint and Yer Man but that performance convinced both trainer and jockey that the next year could well result in a different conclusion.

Towards the end of that year, with the new term well under way, Neale won two valuable steeplechases with Gordon Richards-trained horses: the Mackeson Gold Cup with Pounentes at Newbury and a Doncaster feature event, the Freebooter Novices' Chase, with the highly promising youngster Noddy's Ryde. It was the latter which was to become his favourite racehorse but in time it would also produce his greatest grief.

Another pleasing success around this time was the one gained with Hallo Dandy in the Timeform 'Chasers and Hurdlers 'Chase over three miles at Ayr. Finishing a good second to Cockle Strand at Kelso the next time out aroused hopes that the gelding was coming along nicely for Aintree in the spring.

After a minor setback in Newbury's Hennessy Gold Cup, when he was pulled up, Hallo Dandy was off the course for almost four months but upon his reappearance at Ayr in early March it was obvious the time had been well spent. Looking the picture of fitness, he jumped splendidly all the way and was only beaten two lengths by Good Crack in what was generally regarded as a good trial for the National.

Three weeks later, Hallo Dandy joined 39 others in the line-up for what was Seagram Distillers Limited's initial sponsorship of the Grand National, a generous involvement which at long last secured the future of the great steeplechase. The day before the big race, Neale Doughty endorsed the fitness of his trainer's team when landing the odds on Noddy's Ryde over the Mildmay Course in the Sporting Life Weekender Novices 'Chase and it was no surprise when on the Saturday the odds against Hallo Dandy in the National tumbled to 13–1. Greasepaint was the 9–1 favourite from such well-backed horses as Broomy Bank, Grittar and Lucky Vane, with Corbiere, Eliogarty and Spartan Missile also well supported.

Away to an even break, the Peter Scudamore-ridden Burnt Oak went off at a cracking pace leading into and over the first fence – which, surprisingly, all 40 runners cleared without mishap. Last of them all at this stage was Hallo Dandy and it appeared that his jockey was quite happy to allow his mount to track the remainder in the early stages. Golden Trix was the first to fall at the third, with Burnt Oak jumping Becher's Brook in fine style well clear of his pursuers. Clonthturtin, Three To One, Doorstep, Hazy Dawn and Midnight Love failed to survive this most famous obstacle. Greasepaint jumped into second place at the Canal Turn, followed by Earthstopper, Spartan Missile, Tacroy and Grittar, and despite making a bad mistake at the 12th fence, Burnt Oak still held a long lead coming back onto the racecourse. Starting to show signs of weakening over the Chair, Burnt Oak's advantage was reduced to just half a dozen lengths as the remainder closed on him and, turning back into the country, there were still 30 runners left in the contest. With Earthstopper, Greasepaint and Grittar moving past the front-runner at the 17th, those following were well strung out and Neale Doughty began to make up ground from the rear on the wide outside of the course. Approaching Becher's for the final time, Eliogarty led narrowly from Greasepaint, Earthstopper, Two Swallows and Grittar. With another fabulous leap over the mighty Brook, Hallo Dandy moved smoothly into sixth place and well into contention. The Penrith-trained gelding was jumping superbly, gaining ground with every leap and, after taking Valentine's again effortlessly, Hallo Dandy joined Greasepaint at the head of affairs. Quickly opening a gap between themselves and the rest, it became a two-horse race crossing the Melling Road for the final time, with Hallo Dandy looking the stronger as they came to the last fence. Landing two lengths to the good with another terrific jump, Hallo Dandy strode away down that punishingly long run to the finish but Greasepaint came up with a strong challenge passing the elbow. With his mount pulling across to the stands side of the course, Neale Doughty really got to work and rode out the finish of his life to pass the winning post four lengths ahead of the very game Greasepaint, with Corbiere a length and a half behind in third place and Lucky Vane, Earthstopper and Two Swallows the closest of the remainder. To the surprise of all, 23 of the original 40 completed the course – a record number of finishers which still stands.

It was an incredible success for all connected with Hallo Dandy: for Neale Doughty, whose parents Joyce and Arthur travelled up from South Wales to see their son achieve the most fabulous victory of his career; for the owner Richard Shaw, whose one racehorse turned out to be a National winner; and most of all for that most modest of men, Gordon Richards the trainer. Not only had he discovered and nurtured the young jockey, he had also turned a cast-off racehorse into the hero of Aintree. He ended those three marvellous days at Aintree with four winners – Noddy's Ryde, Little Bay, Hallo Dandy and Jennie Pat – which contributed greatly to his finishing the season in third place of the leading trainers for winning prize money. Neale Doughty also finished in ninth position among the top 12 jockeys with 48 winners.

With such happy memories still to the fore, tragedy struck in the worst possible way in October 1984 when Neale took Noddy's Ryde out as favourite for a small race at Devon and Exeter, a long way from their Lakeland headquarters. After giving the most immaculate exhibition of jumping ever seen at the West Country venue, Noddy's Ryde came to the final fence with an unassailable lead only to slip on landing and break his off-hind leg, which of course ended not just a brilliant career but also his life. Nobody was more distraught at such a terrible end to a horse with such a brilliant career ahead of him than Neale Doughty, who had even named his Doberman after the gelding.

Neale was injured later in the season, which prevented him from partnering Hallo Dandy in the 1985 National, and without him in the saddle the former winner came down at the first fence. Once again, Doughty finished the term in ninth place, this time with 45 winners to his credit.

Neale took the mount again on Hallo Dandy at Aintree in 1986 and finished 12th behind the winner West Tip but, again dogged by injury, he missed the 1987 National. By this time Neale Doughty had been replaced as Gordon

Richards' first jockey and as the 1988 Aintree spectacular drew near he was again without a ride in the race. A last-minute engagement by Salisbury trainer John Fox, however, saw Neale in the Grand National line-up astride the 100–1 outsider Friendly Henry and, though never threatening the leaders, they finished a worthy sixth behind Rhyme 'N' Reason.

Completing the course again in the race 12 months later in seventh position, Neale gave his mount Gala's Image his usual talented assistance and in the 1990 National was back again, representing his old boss Gordon Richards on the promising 13–1 shot Rinus. They finished a respectable third behind Mr Frisk and Durham Edition. Joint second-favourite with Garrison Savannah at 7–1 in the 1991 event, Rinus was going particularly well, disputing the lead when he fell heavily at the 20th.

It was the same combination of trainer Richards and jockey Doughty which produced 9–1 third-favourite Twin Oaks for the Grand National in 1992. After overcoming some pre-race problems with his saddle, Neale rode his customary well-judged race to finish fifth behind Party Politics.

On that sad occasion in 1993, in what will always unfortunately be known as 'the National that never was', Neale Doughty finished sixth with On The Other Hand, proving – if proof were ever needed – that he knew his way around Aintree as well as any rider, and better than most. Of course, with that race being declared void, none of the six who completed it will ever appear in the record books but for Neale Doughty that fact is merely academic. He proved so often over those awesome fences that with the right partner he could never be overlooked and was a very lively contender.

After retiring from the saddle, Neale stayed in the north-west to carve out a future for himself away from the hurly-burly of the racecourse. He is as perceptive out of the saddle as when riding out a strenuous finish against the best riders in the land. Therefore developing and renovating old buildings amid the idyllic surroundings of the beautiful Lake District and then selling or renting them has proved a highly successful enterprise for this man who progressed from sneaking rides on pit-ponies to the highest acclaim any jump jockey could ever hope for.

A regular visitor to Haydock Park and Aintree, Neale is often accompanied by Morgan, his three-year-old son, who, despite showing a distinct interest in rugby and soccer, has recently demonstrated a desire to own a pony. Only time will tell if another generation of Doughtys will ever attain the heights which Neale Doughty rose to but should history repeat itself then young Morgan will have no finer role model than his father, a man who remains a credit to his profession.

Hywel James Davies

Born in December 1956 in Cardigan, Hywel Davies began his riding in the point-to-point field, just like so many other successful jockeys before and since. His first win in this environment was with a stubborn individual by the name of Hampton Boy and among other successes at this early stage of his riding career were Heather's Son, Romany Park and Knight's Queen.

Undaunted by the fact that his brother Geraint was forced to give up race-riding through continuous injuries, Hywel became attached to Josh Gifford's Findon stables in the capacity of an amateur rider and as such won his first race under rules at Fontwell Park in January 1977 on Mister Know All.

Within 12 months Hywel had become a professional jockey and his opening victory among the paid ranks was as a 7lb claimer aboard Josh Gifford's horse Royal Exchange in the three-mile Wyton Handicap 'Chase at Huntingdon in January 1978. His strike rate over the next three years was hardly earth-shattering, achieving a total of 30 winners during that period but, moving on to trainer Rodney Armytage at East Ilsley near Newbury and then to the powerful establishment of Captain Tim Forster at Letcombe Bassett in Berkshire, Hywel began making his way up the steeplechasing ladder.

By the end of the 1979–80 season Hywel's total number of winners for that period had risen to 29, almost as many as his three previous terms put together, and 12 months later he figured sixth among the top jockeys with 52 successes to his credit. Among his most important victories that year were Celtic Ryde in the New Year's Day Hurdle at Windsor; Straight Jocelyn in the Jerry M 'Chase at Lingfield; Shell Burst in the Exp-O-Tel Supersports Long-Distance Hurdle over three miles at Ascot; and Sea Captain at Cheltenham, when he easily took the Three Fives Young Chasers' Final by 12 lengths. It was also in the spring of that year that he came close to recording his first Cheltenham Festival winner when coming a good second on the outsider Bee Sting behind Gaye Chance in the Sun Alliance Novices Hurdle. Another new experience occurred 17 days later at Liverpool, when Hywel took part in his first Grand National aboard the Stan Mellor-trained Royal Stuart. Always in the mid-division, they parted company two fences before Becher's Brook second time round.

Both Celtic Ryde and Shell Burst played an important role in contributing to Hywel's total of 61 victories during the next term, which ended with him in fourth place behind dual champions John Francome and Peter Scudamore. He was again in the National line-up, this time aboard the 50–1 chance Tiepolino, but once more he failed to complete the course when his mount refused at Becher's second time round.

Hywel Davies enjoyed his best period in the saddle thus far during the

1982–83 season, finishing third in the championship chart with 85 triumphs, which included, among others, Approaching in Kempton Park's Charisma Records Gold Cup, Primrolla in the Finale Junior Hurdle and Bold Yeoman at Nottingham in the valuable Nottinghamshire Two-Mile Novices 'Chase. But it was at Aintree that he found the most satisfying moments of his career up to that time.

On the opening day of the Grand National meeting, Hywel gave the outsider Tiepolino a splendid ride round just under one and a half circuits of the big fences to win the Kaltenberg Pils Handicap 'Chase (formerly known as the Topham Trophy) by a comfortable margin. Later that afternoon the Welshman was back in that famous winner's enclosure after another impressive victory on King Or Country in the Tim Brookshaw Memorial 'Chase over Aintree's Mildmay course. Taking the leg-up on third-favourite Spartan Missile in the Grand National two days later, Hywel was excited at partnering the gallant runner-up of two years earlier. Sadly, the gelding was but a shadow of his former self and was labouring when he unseated his jockey at the final Becher's.

Finishing fourth of the top leading riders the following year, Hywel had notched up a brilliant 67 wins by the season's end and although he failed to secure a ride in that year's Grand National he had found a recent addition to Captain Forster's team, a gelding named Last Suspect which gave him a strange feeling of immense possibility.

A former winner of the prestigious Leopardstown Steeplechase when trained by Tom Dreaper, Last Suspect was owned by Her Grace Anne, Duchess of Westminster, best known in equestrian circles for her unique success with the mighty triple Gold Cup winner Arkle. There could never be any comparison between the champion of the 1960s and the son of Above Suspicion, who was transferred to Tim Forster's care, the gelding having already acquired a reputation as something of a wayward character with a very definite mind of his own.

A renowned tail-swisher, usually a sign of contrary behaviour, Last Suspect could be good when very, very good but when he was bad he was very, very bad. Yet something about the animal appealed to Hywel Davies. At Worcester in October 1984, after some up and down performances, Last Suspect behaved himself sufficiently to win the Mitchells and Butlers Brewery Handicap 'Chase after most considerate guidance from Hywel Davies. Behind him that day were such worthies as Hallo Dandy, King Or Country and a promising newcomer named Little Polveir.

His jumping was good but Last Suspect's determination too obviously left something to be desired. Later, though off the racecourse for almost four months, there was a certain reluctance about his run into second place behind Mid Day Gun at Warwick over three and a half miles on 5 February 1985.

The jockey's steady flow of winners did not come without some painful reminders of the dangers inherent in his profession. He broke his pelvis at Chepstow, his jaw at Southwell and came frighteningly close to being fatally injured when involved in an horrific fall at Doncaster. It was only the quick response of a doctor standing nearby, who gave him mouth-to-mouth resuscitation, which saved Hywel's life.

Already entered for the 1985 Grand National, an appointment Hywel Davies looked forward to with great anticipation, Last Suspect blotted his copybook once too often when, as 3–1 favourite for the Crudwell Cup at Warwick, the horse literally pulled himself up in such a flagrant manner that his owner immediately decided to withdraw him from his Aintree engagement.

When made aware of this decision, Hywel Davies at once approached Captain Forster beseechingly, to avert what he considered an unwise move. Convinced by the trainer that the Duchess of Westminster had emphatically made up her mind, the resolute Welshman took it upon himself to approach Her Grace in an attempt to persuade her to reconsider her judgement. With the cheek of the devil himself, Hywel Davies tracked the Duchess down to a ladies' hairdressers and, with a charm unique to the Celts, prevailed upon her to reconsider running Last Suspect in the National. It speaks volumes for his powers of appealing to the gentler sex that Hywel directed the noble lady's mind to his way of thinking. On 30 March 1985, he was faced with the task not just of tackling the terrors of Aintree but also justifying his impromptu insistence.

With such outstanding performers as Corbiere, Hallo Dandy, Greasepaint, Lucky Vane and the highly promising newcomer West Tip lined up against them, Last Suspect and his persistent jockey, Hywel Davies, who put up 6lb over weight, were almost completely ignored in the betting at 50–1.

A groan of despair reverberated from the first fence when last year's winner Hallo Dandy fell, as did Bashful Lad, Solihull Sport and Talon. By the time they reached the Canal Turn, no less than 11 had departed from the contest. Dudie, West Tip, Corbiere and Greasepaint had been prominent from the start and were still to the fore approaching the halfway stage. Over the Water Jump and back out on the final circuit, Dudie was beginning to put out distress signals as Rupertino took up the running from West Tip, Corbiere and the improving Last Suspect racing on the outside. Becher's Brook caught out West Tip, Tacroy and Hill Of Slane and with Corbiere jumping into the lead at the Canal Turn a second victory for Mrs Pitman's runner appeared very likely. Chased all the way back to the stands by Rupertino, Last Suspect and Greasepaint, Peter Scudamore on Corbiere held a four-length lead when coming towards the second-last fence. Suddenly all eyes became centred on Mr Snugfit, who had made ground rapidly over the previous four fences and it was he who struck the front shortly before landing clear over the final fence. Striding away impressively from his pursuers, Mr Snugfit had raced some five lengths clear at the elbow and seemed assured of victory when Hywel Davies came with a terrific run on the tail-swishing Last Suspect. Such was his superior finishing speed that the Tim Forster-trained gelding got up close home to win by a length and a half from Mr Snugfit, Corbiere and the staying-on Greasepaint.

It was a first victory in the race for both jockey Hywel Davies and owner the Duchess of Westminster, but the contrary Last Suspect provided Tim Forster with a hat-trick of Grand National training successes. With John Francome winning the jockeys' championship that year, Hywel was a respectable fourth behind with 50 victories and 12 months later upped that total to 58, finishing again fourth in the table this time behind champion Peter Scudamore.

What promised to be another exciting campaign for this Grand National winner petered out disappointingly, for after winning his first two races over extended distances at Chepstow, Last Suspect reverted to his old mulish behaviour when returning to Aintree. Hywel pulled the horse up at the beginning of the second circuit after his mount had more or less tailed himself off. The Welshman did, however, score a brilliant success on the first day at Aintree that year, riding Beau Ranger to a shock 40–1 victory over the recent Gold Cup hero Dawn Run in the Whitbread Gold Label Cup.

Recurring injuries cost Hywel his regular high percentage of winners during 1987, also resulting in his missing that year's National, and things were little better the next term. When riding the 50–1 chance Northern Bay in the big race at Aintree in 1988, he pulled up when a long way behind the leaders before reaching the 19th.

Back among the leading jockeys during the 1988–89 season, Hywel Davies rode 50 winners, which gave him eighth position in the table but in the National he once more failed to complete the course when falling with Friendly Henry at the open ditch after Valentine's on the first circuit.

At the Cheltenham Festival in 1990, Hywel secured a double victory, on Katabatic in the Grand Annual 'Chase Challenge Cup and Barnbrook Again in the Queen Mother Champion 'Chase. The next big step that year was Aintree. Hywel had to put up 3lb over weight to ride the American-bred and owned Maryland Hunt Cup winner Uncle Merlin, and he was fully aware that the last winner of that race prepared for the National by his boss Tim Forster was the 1980 Aintree hero Ben Nevis.

Straight from 'the off', Uncle Merlin set a furious pace at the head of affairs, jumping splendidly and giving Hywel a winning feel. Closely tracked by the Kim Bailey-trained Mr Frisk, the American challenger swept easily over Becher's, the Canal Turn and Valentine's, by which time he already had the remainder strung out over a considerable distance behind. Mr Frisk, Star's Delight, Polyfemus and Gee-A were in close pursuit of the leader, who went on powerfully over the Chair, the Water and back into the country still full of running. Approaching Becher's for the final time, Uncle Merlin was two lengths clear of Mr Frisk, maintaining a very fast gallop and enjoying himself, when, after a perfect leap over the Brook, he landed awkwardly and unshipped his jockey. It was dreadful bad luck for both horse and rider and from there on the race became something of a procession, Mr Frisk eventually winning somewhat comfortably and setting a new time record for the race.

Hywel again finished high up in the jockey's table in sixth position, with a total of 60 winners, and in his last two seasons before retiring he finished 11th with 51 winners and 12th with 44 winners respectively. During that period he partnered Blue Dart in the 1991 National when again he was unseated at Becher's Brook second time round. In his last Grand National, the 1992 race, Hywel Davies finished 11th with Ghofar, behind the winner Party Politics, and later that year hung up his boots.

Hywel Davies' tremendous ability is evidenced by the fact that, although never becoming champion professional rider, he still rode over 700 winners during his highly distinguished career. As a part-time racing correspondent for BBC Wales, Hywel is still a regular and welcome visitor to Aintree for the Grand National and runs a very successful horse feed business at Ashbury, near Swindon.

Thomas Richard Dunwoody MBE

Over the past 25 years the most outstanding jockeys to repeatedly win the championship for leading National Hunt rider have been John Francome, Peter Scudamore, Richard Dunwoody and Tony McCoy. All are brilliant and dedicated horsemen, constantly in demand for their uncanny ability to bring out the best in any 'chaser or hurdler. It is therefore surprising to find that only one of this magnificent quartet has added victory in the Grand National to their memorable achievements. Richard Dunwoody gained the first of his Aintree victories quite early in his career and such was his dynamism that he repeated that magical process eight years later.

Born in Northern Ireland in January 1964, Richard followed his father

George's footsteps into horse racing without encountering the objections George had experienced from his parents many years before. George Dunwoody had actually run away from home in his quest to become a jockey and eventually gained a position with the Curragh trainer Cecil Brabazon. Having ridden well over 100 winners, George took up training. Even at the tender age of two and a half, Richard Dunwoody faced an appreciative audience riding a grey pony at the Newtownards Horse Show.

Richard was in the hunting field when just six years old and, inheriting his father's passion for horses, Dunwoody junior progressed rapidly. Like his dad before him, he could hardly wait for the time when he could enter the world of racing.

In December 1982 Richard joined the training headquarters of Captain Tim Forster at Letcombe Bassett as an amateur and a little over five months later he rode his first winner. This was at Cheltenham in 1983, in the two-and-a-half-mile Novice Hunter 'Chase. Giving his mount Game Trust a highly competent ride, he won by two and a half lengths from rivals. By the end of the following season the young Ulsterman had begun to make his mark, finishing in third place with 24 successes behind Simon Sherwood and Dermot Browne in the amateurs' table and during that period he also took his first taste of the Cheltenham Festival. Richard finished sixth in that year's Kim Muir Memorial Challenge Cup on Bashful Lad and later that afternoon got his mount Oyster Pond within two lengths of the Jonjo O'Neill winner Mossy Moore in the Cheltenham Grand Annual 'Chase. Making his Aintree début a fortnight later aboard Silent Echo in the Sporting Life Weekender 'Chase, 'Mr' Richard Dunwoody finished third behind the brilliant young 'chaser Noddy's Ryde.

A major turning point in Richard's career came during the 1984–85 campaign when, then 'riding for hire' as a professional, he scored a fabulous double victory at the Cheltenham Festival with Von Trappe in the Coral Golden Handicap Hurdle and West Tip in the Ritz Club National Hunt Handicap 'Chase. It was West Tip who provided him with his introduction to the Grand National at the end of March 1985 and as the winner of four good steeplechases in the period the Michael Oliver-trained gelding started 13–2 joint favourite with the popular Irish challenger Greasepaint.

Jumping superbly from the start, West Tip was up with the leaders for most of the way and with the contest entering its final stages was well in contention alongside Corbiere and Rupertino over Becher's second time. Although he landed too steeply, Richard's horse looked as if he would recover until a riderless horse cannoned into him from behind and West Tip was out of the race. It was a most disappointing conclusion to what could well have been a very successful effort, for West Tip was still on the bridle at the time of his fall. Some consolation did come at the season's close, when Dunwoody finished among the leading riders with 46 winners.

His winning ways continued with more regularity in 1986 with such major victories as the Mackeson Gold Cup on Very Promising, the Cheltenham Grand Annual with French Union and the Whitbread Trophy (formerly the Topham) over the big fences at Aintree aboard the Terry Casey-trained Glenrue. Again engaged to ride West Tip in the National by Michael Oliver, Richard looked forward to improving greatly on their performance last year.

Second in the market at 15–2, behind the runner-up 12 months earlier Mr Snugfit, West Tip had been trained with the 1986 Grand National as his main target and among his 39 opponents were three former winners of the race: Last Suspect and Corbiere were both on the 14–1 mark, while Hallo Dandy, now reunited with Neale Doughty, went off at 16–1.

From a good start, the 40 runners raced into the country to the first fence, where the only faller was Door Latch, and from there Doubleuagain led from Tacroy, Essex, The Tsarevich and West Tip. Much to everyone's surprise, the usually sure-footed Corbiere came down at the fourth and with Becher's for once trouble-free they swept on to the Canal Turn and beyond with a good number still well in the hunt. Never out of the first eight, West Tip was given a perfect ride round by Richard, who positioned his mount well at every obstacle. Back on the second circuit, Classified, Kilkilowen, The Tsarevich, Young Driver and Northern Bay were all vying for the lead and, jumping Valentine's Brook, there were at least eight of them still in the race with a chance. Crossing the Melling Road for the two remaining obstacles, West Tip made a determined forward run to move into third place behind Young Driver and Classified and with another bold leap at the final fence Young Driver landed on the flat a good two lengths ahead of West Tip. With a brilliantly judged challenge, Richard Dunwoody took West Tip into the lead passing the elbow, holding off a renewed effort from Young Driver by two lengths with Classified a long way back in third place and the favourite Mr Snugfit fourth.

It was a tremendous success for all concerned, particularly Richard, whose stylish performance in only his second season as a professional brought admiration from all sections of the racing community. Great things were forecast for him from some of the most knowledgeable personalities of the turf. Over the next 11 years the predictions proved correct.

Every year from that terrific term in which he netted 55 winners his winning tally increased – to 70 the following year, 79 the one after that and 91 at the end of the 1988–89 season. His percentage of winners rose at a staggering rate year by year and Richard Dunwoody gained his first championship crown with 173 successes in 1992. His Cheltenham record was also an ongoing success story. He partnered Kribensis to victory during that time to win the Champion Hurdle in 1990 after winning with the horse the 1988 Daily Express Triumph Hurdle. These triumphs were for trainer Michael Stoute, while for his principal retainer, David Nicholson, Richard won the 1988 Cheltenham Gold Cup with Charter Party, the Arkle Challenge Trophy on Waterloo Boy and the Ritz Club National Hunt Handicap 'Chase aboard Bigsun. Many other Festival triumphs were gained with Remittance Man, Thetford Forest and Montelado, while at Aintree his National record was exceptional – even without winning. Riding West Tip, Dunwoody finished fourth in 1987 and 1988 and second in 1989 and with Bigsun he completed the course in sixth place behind Mr Frisk in 1990. He pulled the same horse up the next year and in 1992 took a heavy fall with Brown Windsor.

Capturing the jockeys' championship again in 1994 and 1995, Richard had by this time become first jockey to the leading National Hunt trainer Martin Pipe, although he elected to ride Nicky Henderson's appropriately named Wont Be Gone Long in the 1993 National which was declared void.

Engaged in a tremendous struggle to retain his championship through the entire 1993–94 campaign against the rising star of the jumping scene, Adrian Maguire, Richard chose one of Martin Pipe's five representatives in that year's Grand National, the 11-year-old Miinnehoma. Favourite for the race at 5–1 was the mount of his closest rival for the leading jockey spot, Adrian Maguire, on Moorcroft Boy, with the brilliant hunter-chaser Double Silk just one point behind as the next-best-backed contestant. The Cheltenham Gold Cup winner, French-bred and trained The Fellow, was strongly supported at 9–1, together with the improving Master Oats. Miinnehoma was at 16s with Mr Boston, Young Hustler and Zeta's Lad.

Very heavy rain in the days preceding the race plus a substantial fall of snow overnight resulted in heavy going at Aintree on the big day, to such an extent that an early morning inspection was performed by the stewards to determine if racing should take place. Given the go-ahead, the 36 runners paraded in front of the stands in the most atrocious conditions experienced at the racecourse for many years.

Away to a first-time start, Double Silk led over the first fence, at which Elfast, Fourth Of July and Henry Mann all fell. With the field already starting to spread out, Double Silk held his position in front with a fine leap over Becher's. Riverside Boy, Young Hustler, Topsham Bay and The Fellow were well to the fore at this point but the Brook caught out Its A Cracker, New Mill House and Laura's Beau. Between the Canal Turn and the Chair falls were plentiful, with Young Hustler and Southern Minstrel making their exit at the 11th and the 13th proving very unlucky for Double Silk, Topsham Bay, Mighty Falcon, Mister Boston and Master Oats. Only 17 survivors cleared the Water Jump before turning back for the final circuit and these were well strung out, with Riverside Boy the new leader from Garrison Savannah, the improving Miinnehoma, Ebony Jane and The Fellow. At the 17th, however, both Garrison Savannah and Run For Free were eliminated by a loose horse turning broadside into them and Riverside Boy refused at the next. The latest upsets left Miinnehoma at the head of affairs, probably sooner than Richard Dunwoody would have wished, but in the prevailing conditions the jockey decided there was little else to do but make the best of their way home. With his mount beginning to idle in front, Richard was relieved when Ebony Jane moved past them on the run to Becher's. Landing steeply at the mighty obstacle, Miinnehoma pecked so badly that he came down on one knee and his head brushed along the ground. With an instant display of perfect horsemanship, Richard sat perfectly still in the saddle, allowed the gelding to right himself and unbelievably stayed in the race. The French challenger, The Fellow, also made a mistake at Becher's and again at the next fence before falling at the Canal Turn, where Miinnehoma led from Ebony Jane and the improving Just So. Back on the racecourse with just two fences left, Adrian Maguire suddenly loomed up with Moorcroft Boy and jumped to the front over the second last before going on to the final fence, over which he landed with a two-length advantage. Still in front at the elbow, Moorcroft Boy began to flag and, seizing his chance, Richard took Miinnehoma smoothly forward towards what appeared to be a comfortable victory. In the last 150 yards, Simon Burrough suddenly appeared with a very determined late challenge on Just So but Miinnehoma held on well to win by a length and a quarter.

Trainer Martin Pipe was over the moon with the result, revelling in the delight of leading in his first National winner. Richard Dunwoody, although relishing a second success in the race, still had a title to defend. He ended the term with 197 winners to win his championship, just three ahead of his nearest rival, Adrian Maguire.

When partnering Miinnehoma in the National the following year, it was soon clear that there would be no double victory with the gelding, who, after making a mistake at the first fence and again at Becher's, was soon tailed off and eventually pulled up. Richard's list of big-race successes continued to grow, however, even after he split with Martin Pipe and became a freelance jockey. The names of the horses he rode to victory read like a *Who's Who* of racing's greats. Desert Orchid, Chief's Song, One Man, Viking Flagship, Rough Quest, Florida Pearl, Hanakham, Ventana Canyon and Paddy's Return are just a few of those successes and they are still considered some of the greatest horses seen in action during the second half of the twentieth century.

In the 1996 Grand National, Richard rode Jenny Pitman's Superior Finish into third place behind the winner Rough Quest and when riding the same trainer's Smith's Band the next year was there with leaders until falling at the 20th. In 1998, Samlee carried Dunwoody into third place again at Aintree behind Earth Summit and in his final appearance in the race Richard was third again with another appropriately named horse – Call It A Day.

His long and tremendously successful career came to an end after that 1999 Grand National, when he announced his retirement. His total number of winners up to that point in the season was just 12, the smallest number since his term as an amateur. Richard's combined number of winners during that illustrious time when he thrilled racegoers everywhere was an incredible 1,699. In ten consecutive seasons he rode over 100 winners each year.

At the annual awards ceremony, The Lesters, Richard was voted National Hunt Jockey of the Year on five occasions by his fellow jockeys and at Aintree's Grand National meeting in April 2000 had his leg pulled ceaselessly by his former colleagues when interviewing them in his new role of BBC correspondent. It can truly be said that Richard Dunwoody is a very hard act to follow in the world of steeplechasing, especially in terms of consistency over Aintree's enormous obstacles, but, above all else, he has set a wonderful example of sportsmanship, integrity and commitment for all who follow him.

EIGHT

Steven Charles Knight

Born in February 1955, Steve Knight became an apprentice to Richard
Hannon at East Everleigh stables, near Marlborough in Wiltshire, after leaving
school and rode his first winner, Sid, on the flat at Ascot in October 1971.
Increasing weight forced him to turn to the jumping side of the sport and
Steve became attached to Bob Turnell's sizeable yard at Ogbourne Maisey
Lodge in Marlborough.

With Andy Turnell, the trainer's very talented son, taking the major role as
the stable's jockey, Steve Knight's progress was rather slow to begin with but
in 1975, while still claiming a rider's allowance, he took the mount on
Turnell's April Seventh in the valuable Whitbread Gold Cup at Sandown Park.

Giving the nine year old a beautiful ride all the way, Steve took April
Seventh past the post, the length-and-a-half winner from Captain Christy and
Barona. That victory gave him only his fourth success of the season but to win
such a prestigious event while still only 20 years old was a great boost for him.

Five years later in 1980 his total for the season was 20 wins, still well below
his expectations although, yet again, included among those victories were
some fine prizes. He won the Panama Cigar Hurdle Final at Chepstow on Run
Hard and went on to score a brilliant double at the Cheltenham Festival.
Making a procession of the contest for the Sun Alliance 'Chase, Steve rode
Lacson to a distance victory and the next day scored an equally easy success
when partnering Prince Of Bermuda in the County Handicap Hurdle.

Upon the sudden death of Bob Turnell in 1982, Steve Knight was promoted
to first jockey for the yard, as Andrew took over his late father's licence, and
over the next couple of years Steve continued to ride winners without ever
threatening to become a likely entry in the top riders' table. During the
1984–85 campaign he rode just 15 winners, two of which were when
partnering the chestnut Maori Venture and the second of them gave hope for

better things to come, for it was in the Tote Mandarin Handicap 'Chase over three and a quarter miles at Newbury.

Maori Venture provided one of Steve Knight's disappointing total of just seven winners the following season but when later sent over to Fairyhouse for the Jameson Irish Grand National they failed to complete the course.

The only really high point for the jockey during this dismal period was gaining his first ride in the Grand National at Aintree on his own stable's Tracy's Special. Reflecting only too vividly his outsider's long odds of 150–1, the gelding was some way off the pace in the mid-division, when falling at Valentine's Brook first time round.

The find of the season among Andy Turnell's team was without question a young bay gelding named Tawbridge, who won five consecutive novice 'chases during the 1986–87 term and revived Steve Knight's hopes for a change in fortune. Maori Venture also showed improved form early on, finishing third in his first three outings, which included a most impressive run in the Hennessy Cognac Gold Cup at Newbury in November.

Steve Knight rode Maori Venture to a second Mandarin 'Chase victory at Newbury in January but by now the gelding had gained a reputation as a rather chancy jumper and hardly the type who would cope with the perils of Aintree. Having been purchased on Mr Jim Joel's behalf by Andy Turnell upon the death of the former owner, Major Rubin, Maori Venture remained in the care of Turnell. Jim Joel was recognised as the grand old man of the British turf, a gentleman in his nineties who owned the Childwick Bury Stud, where he had bred such outstanding flat-race horses as Fairy Footsteps, Major Portion, Connaught, Welsh Pageant and his Two Thousand Guineas and Epsom Derby winner Royal Palace. Uncertain whether to allow Maori Venture to face the dangers of Aintree, it was his trainer and jockey who eventually persuaded him to let the gelding take its chance, for, despite the obvious dangers, they knew their horse had a good deal of class.

The previous year's winner West Tip started the 5–1 favourite of the 40 runners, with the lovely grey Dark Ivy second choice at 11–2 and Classified, Corbiere, Lean Ar Aghaidh and Smith's Man also well supported. Maori Venture was very easy to back at 28–1.

The usual fast gallop to the first fence was led by Lean Ar Aghaidh, who cleared the obstacle at full pelt, but Lucky Rew and Smartside both ended their journey here. Usually a front-runner, Maori Venture was towards the middle of the field this time and, as feared, made a series of mistakes during the course of his journey. Dark Ivy took a horrifying fall at Becher's Brook, bringing down the American challenger Bewley's Hill, and it was here that Steve Knight performed a brilliant recovery to keep the partnership intact when Maori Venture landed awkwardly, his nose actually scraping the ground. Lean Ar Aghaidh was still dictating the proceedings, followed by Big Brown Bear, Eamons Owen, Northern Bay and Insure. There was little change among the leading group all the way back to the racecourse, while to their rear Maori Venture continued to make the occasional mistake. At the Chair Eamons Owen and Little Polveir came to grief and turning back for the final round, Lean Ar Aghaidh led from Big Brown Bear, You're Welcome, Northern Bay and Insure. Becher's Brook was taken for the final time in the same order, with Maori Venture suddenly appearing in sixth place alongside The Tsarevich and Classified. The pace was still strong for such a late stage in the race and rejoining the racecourse for the last two fences an exciting finish looked likely with eight horses still well grouped behind the leader Lean Ar Aghaidh. Still in front over the final fence, the front-runner was immediately challenged by Maori Venture, with The Tsarevich, West Tip, Attitude Adjuster and You're Welcome all still looking dangerous. Staying on resolutely from the elbow, Maori Venture resisted the strong challenge from The Tsarevich to win by five lengths, with Lean Ar Aghaidh third, in front of West Tip, You're Welcome and the winner's stablemate Tracy's Special.

In what had been a comparatively trouble-free contest, 22 completed the course and for the winning connections the usual congratulations came from every direction. Unfortunately the winning owner, Jim Joel, was not present but was in fact in mid-air somewhere between South Africa and London. The following day, however, he was present at Andy Turnell's stables in East Hendred, Oxfordshire, to welcome home his Aintree heroes.

It was at this celebration that Mr Joel announced the immediate retirement of Maori Venture and gave notice of his intention to bequeath the horse to Steve Knight in his will. It was a gesture from a grateful owner like none before or since in the history of horse racing and when the gallant old gentleman Mr Joel passed away shortly afterwards, Steve Knight became the delighted guardian of the horse which provided his greatest memories of a life in the saddle.

Back at Aintree the following spring, Steve rode Tracy's Special in the National but his measure of good luck had been exhausted and he was forced to pull up at the fence before the second Becher's Brook.

After riding just two winners at the beginning of the 1988–89 season, Steve Knight hung up his boots and returned home to look after the horse which provided his proudest moment.

Brendan Gerard Powell

Irish-born Brendan Powell, in his later years at least, could well be described

as the quiet man of the jockeys' room. That said, however, he was always the
first to offer assistance to any of his brother jockeys, to advise and console any
youngsters suffering nervous pangs of uncertainty, but most of all, he was
always ready to lend a sympathetic ear to anyone troubled or upset.

Born on 14 October 1960, the softly spoken Irishman was from an early
age determined to make his mark in steeplechasing and, like many, he started
his racing career in the ranks of the unpaid as an amateur rider.

Picking rides wherever he could, Brendan was sufficiently proficient in the
art of race riding that such well-established trainers as Jenny Pitman and David
Gandolfo availed themselves of his services. He rode his first winner, Button
Boy, on 30 January 1982 at Windsor for the Minehead trainer Mr Ayliffe and
three weeks later guided the same horse into third place in the Bideford
Handicap 'Chase at Stratford behind the very useful jumpers Badsworth Boy
and Rathgorman.

The following season he was attached to Stan Mellor's yard as a 7lb-
claiming conditional jockey and his strike rate increased dramatically to a tally
of 16 wins by the end of the campaign. Among these was his most valuable
event yet, the Alpine Meadow Hurdle at Ascot on the Les Kennard-trained
Fitzherbert.

Twelve months on, without the benefit of any rider's allowance, Brendan
raised his total to 26 victories, which included a very positive triumph with
Mr Moonraker for Les Kennard in the Welsh Novices Championship 'Chase at
Chepstow. At Aintree the day before the National, he also secured a ride in the
Derby Quincentenary Hurdle, finishing eighth on Ace Of Spies. It was at
Newbury later in the year that Ace Of Spies provided him with one of his
major triumphs of the 1985–86 season when winning the Flavel-Leisure
Hurdle by a short-head from the odds-on favourite Nebris. Another valuable
prize came Brendan's way at Ascot when giving Charcoal Wally a copybook
ride to win the Sapling Novices 'Chase. At Aintree in April, the Irishman
experienced his taste of the National fences in the two-and-three-quarter-mile
Whitbread Trophy. Up with the leaders all the way on Run To Me, they
finished a decent third behind Richard Dunwoody on Glenrue. Brendan ended
that term with his highest number of winners so far, a commendable 45, which
placed him in eighth place behind the champion Peter Scudamore.

Finishing in the top 12 again with 48 wins to his credit at the end of the
1987 jumping period, Brendan enjoyed some memorable, valuable successes
with Saffron Lord at Newbury and Memberson at Sandown. Yet one of his
finest efforts that year was when he was narrowly beaten in the Hennessy
Cognac Gold Cup. Partnering the 50–1 rank outsider Two Coppers, they were
always in the firing line and ran on gamely towards the finish to get within a

length and a half of the very talented Broadheath. A similar distance behind was Maori Venture, a horse Brendan would face again at Aintree the following spring.

Grand National day at Liverpool is always an anxious and tense time for all riders, particularly those facing the enormity of the task in hand for the first time, but Brendan Powell could at least take some comfort from the fact that his conveyance, Glenrue, had won over one circuit of the course. As it turned out, that was a minimal consolation, for they parted company at the first open ditch and Brendan was back in the home straight in time to watch Maori Venture romp to victory.

Unaware of what the new season would bring, Brendan made the acquaintance of a gelding named Rhyme 'N' Reason in the opening weeks of the campaign when booked to ride it by trainer David Elsworth. Second time out the pair made a successful appearance when winning the three-mile Lingfield Park Handicap 'Chase by five lengths from Gainsay and the very useful Playschool. A week later another rich prize came Brendan Powell's way when he rode Panto Prince to a comfortable victory in the Frogmore 'Chase at Ascot and, three days after Christmas, renewed his partnership with Rhyme 'N' Reason. The venue was Chepstow and the contest the stiffest test yet for David Elsworth's eight year old: the Coral Welsh National over three miles and six furlongs.

Well to the fore throughout, Rhyme 'N' Reason jumped perfectly all the way, untroubled by the heavy going, and by the time they turned for home the race had become little more than a duel between Brendan Powell's mount and Playschool. In a stirring finish, Playschool just got the better of the struggle to win by one length from Rhyme 'N' Reason but after such a brave performance there could be no disgrace in defeat. With the New Year hardly begun, Brendan and the game gelding were back in action again, this time in the important Anthony Mildmay, Peter Cazalet Memorial 'Chase at Sandown Park and once more a fluent display brought them a comfortable and well-deserved victory. Returning to the Esher track during the first week of February, they were beaten into second place by future Gold Cup winner Charter Party over a distance considered by Brendan Powell too short for his mount to demonstrate his true ability. Interestingly, though, the horse which finished a neck behind him in third place was the outstanding grey, Desert Orchid.

Reverting to the smaller obstacles at Newbury later that month, Brendan took the mount on another from David Elsworth's yard, Jamesmead, in the very valuable Tote Gold Trophy Handicap Hurdle. Producing his charge at the final flight in a fast-run race, Brendan won by three-quarters of a length from Lorcan Wyer on Buck Up and some other extremely high-class performers.

It was soon back to winning ways again, with Rhyme 'N' Reason at Windsor in the Fairlawn Chase the following week, with a seemingly effortless 12-length victory over Run And Skip and Boland's Cross.

On the crest of a wave, jockey Powell kept up the good work at Kempton Park in the Racing Post Handicap 'Chase at the end of the month, when riding Rhyme 'N' Reason to an emphatic triumph over Lean Ar Aghaidh, Mr Frisk, The Tsarevich and Broadheath. By now the connections of Rhyme 'N' Reason were beginning to think seriously about the forthcoming Grand National and his preparation for the race took on greater meaning.

They came down to earth with a bump, however, when, ambitiously bidding for the Cheltenham Gold Cup, Rhyme 'N' Reason failed to complete the course behind the winner Charter Party. There was a little consolation for Brendan later that afternoon, though, when Private Views carried him to an all-the-way win in the Cathcart Challenge Cup for trainer Nick Gaselee. From that point on, Brendan's every second thought was somehow associated with Aintree.

The customary flood of betting for the Grand National resulted in Sacred Path starting the 17–2 favourite, with Lean Ar Aghaidh and Rhyme 'N' Reason joint-second choices on 10–1 and the evergreen West Tip, the Irish challenger Hard Case, Border Burg, Bucko and Repington also very well supported. With the tension as usual at fever pitch seconds before 'the off', a gasp of exasperation from the crowd signalled the fact that there would have to be a delay when Repington and Gee-A charged the tape and the field was recalled to begin again. When at last the runners were officially sent on their way, Lean Ar Aghaidh repeated his front-running tactics of the previous year, galloping strongly towards the first fence at the head of the other 39 competitors. Favourite Sacred Path over-jumped at the obstacle and crumpled to the ground, together with Hettinger and Tullamarine. There were no further casualties on the run to Becher's, with Big Brown Bear, Insure, Lean Ar Aghaidh, Kumbi and Gee-A all well to the fore. Meeting the Brook on the wide outside, Rhyme 'N' Reason veered to the left and on landing stumbled so badly that his legs went from under him and he slithered for some yards on his belly. In amazement, spectators witnessed probably the most astonishing recovery ever seen in a steeplechase. With remarkable calmness, Brendan Powell sat tight in the saddle and, although he lost an enormous amount of ground, somehow kept the gelding in the race. It must have seemed to Brendan that whatever chance they had was gone completely in those seconds of agony, but although now last of the 33 remaining in the contest, he continued his now forlorn journey. For the remainder of the first circuit the race followed a predictable pattern, with Lean Ar Aghaidh setting the pace closely followed by Gee-A, Eton Rouge, Little Polveir, Kumbi, Course Hunter and, a long way back, Rhyme 'N' Reason. In the same order they took the Chair and with the field now thinning out they then jumped the Water and went back out into the country. To everyone's amazement, as the leaders took the 17th fence, Rhyme 'N' Reason was seen to be moving smoothly up into a useful position. Two fences later, Brendan had moved his mount into fifth place behind Gee-A, Little Polveir, Strands Of Gold and Course Hunter and with the strong pace beginning to affect many, the survivors became fewer. Strands Of Gold came down heavily at the second Becher's, Course Hunter was lucky to survive a serious mistake and West Tip, Gee-A, Rhyme 'N' Reason and the improving Durham Edition were all now well in contention. Little Polveir struck the front jumping the Canal Turn, with Rhyme 'N' Reason now second, in front of Monanore, West Tip, Lastofthebrownies, Durham Edition and Attitude Adjuster. With the race still wide open, Little Polveir parted company with his jockey at the fence after Valentine's, leaving Brendan and Rhyme 'N' Reason in front. Despite misjudging the last ditch, where Attitude Adjuster and Lastofthebrownies fell, Rhyme 'N' Reason held his advantage coming back across the Melling Road, with West Tip, Monanore and Durham Edition in close attendance. With Durham Edition moving strongly into a challenging position, he and Rhyme 'N' Reason began to draw clear of the remainder and with the latter making another mistake at the penultimate fence Chris Grant took Durham Edition to the front. With Brendan Powell hard at work on his mount coming to and going over the last fence, the race looked in the bag for Durham Edition, but rallying courageously coming to the elbow Rhyme 'N' Reason came up with a terrific burst of speed in the final 100 yards to win by four lengths, with Monanore 15 lengths further back and West Tip fourth of the nine which completed the course.

The amazing turn of events which gave Rhyme 'N' Reason victory after such an apparently devastating collapse so early in the race was further compounded when the announcement was made that there was to be a stewards enquiry. It hardly seemed possible that after such a heroic performance Brendan Powell should suffer the indignity of being carpeted. The concern of the officials applied to the number of times the jockey had used his whip before and after the final fence but the result of their deliberations led to nothing more than a caution and, as a final aside, the congratulations of the stewards for his unique display of horsemanship and determination.

Rounding off what had been a truly fabulous period of his career, Brendan won the Motor Import Handicap 'Chase at the Punchestown Festival at the end of April on Flying Ferret for the Kildare trainer Redmond. Again among the leading riders with 38 winners, Brendan Powell fully deserved all the plaudits heaped upon him.

That Grand National success in such unbelievable circumstances was the highlight of Brendan Powell's career in the saddle and although he became an elder statesman of his trade, continuing for another 12 years, nothing could ever equal that unforgettable day at Aintree with Rhyme 'N' Reason. But there were wonderful moments in other great races, with the likes of Dublin Flyer at Cheltenham and in the John Hughes Memorial at Aintree; Nomadic Way in the Irish Champion Hurdle; Monsignor at Cheltenham; Amlah in the Galway Plate; and a stupendous success on Roll A Joint in the Scottish National – and these form an impressive testament to his ability.

In those remaining 12 seasons it seems incredible that Brendan competed in only five more Nationals but such is the nature of sporting endeavour – with each passing year a new generation of talent emerges and so many heroes of the past too quickly become yesterday's men.

Following his success with Rhyme 'N' Reason in the National, he rode Stearsby in the 1989 race, when he refused at the 11th; he finished 14th on Ghofar the following year and then waited five years before Jenny Pitman engaged him to partner one of her six runners in the 1995 event. After showing prominently for most the way, Brendan and Do Be Brief fell at the 20th. Another four years elapsed before his services were again required in the National. Riding the Philip Hobbs-trained Mudahim in 1999, Brendan parted company with his mount at Becher's Brook first time round.

Brendan Powell's farewell to Aintree, and to the race he so enriched with such an unforgettable performance, came in the year 2000 when riding the Yorkshire-trained and strongly fancied Young Kenny. With probably more media attention directed his way on that occasion than ever before, the fairytale ending was not to be, with Young Kenny and Brendan falling at the fence after Valentine's Brook on the first circuit. As one privileged to have been present in the jockeys' room that day when Brendan returned from the long walk back from the country and received the applause of his peers, I find it easy to understand why this modest, likeable gentleman of the turf generated the respect and affection of all he came into contact with.

Within months of his retirement, Brendan Powell had achieved his three major ambitions: to win the Grand National, to acquire plenty of rides and to become a racehorse trainer. But more importantly, he had built a family of which he could always be proud. He married Rachel (who had looked after Mr Frisk at the time of his 1990 Grand National victory) and produced Brendan junior and Jenny. With Brendan already having saddled a steady supply of winners, it is surely only a matter of time before a new generation of Powells appears at Aintree.

James Douglas Frost

Born the son of Devon 'permit holder' Richard Frost on 31 July 1958, Jimmy Frost was in the saddle almost as soon as he could walk and, quickly equipping himself well for the demands of horsemanship, nothing could have been more assured than the fact that his future would lie in the world of horse racing.

He rode his first winner in a point-to-point at Lemalla in Cornwall on Doctor Fred at the age of 13 and between such events he spent every moment assisting his father with the multitude of jobs to be found in any stable. Upon leaving school, Jimmy began the long process of trying to establish himself as a conditional jockey and, despite his background, it was for many years a hard struggle.

By the age of 26 he had ridden a total of just 31 winners in five years as a professional, most of these when partnering his father's horses, but during the 1984–85 season Jimmy passed the winning post for the first of a future 22 occasions.

Like many in his profession, he was unfortunate to be of a generation so rich with such outstandingly talented jockeys such as Peter Scudamore, Richard Dunwoody, Chris Grant, Simon Sherwood, Steve Smith Eccles and Graham Bradley. Unlike most, however, Jimmy Frost benefited from being a trainer's son, which meant he earned a living acting as assistant trainer to his father when not required on the racecourse, but the realisation that he was never going to be among the jockeys most in demand was obviously a huge disappointment to the West Country rider. One important development in his career did occur in 1986, when he partnered the former Grand National leading fancy Lucky Vane to victory in a long-distance steeplechase at Sandown Park for Toby Balding.

In December 1987, Jimmy was again engaged by the Weyhill trainer to ride Salehurst in the valuable BMW Series Final Handicap 'Chase at Cheltenham. Riding a waiting race over the testing three-mile, one-furlong Prestbury Park course, he brought his mount with a perfectly timed challenge to win with plenty in hand from Lucky Rascal and Alexandra Palace. Other opportunities came from the Balding establishment and at the end of that term he recorded his highest total of winners so far, 30 in all.

His first major success of the next campaign came in the Scilly Isles Novices 'Chase at Sandown Park on 4 February 1989, when getting up close home on The Bakewell Boy for a head victory over Simon Sherwood on Southernair. The fact that this winner was trained by his dad Richard gave Jimmy particular satisfaction and, although he could never have guessed it, there was even better yet to come.

Some five weeks before the 1989 Grand National, Toby Balding purchased a gelding named Little Polveir on behalf of Edward Harvey, who wanted an old 'chaser to give his son Alex a safe passage in Sandown's Grand Military Gold Cup. The horse justified the purchase by finishing fourth in that amateur riders' event and, realising that the purchase of the 12 year old included an entry for the 1989 National, Jimmy Frost pestered Balding to persuade Harvey into allowing the horse to take his chance at Liverpool.

It was a most difficult decision for both the owner and trainer, bearing in mind that the horse had already run three times in the race without success. Frost was quick to point out, though, that in the previous year's race, Little Polveir was going very well in the lead until meeting the fourth from home completely wrong and falling. He also emphasised the fact that two years earlier the gelding had decisively won the Scottish Grand National at Ayr in the hands of Peter Scudamore. The jockey's appraisal was considered sound and with the decision to run in the greatest test of all taken it was also agreed that Jimmy Frost should take the mount.

That dreamt-of, yet seemingly impossible prospect of riding over the most demanding and historic of all steeplechasing locations brought an anguish to Jimmy Frost that he had never before encountered, but with great fortitude the jockey put all qualms aside to concentrate on the tremendous trial awaiting him.

Trainer Toby Balding had a number of runners competing at Aintree's Spring meeting and on the opening day his selected jockey Jimmy Frost rode General Chandos in the John Hughes Memorial Trophy 'Chase over one circuit of the National fences. Although Jimmy was given a fine ride over those mighty obstacles, the horse was never a danger to the two favourites which filled first and second places. Jimmy finished in fourth place behind Villierstown, Eton Rouge and Red Columbia. Under the circumstances, it was good experience for the jockey on his first journey over those notorious fences but the following two days must have seemed endless as the seconds slipped slowly by to his date with destiny.

A full complement of 40 runners assembled at the start for the 1989 Grand National with Dixton House the 7–1 favourite ahead of Durham Edition, Bonanza Boy, the former Cheltenham Gold Cup winner The Thinker, Stearsby and West Tip. A late rush of money brought down the price of Little Polveir from 50–1 to 28–1. Putting up 3lb over weight – which took his mount's weight to 10st 3lb – Jimmy Frost survived the tense preliminaries like a true professional, aware the soft ground was well to the liking of Little Polveir.

Away to an even start, they charged down to the first fence well-bunched. With Ceriman falling here and Cranlome dropping out with Bob Tisdall at the next, they raced on towards Becher's Brook. Stearsby led the way over the Brook, closely followed by West Tip, Newnham, Mr Chris and Little Polveir but Dixton House collapsed on landing. Other casualties here included Hettinger, Brown Trix, Seeandem, Sir Jest and Sergeant Sprite. At the big ditch after Valentine's the leader Stearsby refused and Friendly Henry fell, as did Perris Valley, and from there on Newnham led from West Tip and Little Polveir. In this order they returned to the racecourse and at the Chair the leaders were joined by Mithras, with The Thinker and Team Challenge making steady progress from the rear. With his mount running with a zest which belied his years, Jimmy Frost allowed Little Polveir to take up the running on the way back to Becher's, where he put in a super leap which increased his advantage to some five lengths. Rounding the Canal Turn he still led from the improving Bonanza Boy, Gala's Image, Lastofthebrownies, West Tip, Durham Edition and Team Challenge but it could be clearly seen that they were all struggling to keep pace with the leader. Still in front at the fourth-last Little Polveir was now closely attended by the riderless Smart Tar, with his nearest mounted rivals Team Challenge and Durham Edition still three lengths in arrears. Coming to the final fence, Chris Grant brought Durham Edition up with a dangerous-looking challenge and as Little Polveir cleared the fence perfectly with the loose Smart Tar upsides, The Thinker also began a forward move. As Durham Edition weakened passing the elbow, both The Thinker and West Tip put in determined efforts to make ground on the leader. But, staying on extremely well in the soft ground, Little Polveir passed the post seven lengths ahead of West Tip, with The Thinker in third place in front of Lastofthebrownies, Durham Edition and Monanore.

The scenes of joy in the winner's enclosure matched any ever seen and when interviewed after weighing-in Jimmy Frost paid tribute to his horse with the following statement:

> I thought he might be one of those old 'chasers who came alive in the supercharged atmosphere of Grand National day and I was proved right. He got himself really revved up going to the start and by the time there had been a little delay while one of the horses was re-shod, he was really buzzing. He gave me a cracking ride all the way round and actually jumped the Canal Turn so fast that the saddle slipped! I soon got it back into place because it didn't weigh that much and he went on and won, simply because he loved the place.

His day's work still not completed, Jimmy Frost went out just over an hour later on Toby Balding's Morley Street to win the Mumm Prize Novices Hurdle, putting the icing on the cake for an unforgettable day.

Jimmy ended that term with 41 winners and achieved a well-earned 12th place among the leading jockeys. Little Polveir retired after his Aintree victory and Jimmy Frost rode Martin Pipe's Torside in the race in 1990 but was forced to pull up before reaching Becher's Brook; it was a similar story 12 months later. This time aboard the David Barons-trained Bumbles Folly, they were hampered at the seventh fence, became tailed-off and the jockey called it a day after jumping the 20th.

While continuing to provide a regular supply of winners over the next couple of years, Jimmy had to wait until 1994 before again appearing in the Grand National and that year once more represented David Barons on Topsham Bay. Well up with the leaders for most of the first circuit, a loose horse cut across them at the 13th and the rider was unseated. His final ride in the race came five years later when finishing ninth behind the winner Bobbyjo in 1999 with the 200–1 shot St Melion Fairway.

Jimmy now commands as much respect as ever from his fellow jockeys, as the oldest still riding over jumps. His intention is to carry on for a few more years before taking over full-time from his father and, as the Peter Pan of his profession, it is not beyond the bounds of possibility that he could yet again appear in the race he won with Little Polveir. His long and productive career has enriched the jumping scene throughout his involvement and to date he has ridden 496 winners.

Marcus David Armytage

Born on 17 July 1964, the son of East Ilsley trainer Roddy Armytage, Marcus initially combined his inbred riding skills with his talent as a journalist in a highly successful manner. Entering the competitive world of steeplechasing as an amateur rider in 1982, he rode his first winner in April of that year on Brown Jock at Plumpton, adding another success to his first term's total before the season's end. A blank period the next year was followed by another two victories in 1984 and twelve months later, Marcus enjoyed his most profitable term thus far when winning seven races and achieving ninth place among the leading unpaid riders. The most memorable of these successes came on Grand National day 1985 when, just over an hour after Last Suspect provided Hywel Davies with his greatest triumph, Marcus rode the five-year-old Seagram to a most impressive eight-length victory in the two-mile White Satin Handicap Hurdle. His writing career was far from neglected during this time, for he was by now the racing correspondent for the *Newbury Weekly News*, as well as editor of the Jockeys' Supporters' Association journal, *Kick On*.

With just one winner to his credit the following year, Marcus did, however, experience for the first time the rigours of the National fences. Riding the Roddy Armytage-trained grey Rocamist in the R.E.A. Bott Foxhunters' 'Chase, Marcus enjoyed a clear round to finish in sixth place behind the winner Eliogarty. Just two in front of him at the winning post was Gala Prince, another gelding prepared by his father and ridden by the extremely talented lady rider Gee Armytage, his own younger sister.

Throughout the 1986–87 season, the friendliest sort of sibling rivalry was seen between these two amongst the amateur ranks of riders, with Marcus and his sister both notching up a respectable number of winners, but his nine victories were doubled by Gee, who gained eighteen and thus second place in the table. Her performance that year was nothing short of phenomenal and at the Cheltenham Festival she won the Kim Muir Memorial Challenge Cup on The Ellier, following it up 24 hours later with a surprise victory in the Mildmay of Flete Challenge Cup with the appropriately named Gee-A. Marcus again took part in Aintree's Hunters' 'Chase on another from his father's yard, Applalto, finishing 14th of the 20 runners. The following day he took the leg-up from his dad on Brown Veil in the Grand National. On the fast ground that day, the leaders left Brown Veil some way behind on the first circuit and after jumping well for two-thirds of the journey, Marcus pulled his mount up after the second Becher's.

The media had a field day on the run-up to the 1988 Grand National, with the realisation that there was every likelihood of a brother and his sister taking part in the race for the first time ever. Gee was engaged to partner her Cheltenham winner Gee A by trainer Geoff Hubbard, but sadly Marcus received an injury shortly before the race and was unable to compete. Gee Armytage gave a splendid performance on Gee A, disputing the lead through the first circuit and still well in contention after jumping Becher's for the second time. Unfortunately she had received an injury to her back when clearing the 19th and, unable to continue in the closing stages, pulled up four from home.

For Marcus, apart from the injury which cost him his National ride, the season was one of his most pleasing yet, finishing second to Tim Thomson Jones in the table with 12 winners and finishing third with Acarine in the Christies Foxhunter Challenge Cup at Cheltenham. Without appreciating the significance of it at the time, he also won the Sheila's Cottage Handicap 'Chase at Doncaster on a chestnut gelding trained by Kim Bailey named Mr Frisk.

Taking fewer rides as his journalism thrived, Marcus partnered seven winners the next year, came sixth in Cheltenham's National Hunt Cup 'Chase with Friendly Henry, failed to get round with Liverpool Rambler in the Foxhunters' 'Chase at Aintree and rode Sharp Jewel into second place at Stratford in the Horse and Hound Cup.

By now a highly respected journalist contributing to the *Daily Telegraph*, *Horse and Hound* and the *Racing Post*, Marcus was mostly at the races in this capacity and found less time for actual competition. Accordingly, his efforts in the saddle brought only six winners, three of those with the same horse, but the events of that season will remain forever in his memory.

Teaming up again with Kim Bailey's Mr Frisk at Taunton in November 1989, the pair romped home 30 lengths clear of their nearest rivals over three miles. Later that month they renewed the partnership in Newbury's Hennessy Cognac Gold Cup. Foot-perfect the entire way, they were headed on the run-in and, failing to quicken, finished a good third, just under three lengths behind Ghofar and Brown Windsor.

Third again at Doncaster early in December, Mr Frisk was given a well-earned winter break before appearing at the Cheltenham Festival in March 1990. In a very competitive field for the Kim Muir Memorial Challenge Cup, Marcus and Mr Frisk figured prominently throughout, jumped well all the way and were chopped for speed coming to the final fence to finish a decent fourth behind Master Bob, Golden Minstrel and Dudie. Riding the veteran West Tip later in the meeting, Marcus survived serious interference at the last to come third in the Christies Foxhunter 'Chase Challenge Cup behind Call Collect and Old Nick. From there on, all the rider's thoughts revolved around Aintree and the Grand National.

Of the 38 runners for the big race that day, Brown Windsor was the 7–1 favourite from Bigsun, Durham Edition, Rinus, Ghofar and Call Collect, with Mr Frisk receiving some late attention before going off at 16–1. Away promptly, they raced out into the country and straight away it was apparent that the firm ground and the pace they were setting was very likely to result in a fast time. An unusual aspect of the contest was that the two trailblazers, Uncle Merlin and Mr Frisk, were both owned by American ladies. For much of the way each owner was on her toes with excitement. Taking up the running from the first open ditch, Uncle Merlin simply galloped most of the opposition into the ground, his nearest rivals being Mr Frisk, Polyfemus and Brown Windsor as they approached Becher's Brook for the first time. Putting in a very long jump at the Brook, Uncle Merlin dipped noticeably on landing but he was soon back into his stride and led them around the Canal Turn, where Roll A Joint came down heavily. Several lengths ahead of their pursuers, Uncle Merlin and Mr Frisk took the Chair brilliantly and returning to the country were still going strong and jumping superbly. Rinus began making a forward move as they jumped the 19th and Chris Grant also increased his pace on Durham Edition. Now galloping on the inside of the course, Uncle Merlin came to Becher's again with a length lead over his nearest rival but, landing awkwardly there, where the drop is most pronounced, he unseated his rider, leaving Mr Frisk with a clear advantage. With Marcus Armytage riding one of the most confident races seen at Aintree, he measured his fences perfectly and made full use of his mount's bold jumping while ensuring the horse had something left for the punishing final stages of the race. As Brown Windsor began dropping back after Valentine's Brook, Durham Edition edged ever closer and looked still full of running. Rinus was staying on well in third place, followed by Bigsun, Call Collect, Lastofthebrownies and Sir Jest. Two lengths to the good over the last fence, Mr Frisk landed running but was immediately challenged by Durham Edition and the pair were almost together passing the elbow. Riding his mount out superbly with hands and heels over the final furlong, Marcus Armytage held on with Mr Frisk to be worthy winners by three-quarters of a length from Durham Edition, with Rinus third in front of Brown Windsor, Lastofthebrownies, Bigsun and Call Collect.

As was forseen, the time for the race was a record, being run in 8 minutes and 47 seconds but the statistics of the event meant little to the winning connections and in banner headlines on the following Monday the *Racing Post* presented a unique description of the triumph by Marcus Armytage himself, entitled 'How I Won The National'.

At Sandown Park three weeks later, Mr Frisk was again brilliantly ridden by Marcus to a record-breaking victory in the Whitbread Gold Cup in a finish reminiscent of the Grand National one, with the runner-up again the brave Durham Edition.

At Aintree in 1991 Mr Frisk was pulled up by Marcus before the second Becher's, some way out of touch with the leading group. Later that year, Marcus Armytage published his first book, *Generous*, the story of the Derby winner of that name.

At the Cheltenham Festival in 1992, Marcus rode a brilliant double – with Tug Of Gold in the Kim Muir Challenge Cup and Keep Talking in the National Hunt Challenge Cup.

He was without a ride in the 1992 National but partnered Travel Over in the void race the next year and in 1995 he dead-heated for fifth place in the race on Romany King alongside Into The Red. His final ride in the race was aboard Bishops Hall in 1996, when he was unseated at the first fence.

In 1997 his book *Hands and Heels* was published and it provides some of the finest descriptions of the best horses he and Richard Dunwoody have encountered during their illustrious careers.

NINE

Nigel John Hawke

Another son of the West Country, whose life became deeply involved in the captivating world of steeplechasing from an early age, is Nigel Hawke. He was born on 13 January 1966 and his first employer was David Barons at his stables in Kingsbridge, Devon.

The youngster's first winner came quickly, at Wincanton on Boxing Day 1987, with the Somerset trainer Kevin Bishop's Redgrave Devil. Uniquely for a conditional jockey, Nigel rode this horse the following March at the Cheltenham Festival, finishing unplaced in the County Handicap Hurdle. That first term brought a promising 12 winners for Nigel and he increased that total to 18 the following season, which more importantly brought him into contact with his stable's Seagram. The New Zealand-bred gelding was, within a very short time, to put Nigel firmly in the public eye.

At Newton Abbot in August 1989, Nigel Hawke gained his initial success of the new term when riding Imadyna to victory and quickly followed this up with another win aboard Handy Lane at Worcester. Riding Hellovastate at Devon and Exeter, Sea Flower over three miles at Chepstow and Rocktor, some way from home at Market Rasen, all kept the 23 year old in winning form even before Seagram was brought into action again.

When he was at Devon in late October the gelding made a promising start to his campaign, finishing second behind Panto Prince in a steeplechase much too short to do him justice. Second again to the very useful Rowlandson's Jewels over an extended three miles at Sandown Park proved Seagram had not lost his appetite for jumping and at Ascot he won the valuable Rip Handicap 'Chase by a short-head after a dour battle with Black Spur.

In the meantime, Nigel's tally of winners steadily increased with other members from David Barons' team. Searcher, Cock A Leekie, Thatcher Rock and a particularly good win at Cheltenham with Auction Law all added to the growing reputation of the 3lb-claiming jockey. Getting the better of another stirring finish at Haydock Park soon afterwards, Nigel Hawke gave another commendable performance, again with Auction Law, to win the valuable Coral Golden Hurdle.

After another workmanlike display gained Seagram third place at Cheltenham, they returned with high hopes to Ascot for the SGB Handicap 'Chase, only to prove most disappointing when, after a number of errors, Nigel was forced to pull the horse up. A short break from routine was decided for the horse and, while awaiting his return to competition, Nigel continued to catch the judges' eye with such good winners as Just As Hopeful and Ever Hopeful.

Returning to the racecourse after a two-month lay-off, Seagram performed splendidly at the end of February to finish third in Kempton's Racing Post 'Chase behind the brilliant Desert Orchid and a few weeks later the decision was taken to let him take his chance in the Ritz Club National Hunt Handicap 'Chase at Cheltenham.

As always, this highly competitive event attracted some of the finest three, milers from both sides of the Irish Sea and, rising to the occasion, both Seagram and his jockey gave a brilliant display. Close up with the leaders all the way, Nigel allowed his mount to take up the running at the third from home and leading over the last fence looked sure to win. In the final strides of the race, however, Richard Dunwoody brought Bigsun with a terrific burst of speed to snatch victory from defeat by a head.

With one ride on each of the first two days at Aintree's Grand National meeting, Nigel was particularly optimistic that the second of these, Seagram, would at last collect a worthy prize. His first mount, Thatcher Rock, ran a good race after a long lay-off to finish 8th of 20 and Nigel looked forward to seeing how Seagram would cope with the Mildmay fences the next day.

Carrying top weight, Seagram ran his usual brave race, making most of the running and jumping really well. Despite being joined up front by One More Knight at the third-last, he stuck well to his task. Once again, though, they were caught on the run-in and beaten by a length. Returning home that evening somewhat dismayed, Nigel received some consolation the next day at Hereford, when riding Beaconside to a comfortable 15-length victory in the Mitchell & Butlers Handicap 'Chase.

The Whitbread Gold Cup at Sandown on the last Saturday in April was Seagram's last race of the season and in a very fast-run contest, he finished in ninth place behind the National winner Mr Frisk.

A similar programme as before was mapped out for Seagram by David Barons, the main intention being for the gelding to be at his fittest and strongest for the plum prizes on offer in the spring. Roddy Greene rode him on his first appearance of the 1990–91 season, coming third at Ascot. With the same jockey in the saddle at Cheltenham, he ran well to finish second behind Sam Da Vinci. In the Hennessy Cognac Gold Cup, they finished well to the rear behind the Jamie Osborne-ridden winner Arctic Call and, still with Roddy riding, Seagram ran second again at Cheltenham behind Master Bob in early December.

On New Year's Day, Nigel Hawke resumed his association with Seagram in the four-mile ASW Handicap Steeplechase at Cheltenham. Despite pulling hard, the gelding gave a superb exhibition of jumping to outstay his rivals and win running on, very comfortably. Behind him that day were such well-seasoned performers as Bonanza Boy, The Langholm Dyer, Mister Christian and Bigsun.

A short break from racecourse activity seemed not to suit Seagram, though, who next time up at Wincanton gave a completely lacklustre account of himself when finishing third of three behind Cool Ground.

Three weeks later, however, all the hard work and patience with the horse was fully rewarded when Nigel took him on to the track at Prestbury Park for the start of the Ritz Club National Hunt Handicap 'Chase. With a simply superlative display of fencing and perfect assistance from the man in the saddle Seagram just jumped the opposition ragged to win by 5 lengths from the Irish champion Cahervillahow and Outside Edge 20 lengths further back.

Nigel Hawke went back to Aintree, but this time he was required for all three days, especially Saturday 6 April, Grand National day. Quickly getting prepared for all that may follow, Nigel rode Rocktor into second place on the opening day in the White Satin Novices Hurdle. Day two brought him a third place on Southover Lad in the Martell Handicap Hurdle and a fourth with Jump Start in the last race of that day.

Seagram and his jockey, both newcomers to Aintree's huge obstacles, still received plenty of support from the punters, largely as a result of his recent Cheltenham success and, as they paraded before the start, were prominent in the betting at 12–1. The favourite was the Peter Scudamore-ridden Bonanza Boy at 13–2, with the Cheltenham Gold Cup winner Garrison Savannah jointly occupying second spot in the market with Rinus at 7–1. Bigsun, Ten Of Spades, Docklands Express and Master Bob were among the best backed of the remainder.

After an eight-minute delay, the 40 runners began their journey into the unknown with the customary cavalry-like charge across the Melling Road to the first fence, at which the only casualty was Docklands Express. Run And Skip went at the second and Envopak Token was pulled up before reaching Becher's Brook, where Golden Freeze led over from the French entry

Oklaoma II and Garrison Savannah. Close on the heels of the leaders jumping the Canal Turn were Leagaune, Over The Road, Ballyhane, Ten Of Spades, Mr Frisk and Team Challenge. Jumping Valentine's, Seagram was to the rear of the mid-division but at the 12th he blundered badly and lost a good deal of ground. Jumping the Water at the halfway point, Golden Freeze, Garrison Savannah and Team Challenge were all well to the fore, bringing a smile to the face of Mrs Jenny Pitman who trained all three. Back in the country, the race began in earnest, with the field now becoming well strung out. Still Golden Freeze led from a group consisting of Rinus, Over The Road, Garrison Savannah, Auntie Dot, Ballyhane and General Chandos. After jumping the 17th, Nigel made a forward move on Seagram, carefully picking his way through the stragglers and when Rinus made a mistake two fences later, they moved into sixth place. Neale Doughty fell with Rinus at the next, leaving Golden Freeze clear of Garrison Savannah, New Halen, Auntie Dot and the still improving Seagram. Over Becher's, Garrison Savannah was but a length behind Golden Freeze, with New Halen blundering just behind and Auntie Dot, Seagram and Over The Road still going strong. As this group drew clear of the remainder jumping the Canal Turn, nothing was going better than Mark Pitman's mount Garrison Savannah and Jenny Pitman looked set for a second National victory. Back on the racecourse and lining up for the second-last fence Garrison Savannah now held the upper hand, with his nearest rivals now reduced to just Auntie Dot and Seagram, but a splendid leap over that fence gave the leader a distinct advantage of some five lengths. With Auntie Dot obviously flagging, Seagram was the nearest to the Gold Cup winner, who again outjumped Nigel Hawke's mount at the final obstacle. Quickly into his stride, Garrison Savannah looked certain to emulate Golden Miller's 1934 record as the only horse to win the Gold Cup and Grand National in the same year. With the benefit of the inside rail, he galloped on seemingly unbeatable but at the elbow he began to falter and with every stride up that punishing home stretch Nigel Hawke drove Seagram ever nearer. One of the most amazing turnarounds in the history of the race was then enacted before everyone's eyes. Running on with near fanatical determination, Seagram and his young jockey reached and then passed Garrison Savannah to pass the winning post, the victors by a remarkable five lengths. Auntie Dot was eight lengths behind the gallant Garrison Savannah in third place, followed by Over The Road, Bonanza Boy, Durham Edition and 11 other finishers.

The result was a tremendous publicity success for the race sponsors, Seagram, who played down the fact that the little New Zealand horse had twice been offered to their Company Chairman, Major Ivan Straker, who to his everlasting regret declined the purchase. Purely by chance, that was the last

KINGS FOR A DAY

Grand National to be run which carried the Seagram prefix, for the Seagram Company then handed over future sponsorship of the event to one of their subsidiary associates, Martell.

In their final race of that glorious season, Seagram and Nigel finished fourth in the Whitbread Gold Cup behind Docklands Express, Cahervillahow and Wont Be Gone Long.

Only a shadow of his former self the next year, Seagram did little of account in any of his races. In the 1992 Martell Grand National he was never in the hunt and was tailed-off when Nigel pulled him up before the third-last fence.

Sadly that was the last time either Seagram or Nigel Hawke were seen in action over the National fences, the horse being retired soon after Sandown. Nigel obviously still had a very successful riding career ahead of him. Cruelly he had that opportunity snatched away in the most tragic manner. After receiving serious head injuries in a fall at Newton Abbot, it was discovered that Nigel had a blood clot on the brain and his riding career was most cruelly brought to an end. His gradual recovery took a long time, during which he was forbidden to a drive a car for four years, but in 1995 he bravely began a new career as a trainer. His first winner came the following season and although establishing himself in this new capacity has taken time, he turned out the beautiful grey gelding Kendal Cavalier to win the Welsh National at Chepstow in December 1998. Subsequently the horse ran well to finish a respectable seventh in the real thing at Aintree in 1999 and hopefully Nigel will be back to emulate the handful of men who have both ridden and trained a Grand National winner.

Carl Llewellyn

Like his fellow countryman Hywel Davies, Welshman Carl Llewellyn learned his craft riding in point-to-points across the Welsh countryside, securing his first success in this environment at a Pembrokeshire event aboard Kilpeck in a dead-heat also involving Kate's Sister.

Carl was born on 29 July 1965 in Pembrokeshire and both he and his brother David were involved in riding from their earliest days. So competitive was their equestrian relationship that Carl sought to repeat David's win at the Llangeinor Hunt point-to-point, achieving it when winning the maiden race on Yukon in 1985.

It was at this juncture that he decided to make racing his profession and began as an amateur under the guidance of trainers Stan Mellor and Jim Old. He rode his first winner under rules at Wolverhampton in March 1986 on the Scarborough trainer William Roy Robinson's Starjestic. In the ensuing months, Carl Llewellyn demonstrated his natural talent as a horseman on such jumpers as Lefrak City, Rattling City and Brave Hussar, contributing greatly to his winning the conditional jockeys' championship in the 1987–88 season with 41 winners.

During 1986 Carl became attached to Captain Tim Forster's Letcombe Basset training headquarters and it was on the Captain's Pegwell Bay that he won the 1988 Geoffrey Gilbey Memorial at Newbury. Later that year he achieved his first Festival success in the Mildmay of Flete Challenge Cup on Smart Tar and at Aintree in April Carl took his first close look at the National fences.

Riding the 'Ginger' McCain-trained Kumbi in the race so dramatically won by Brendan Powell and Rhyme 'N' Reason, they took a crashing fall at Becher's on the second circuit.

Among his 20 winners the following year were Pegwell Bay in the Glynwed International 'Chase, Eastshaw providing him with a second successive victory in the Geoffrey Gilbey Memorial, and Smart Tar in the Piper Champagne Golden Miller 'Chase at Cheltenham. It was with the last of these that Carl made a second attempt in the Grand National in 1989. After blundering badly at the first fence, Smart Tar recovered sufficiently to accompany the leaders for most of the first circuit. They were still in contention going back to Becher's for the final time but fell at the 20th.

It was another three years before Carl Llewellyn's name was again listed alongside a Grand National runner and during that period his reputation as a highly competent jockey increased tremendously. Nineteen wins during the 1989–90 campaign were followed by an impressive 32 the following year, during which Carl also finished third in Aintree's John Hughes Memorial Trophy over the National fences with Tom Caxton.

His initial major success of the 1991–92 jumping period came in the valuable Steel Plate and Sections Young 'Chasers Championship final at Cheltenham in November when bringing home the Nigel Twiston-Davies-trained Tipping Tim three lengths ahead of Peter Scudamore on Sea Island. It was an excellent start to what was to be a momentous year and at the Cheltenham Festival in March Carl Llewellyn caused something of a shock when winning the Ritz Club National Hunt Handicap 'Chase again on Tipping Tim but this time at 20–1.

Retained by the Lambourn trainer Nick Gaselee as a late replacement for his injured jockey Andy Adams, Carl welcomed the opportunity of partnering Party Politics in the 1992 Grand National and also his old friend Tipping Tim on the opening day of the meeting.

The 14–1 outsider of eight runners in the Martell Cup over three miles and one furlong of the Mildmay course, Tipping Tim gave a very good account of himself to finish second behind the speedier King's Fountain. Over the same distance the next day, Carl took the mount on the promising youngster trained by David Nicholson, Barton Bank, in the Heidsieck Dry Monopole Novices Hurdle. The least fancied of Nicholson's two runners in the race at 20–1, Barton Bank was given a well-judged waiting race by Carl Llewellyn, who brought the gelding gradually through the field to lead over the final flight of hurdles and win by six lengths from their 4–1 stable companion Bishops Island.

Kim Bailey's Docklands Express, ridden by champion jockey Peter Scudamore, was the 15–2 favourite for the National, with Brown Windsor and Twin Oaks the next-best backed. There was also plenty of money for the Cheltenham Gold Cup winner Cool Ground at 10–1, Auntie Dot on 12s, with Laura's Beau and Party Politics on offer at 14–1.

With only a two-minute delay at the start, the 40 runners galloped away into the country with Golden Minstrel blazing a trail ahead of Willsford, Brown Windsor, Hotplate and Forest Ranger, with the rest closely bunched. At Becher's Brook Brown Windsor collided with Forest Ranger, which put the former out of the race. With the leading group still closely bunched, they headed back in the direction of the racecourse after jumping the Canal Turn. As Golden Minstrel began to lose ground, Willsford took up the running to lead the unusually large number of 33 other survivors back towards the Chair. With the race still wide open at the end of the first round, Willsford and Golden Minstrel led the way back out into the country again, followed by Ghofar, Hotplate, Party Politics and Forest Ranger with Cool Ground making rapid progress from the rear, together with Romany King. Stretching out well over Becher's, Hotplate led by two lengths from Ghofar, Golden Minstrel, Romany King and Party Politics but Cloney Grange and Mister Ed both fell here and Jamie Osborne made a remarkable recovery on Whats The Crack. Richard Guest struck the front with Romany King at the Canal Turn, leading the well strung-out survivors over Valentine's and back towards the racecourse. Romany King was overtaken at the fourth-last, however, by the giant Party Politics. The race now entered its final stage and was on in earnest. Crossing the Melling Road these two were closely attended by Stay On Tracks, Docklands Express, Ghofar, Old Applejack, Over The Road, Cool Ground, Twin Oaks, Laura's Beau and Forest Ranger. After jumping the penultimate fence, though, it was definitely a two-horse race, with Party Politics holding the upper hand from the still dangerous Romany King but, keeping his lead over the last, Carl Llewellyn kicked confidently for home. Riding a superb finish at the end of such a long contest, Carl kept his mount hard at work to withhold the sustained challenge of a very brave Romany King by two and a half lengths. Laura's Beau was some way back in third place, followed by Docklands Express, Twin Oaks and Just So. In all there were 22 finishers but for the winning connections the bare statistics of the race mattered little.

Standing over 18 hands high, Party Politics was probably the biggest horse to succeed in the National and as an out-and-out stayer, the extreme distance and severe obstacles suited him down to the ground.

Carl experienced his best season so far, not merely by finishing ninth among the leading jockeys with 53 winning rides, but more satisfyingly by gaining that Aintree success attained by so few.

Early in the new jumping period, Carl resumed his successful association with Tipping Tim, winning a hard-fought tussle with Neale Doughty on Pat's Jester in the Tetley Bitter Charlie Hall 'Chase at Wetherby by a neck. A fortnight later he rode Tipping Tim to a more decisive and important victory in the Mackeson Gold Cup at Cheltenham.

Big race victories came aplenty that season for Carl Llewellyn: the SGB Handicap 'Chase at Ascot with Captain Dibble; Baring Securities Tolworth Hurdle at Sandown on Sun Surfer; again at the Esher track, this time aboard the outstanding Nigel Twiston-Davies-trained youngster Young Hustler in the Scilly Isles Novices 'Chase – and yet again at Sandown in the Agfa Hurdle, a decisive (if shock) victory with 33–1 shot Mole Board.

Improving with every race, Young Hustler romped home impressively in the Arlington Premier Series 'Chase Final at Newbury in mid-February and, most importantly to Carl, Party Politics carried him to victory in the Greenall Gold Cup 'Chase at Haydock. With this success, all connected with the gelding had good reason to look forward to April at Aintree with high hopes.

At the Cheltenham Festival Carl Llewellyn scored another surprise success with another Nigel Twiston-Davies newcomer, the six-year-old Gaelstrom, who ran out an easy winner at long odds in the Sun Alliance Novices Hurdle. At Ascot, during Grand National week, Carl won the Letherby And Christopher Long Distance Hurdle with Sweet Duke, another from Nigel Twiston-Davies' stable.

Completely satisfied with the preparation Party Politics had received, Carl felt confident that they could give another good account of themselves in the National, but sadly for all involved with the race everything went pear-shaped. Carl was caught up with his companions in the humiliating double false start, which led to the race being declared void and nobody was a winner. Indeed, considering everyone's intense commitment through an entire season, everyone was a loser. His final tally of 68 winners, which gained him eighth place among the leaders, was small consolation for the lost opportunity of another glory day at Aintree.

Carl was without a mount in the 1994 National but was back the following year with Young Hustler, although their partnership was short-lived as a result of Carl being unseated at the first open ditch. It was the third fence again 12 months later at Aintree, which brought a premature end to Carl Llewellyn's aspirations when his former champion Party Politics fell with him there.

Enduring that traumatic day of the bomb threat in 1997, which caused the postponement of the National, Carl, along with his fellow jockeys, waited out that long weekend in a manner far more meaningful than the intentions of the perpetrators of the outrage that day. Seemingly without a chance of success, he lined up on that 'mystical Monday' astride the 100–1 outsider Camelot Knight. Given a perfect ride throughout, Camelot Knight responded brilliantly over the final mile to finish a respectable third behind the runaway winner Lord Gyllene and Suny Bay.

In the annals of Aintree's annual marathon the assumption that history has a habit of repeating itself has never been more forcibly endorsed than in the 1998 Grand National. Once again Carl Llewellyn acquired a ride in the race due solely to another jockey suffering an injury. Carl must well have remembered that time six years before when Andy Adams missed out on what would have been the highlight of an otherwise undistinguished career because of a broken leg.

This time round the casualty was Tom Jenks and the horse concerned a high-mileage gelding trained by Nigel Twiston-Davies and owned by a syndicate headed by Aintree's Press Officer, Nigel Payne.

Earth Summit had already proved his ability in jumping and staying long distances by winning both the Scottish National at Ayr and more recently its Welsh equivalent at Chepstow. In between these victories the horse had suffered very severe injuries through a fall at Haydock Park which proved almost fatal. Somehow, Nigel Twiston-Davies restored him, not just to full fitness but to his former effervescent attitude to steeplechasing. A renowned mudlark, the gelding found the heavy going at Aintree on the day exactly to his liking. All things considered, he was a worthy favourite at 7–1 for the 1998 Grand National.

Joint second favourites on the 8–1 mark were Samlee and Him Of Praise, with Challenger Du Luc, Rough Quest, Nahthen Lad and Banjo the best supported of the remainder. The 37 runners got away to a good start, with Greenhil Tare Away and Scotton Banks leading into the first fence, where among the five fallers were Banjo and Challenger Du Luc. At the first ditch, Fabricator fell followed by Do Rightly at the next and Griffins Bar and Celtic Abbey at the fifth. Over Becher's the lead was contested by Greenhil Tare Away, Decyborg and the French challenger Ciel Be Brion. After starting slowly, Earth Summit had by now moved into the mid-division, Carl Llewellyn taking the longest way round on the wide outside. There was little change in the order jumping the Canal Turn and on the run back towards the Anchor Crossing the casualty rate increased with the falls of Dun Belle at Valentine's and Damas two jumps later at the open ditch. Nahthen Lad unseated his rider and General Crack was pulled up a long way behind the field. With two riderless horses threatening trouble approaching the Chair, Ciel De Brion, Greenhil Tare Away and Decyborg still cleared it well, closely pursued by St Mellion Fareway, Go Universal, Scotton Banks and the rapidly improving Earth Summit. Three stragglers pulled up early on the second circuit but Rough Quest and Suny Bay made tremendous improvement from the rear and as Greenhil Tare Away regained the lead he was followed over Becher's by Ciel De Brion, Earth Summit, Suny Bay, Brave Highlander, St Mellion Fareway and Rough Quest. The striking grey Suny Bay appeared the stronger as he jumped into third place at the Canal Turn. With Brave Highlander dislodging his jockey here and Ciel De Brion coming down at the fence after Valentine's, there were now only a handful left in the contest. Beginning to tire, Greenhil Tare Away was easily passed by Suny Bay and Earth Summit just before falling at the 27th. With the race now just between Suny Bay and Earth Summit, they drew ever further away from the few struggling behind, crossing the Melling Road side by side, their jockeys intent on jumping the last two fences safely. Still together when touching down after the last fence, Carl Llewellyn immediately took Earth Summit ahead to race clear and win with something in hand by 11 lengths from the gallant top-weight Suny Bay. A long way back in third place came Richard Dunwoody on Samlee, followed by St Mellion Fareway, Gimme Five and Killeshin, the only others to get round.

It had been a very exhausting race for all competitors but with Earth Summit revelling in the mud and his jockey riding a tactically brilliant race there can be no doubt that even with a big weight concession from the runner-up, the best horse won on the day.

Continuing to partner winners on a regular basis again the following season, Carl again took the mount on Earth Summit in the 1999 Grand National happy in the knowledge that the gelding had shown his well-being earlier that term when winning Aintree's Becher's 'Chase. This time, though, they didn't have ground that suited them and after jumping well through the entire journey could only finish in eighth place.

Weighing-out for the 2000 National, Carl Llewellyn this time rode a complete outsider, the 100–1 grey gelding Senor El Betrutti but, living up to his long odds, the 11 year old came down at the first fence.

Riding the top-weight Beau for Nigel Twiston-Davies in the 2001 Grand

National, Carl was again teaming up with a recognised mudlark but the going was more demanding than when he won on Earth Summit. In the worst conditions witnessed at the course since 1955, a colossal pile-up at the Canal Turn decimated the field and, as Beau led into the Chair, he was cannoned into by another horse. Only through a brilliant piece of horsemanship did Carl Llewellyn keep the partnership intact but in the process both his reins finished up on the same side of his mount's neck and from there on Beau was completely without steering. Over the Water Jump and back into the country, in what must have been a nightmare experience for Carl, Beau still led a pitifully small number of weary survivors until at the 19th Beau lost his rider when pecking badly. Despite brave attempts to remount, Carl was unsuccessful as the riderless Beau proceeded to chase the few still in the race.

Still among the leading prize-money-earning jockeys, Carl Llewellyn is a popular figure on racecourses throughout the land and with two National victories already in the bag it is not beyond his outstanding capabilities to make it three before he decides to hang up his boots.

Jason Titley

Born in Shannon, County Clare, on 2 March 1971, Jason Titley rode his first winner at Limerick on Cupincur in 1988 and the young man soon notched up a steady run of victories in his homeland.

It was not until 1992 that his career really began to take off, though, with a series of big wins which quickly increased demands for his services. In January at Leopardstown, Jason rode the 20–1 shot How's The Boss for trainer Brassil to a sparkling win in the Ladbroke Limited Extended Handicap Hurdle, leaving such established jockeys as Charlie Swan, Mark Dwyer, Graham McCourt and Peter Scudamore trailing in his wake.

Again with a long-priced outsider, My View, the youngster stormed to victory in the Coral Golden Hurdle Final at the Cheltenham Festival for the Irish trainer Michael Purcell. At Fairyhouse in April he won the Jameson Irish Grand National, giving Vanton an intelligent and powerful ride. He finished a brilliant term on Natalie's Fancy in the Galway Hurdle and his impressive displays were considered by many a foretaste of greater things to come.

Sadly, however, that which was so confidently predicted somehow failed to materialise and for no apparent reason Jason seemed to have lost the winning touch and, worse still, was now finding it difficult to get rides.

At the Aintree spring meeting in 1994 Jason managed to secure a ride on Shawiya, which he had previously ridden to victory in Ireland. In running they gave a reasonable account of themselves to come sixth behind their exceptional countryman Danoli in the Martell Aintree Hurdle. Jason Titley filled the same position in the Stakis Scottish Grand National at Ayr a little over a fortnight later when aboard Into The Red, behind a gutsy little six year old called Earth Summit.

It would be pure conjecture to guess the circumstances surrounding Jason Titley's emergence from the wilderness, circumstances so often encountered by young and hopeful jockeys. Unquestionably, though, one of the major factors was that in 1995 Mrs Jenny Pitman found herself with no less than six horses still in the Grand National at the five-day forfeit stage. Somewhat late in the day, the 24-year-old Jason was engaged to partner one of the least fancied of the sextet, the 12-year-old Royal Athlete.

As Jenny Pitman herself freely admitted, 'Alfie' (her pet name for Royal Athlete), had been a sheer nightmare to train, suffering one injury after another. Even getting him to Aintree fit enough to compete had developed into a major task. So far as Jason Titley was concerned, the most important thing to him was that at last he would take part in the one race in the calendar which could mean everything to any aspiring jockey.

Of the 35 runners taking part, that proven stayer Master Oats was favourite at 5–1, with the versatile mare Dubacilla second choice on the 9–1 mark and Young Hustler, Country Member, Miinnehoma, Crystal Spirit and Lusty Light also receiving much attention from the gambling public. Probably the least heard of among Mrs Pitman's jockeys that year was Jason, with Peter Niven accompanying her Superior Finish, John White on Esha Ness, Rodney Farrant riding Lusty Light and Warren Marston and Brendan Powell in charge of Garrison Savannah and Do Be Brief respectively. With Lusty Light the most fancied of her representatives at 12–1 and the already proven Aintree performer Garrison Savannah on 16s, the rest of her contingent received scant regard and Royal Athlete went off at 40–1.

Away to a good start at the first time of asking, Camelot Knight, Master Oats and Into The Red took their 32 opponents on to unknown consequences, with the first fence again putting paid to the chances of too many. Errant Knight, Lusty Light, Bishops Hall, The Committee, Country Member, Tinryland and Jumbeau all fell victim to the very first obstacle. Leading over Becher's Brook, Master Oats jumped it well on the outside of the course but was headed two fences later when Superior Finish took up the running with a fine leap at the Canal Turn. Closely followed by Into The Red, Garrison Savannah, Riverside Boy and another of Jenny Pitman's runners, Do Be Brief, Superior Finish lost his jockey when blundering at the jump after Valentine's and from there on the lead changed a number of times on the way back to the racecourse. Clearing the Chair well, Do Be Brief held a narrow advantage over Crystal Spirit, Camelot Knight, Ebony Jane and Master Oats, with plenty still well in touch. Jason Titley, having settled his mount early on, could now be seen making ground fast on Royal Athlete and, after jumping the Water Jump within easy reach of the leaders, struck the front at the first fence back in the country. Topsham Bay, Master Oats, Into The Red, Do Be Brief and Over the Deal were all in hot pursuit of Royal Athlete on the way back to Becher's but at the fence before the Brook Camelot Knight and Desert Lord fell. Giving his horse a tremendous ride, Jason was still dictating the pace over the Canal Turn and when joined by Master Oats at Valentine's these two opened up a gap between themselves and those behind. Getting the measure of Master Oats at the last ditch, Royal Athlete drew steadily away. He jumped the final obstacle with a commanding lead and easily withheld the late challenge of Party Politics to win by seven lengths. He was followed home by Over The Deel, Dubacilla, Into The Red, Romany King and nine others, which included the favourite Master Oats and Garrison Savannah.

Both trainer Jenny Pitman and her assistant Mark Pitman were generous in their praise of Jason Titley's handling of the winner, declaring that, 'Jason gave that horse the most wonderful ride and, yes, we will be happy to use him again on our horses in the future.'

The jockey himself appeared a little surprised by all the attention he received and when interviewed simply remarked,

> I walked the course this morning with Mark Pitman, who gave me
> some valuable advice from his rides at Aintree and Royal Athlete gave
> me a tremendous ride. You ride every fence as they come, there were
> hardly any hiccups and, although he fiddled a bit at the last, he was
> brilliant. I could hear Party Politics somewhere on the run to the post
> but I didn't look round.

In the 1996 National Jason rode Nick Gaselee's Bavard Dieu but was unseated when the horse landed badly at the first fence. The following year he was again booked by Jenny Pitman to partner her promising eight-year-old Nahthen Lad. That year's runaway winner Lord Gyllene left his 35 opponents trailing from the early stages of the contest and Jason finished in ninth place of the 17 finishers.

A few weeks later in his homeland at Fairyhouse Jason Titley repaid Mrs Pitman's confidence when winning the Irish Grand National on her Mudahim. Shortly afterwards he became first jockey to Henrietta Knight but eventually moved back to Ireland where he continued his riding career. Without a National ride in either 1998 or 1999, Jason returned to Aintree for the 2000 race to partner the well-fancied Willie Mullins-trained Micko's Dream but the pair fell at the first fence.

Still riding plenty of winners in his native land, it is only on rare occasions that Jason Titley competes in Britain but the memory of that glorious victory on Royal Athlete at Liverpool in 1995 will remain with him always.

Michael Anthony Fitzgerald

Born in Cork City in May 1970 and raised in Camolin, County Wexford, Mick Fitzgerald learned an early lesson from his father Frank, who told him on many occasions, 'If you want something, you've got to go out and earn it. It won't just happen, you've got to make it happen.' Very wise words indeed, which were accepted without question and to which even now, as a highly successful practitioner of his trade, Mick still strictly adheres.

Blessed with very supportive parents, Mick rode from his earliest years in local shows. He frequently went hunting but it was the availability of the many ponies he helped break with his father which imbued him with the perfect credentials for the profession he so desperately wished to enter – that of a professional jockey.

His first break into racing came when his father was repairing a client's car and the customer noticed young Mick riding a pony close by. A friend of Coolgreaney trainer Richard Lister, the client mentioned that there could well be a position for the youngster at those stables. Mick was soon employed there and Frank Fitzgerald ferried his son to and from the training establishment for the next 12 months. Mick at once knew there could be no other future for him but within horse racing.

Upon leaving school at the age of 15 he was employed full time at the yard and at Gowran Park in 1985 he took part in his first race in which he finished fourth on Being Bold. Still riding on the flat at 7st 6lb, Mick competed in a further 21 races without riding a single winner. When he moved to the stables of trainer John Hayden, things not only failed to improve but Mick's stature increased an extra four inches – and with it grew his weight.

Fully aware that a future of any kind in flat racing was now out of the question, he decided the National Hunt side of the sport was his only hope of making anything of himself as a jockey. With a view to taking a chance across the Irish Sea, he telephoned the Royston trainer John Jenkins and was over the moon when offered the position of being his conditional jockey. Soon he was on the move again, though, and, realising the opportunities for rides would be more plentiful at a smaller yard, he successfully applied for a job with the Devon permit-holder Richard Tucker.

Inside a month of joining the yard Mick at last experienced the thrill of riding his first winner, Lover's Secret, at Ludlow on 11 December 1988, and a couple of weeks later he boosted his confidence when scoring a second victory. It was to be another 18 months before he again enjoyed the sensation of riding into the winner's enclosure and towards the end of that frustrating period Mick began to consider going off to try his luck in New Zealand. A chance ride from another permit-holder, Ray Callow, resulted in that long-awaited third winner on a horse called Sunset Sam in the Holiday Selling Hurdle at Ludlow on the 16 April 1990.

Moving on to another trainer, Gerald Ham at Axbridge in Somerset, things improved dramatically for Mick and all thoughts of travelling to the other side of the world left his mind. A win at Sandown Park on Rafiki went a long way to restoring his confidence and the best stroke of luck to come his way since leaving Ireland was when he was offered the job riding Mrs Jackie Retter's horses.

A lady trainer based in Exeter, Mrs Retter had around 20 horses in her care and was making a reputation for herself as a skilful trainer. Appointing a 7lb-claiming jockey such as Mick Fitzgerald paid him a huge compliment.

The success they shared on the racecourse is reflected in Mick Fitzgerald's winning figures for the 1991–92 season, when he was led into the winner's enclosure on 38 occasions, most of these on horses prepared by Jackie Retter. His total for the previous three terms of activity had been a mere 14. Another milestone that year for the young Irishman was making his début over the National fences when riding Skinnhill for Tim Thomson Jones in the John Hughes Memorial Trophy, finishing tenth behind The Antartex.

By the end of the following period of jumping, however, Mick could justifiably say that he had arrived, for with 54 successes to his credit he filled 11th place among the leading riders. It was also in that year that he came very close to achieving his first Cheltenham Festival victory when finishing second on Smartie Express behind Sacre D'or in the Mildmay of Flete Challenge Cup. Also that year he made his second attempt at the big Liverpool fences. Riding the Paul Nicholls-trained Wellknown Character in the John Hughes Memorial Trophy 'Chase, they failed to complete the course in the contest, which was won by Adrian Maguire on Sirrah Jay.

Having caught the attention of the trainer Nick Henderson, Mick Fitzgerald could look forward to an abundance of runners for the foreseeable future but, like all in his profession, he still had to produce a regular supply of winners and to do that, of course, he had to steer clear of serious injuries. This is no mean task when jockeys risk life and limb every time they mount a horse.

His most productive period on the racecourse up to this point came during the 1993–94 jumping fixtures, by the end of which he had amassed 68 victories, earning sixth place in the table behind the champion Richard Dunwoody. Among his most important wins were Light Veneer in the Steel

Plate and Sections Young 'Chasers Championship at Ascot and a milestone Cheltenham Festival success on Lady Lloyd Webber's Raymylette in the Cathcart Challenge Cup. The win at Cheltenham firmly cemented his association with Nicky Henderson and Mick made his presence well felt as that trainer's retained jockey at Severn Barrows in Lambourn. To the delight of all concerned, the partnership of Henderson and Fitzgerald proved more successful than anyone could have hoped, with Mick regularly putting the triumphant finishing touches on the racecourse to Nicky's diligent preparations. Their similar personalities also added admirably to the relationship and through their joint efforts Mick Fitzgerald steadily climbed ever closer to the top of that envied jockeys' championship table. An added bonus for the Mick came in April 1995 when he got the leg-up from Nicky Henderson on Tinryland for the Martell Grand National. Although falling at the first fence, he felt confident that more opportunities in the big race would come his way.

Ironically, though, the greatest moment of his career was provided by another handler of horses, Terry Casey, who operated from his stables at Dorking in Surrey. A fellow son of the Emerald Isle, William Terence Casey spent most of his life as a jockey in Ireland after having served his jockey's apprenticeship with the great Aubrey Brabazon. Failing to set the world alight in that capacity, Terry turned his to attention to training after serving as Head Lad to both Paddy Mullins and Frank Gilman.

Terry Casey had already tasted the thrill of success at Aintree in 1986 when he turned out Glenrue to win the Whitbread Trophy 'Chase over the famous obstacles and now, ten years later, he had another diamond in his care, the ten-year-old bay gelding Rough Quest.

After finishing third on Big Matt in the Mackeson Gold Cup at Cheltenham in November, Mick rode him to victory at Ascot in the Victor Chandler 'Chase and recorded another big race success aboard Amtrek Express in Sandown's Agfa Diamond Steeplechase some weeks later. In the interim period he had taken the mount on Terry Casey's Rough Quest at Newbury in the Hennessy Cognac Gold Cup, finishing a reasonable second behind Dean Gallagher on Couldnt Be Better. So early in the campaign, little thought could be given to what glories may lie ahead. At Kempton Park towards the end of February Mick Fitzgerald was committed to riding his stable's Amtrek Express in the Racing Post 'Chase and was unseated during the contest. The winner that day was Rough Quest, with Richard Dunwoody in the saddle.

A spare ride for Guy Harwood on Amancio in Sandown's Imperial Cup brought some consolation and then at the Cheltenham Festival he regained the ride on Rough Quest in the feature race of the meeting, the Tote Cheltenham

Gold Cup. Always up with the pace, Mick gave the Casey horse a superb ride and in with a great chance at the last fence, was beaten for speed on the run to the line by that very good Irish horse Imperial Call. It was only afterwards that it was discovered Rough Quest was suffering from a muscle enzyme problem and with the gelding already promoted as favourite for the Grand National by the bookmakers Terry Casey was forced to warn punters that Rough Quest must be considered a doubtful runner at Aintree.

It speaks volumes for the trainer's expertise that his Gold Cup runner-up was in the line-up for the National on 30 March 1996 and that the man in the saddle was Mick Fitzgerald. Sent off 7–1 favourite of the 27 runners, Rough Quest was up against some outstanding staying jumpers that day and, as was always the case with a newcomer to the Grand National's obstacles, there had to be a question as to how he would cope with them.

According to the betting, Fitzgerald had most to fear from Young Hustler, Son Of War, Superior Finish, Party Politics, Life Of A Lord and Deep Bramble but at the end of the day it would be courage and ability which counted more than mere statistics.

Away to a good start, the 200–1 outsider Sure Metal, trained by 'Ginger' McCain and ridden by his son Donald, led them all a merry chase down to and over the first fence. Young Hustler and Three Brownies were also well up with the pace but Bavard Dieu and Bishops Hall both lost their jockeys at the first and Party Politics fell two fences later. A beautiful leap at Becher's carried Sure Metal well over ahead of Three Brownies, Over The Deel, Sir Peter Lely and Young Hustler, with Rough Quest jumping well further back alongside Antonin, Far Senior and Riverside Boy. Over and around the Canal Turn there was little change in this order and returning to the racecourse, the race was still anybody's. Three Brownies held a fractional advantage jumping the Chair ahead of Sure Metal, Young Hustler, Greenhill Raffles, Superior Finish, Sir Peter Lely and Over The Deel. On the run back to Becher's Brook, Mick Fitzgerald gradually improved his position and was in ninth place jumping the Brook. So far the jockey's knowledge of his mount had served him well. He understood perfectly that it was essential to hold Rough Quest up, for once the horse struck the front he began to idle, thinking his job was done. Over the Canal Turn again, Young Hustler had assumed command from Sir Peter Lely, Three Brownies, Encore Un Peu and hot on their heels came Rough Quest and Life Of A Lord. Three from home, Encore Un Peu drew alongside Young Hustler and, after crossing the Melling Road, went clear of the top weight, whose nearest rivals included Three Brownies and the patiently ridden Rough Quest. Fully five lengths clear of the strongly finishing Rough Quest over the final fence, Encore Un Peu raced away on the flat looking all over the winner. With a little over a quarter of a mile to run, Mick set Rough Quest alight and the response was immediate. Drawing level at the elbow, Rough Quest veered slightly to his left, almost touching his rival but, quickly straightened by his jockey, he forged ahead without making any contact. Staying on in the bravest fashion, Rough Quest resisted the renewed challenge of Encore Un Peu to win by a length and a quarter, with Superior Finish third just ahead of Sir Peter Lely and Young Hustler. In all there were 17 finishers, the last being Sure Metal and young Donald McCain.

Even before they reached the unsaddling enclosure a stewards' enquiry was announced and for the following 15 minutes more anguish was felt by the winning connections than they'd experienced during the whole race. Eventually the all-clear signal was given that the placings remained unaltered, to many sighs of relief. Apart from the winning jockey, probably the happiest man that day at Aintree was another Fitzgerald, Mick's dad, Frank. When he finally caught up with his son he spoke just three words. That simple acknowledgement, 'You did it!', was as great a reward as any son can ever receive from a parent, made all the more valuable by knowing that without those parents' sacrifices nothing would have been possible.

The famous Des Lynam interview with the winning jockey for BBC's *Grandstand* was somewhat delayed due to the officials' enquiry but when it did take place it provided one of the most spontaneous and forever quoted comments ever delivered after a major sporting event. When asked by the genial presenter, 'How does it feel to have won the National?', Mick Fitzgerald's immediate and obviously genuine response was, 'After that, Des, even sex is an anti-climax.'

Accumulating a total of 68 winners that year gained Mick fifth place in the jockeys' list but more personally important was his success in winning the hand of his fiancée Jane in marriage (which, in the light of his comments to Des Lynam, says a great deal for the understanding of the lady).

Going from strength to strength, he continued his career very successfully, sharing famous victories with such outstanding horses as Remittance Man, Travado, Bacchanal, Marlborough, Tiutchev and Stormyfairweather. Mick has enjoyed many triumphs wearing Her Majesty the Queen Mother's colours and, perhaps setting the foundations for a future career when his riding days are over, has proved himself a highly popular and most articulate television pundit.

Adding to his list of many winners from Nicky Henderson's yard, his winning the Cheltenham Gold Cup in 1999 on See More Business was of particular significance to Mick, for the horse was trained by his brother-in-law Paul Nicholls.

In his four Grand National attempts since winning the race with Rough Quest, Mick has surprisingly failed to complete the course; pulling up when on the favourite Go Ballistic in 1997, pulling up again the following year with Rough Quest and falling at the second Becher's when going well in 1999 aboard Fiddling The Facts. Mick fell at the same point again when riding Esprit De Cotte in the 2000 Grand National and 12 months later at Aintree he was set to ride the same horse when an old injury recurred shortly before the race and he was unable to take part.

He did, however, that year achieve a fabulous Aintree victory in the Martell Cup on See More Business and it can surely only be a matter of time before he rides a second Grand National winner. For the last two seasons Mick Fitzgerald has been the leading rider at each Cheltenham Festival. His determination and persistence against all the odds is an example to all would-be jockeys.

Yet, above all this, his most likeable feature is his normality; his down-to-earth acceptance that he is privileged to be doing a job he enjoys very successfully. That ever-ready impish grin, with which he greets everyone, is the hallmark of a very decent man.

TEN

Anthony Dobbin

Born in Downpatrick, Northern Ireland, on May Day in 1972, Tony Dobbin followed the path of many of his fellow countrymen when deciding to attempt a career in horse racing. Such was his fervour that he crossed the Irish Sea at the age of 15 to pursue that dream.

At once involved in the demanding day-to-day running of a racing stable at Neville Callaghan's headquarters in Newmarket, Tony suffered such dreadful homesickness that, with his emotions in a turmoil, he returned home. Such was the lure of the turf, however, that the youngster was soon back in England, this time in the north-west at the stables of the legendary Jonjo O'Neill.

Former champion jump jockey turned trainer, Jonjo had settled in Penrith, Cumbria, after retiring from the saddle. Not just a specialist with horses, that gentle son of Erin must also have possessed the ability to dispense care and consideration to a young man far from home trying to follow in his footsteps. As an apprentice, Tony rode his first winner on the flat in May 1990 at Hamilton Park riding a horse called Stay Awake, and before leaving Jonjo some three years later he rode a further 24 winners for his Penrith yard.

When offered a job by the former Grand National-winning jockey Maurice Barnes, Tony jumped at the opportunity to further his experience and moved the short distance to the Little Salkeld handler's training establishment. It proved a very wise decision for by the end of that 1994 season Tony had made his mark in the best possible way by finishing in 11th place among the leading riders with 45 successes to his credit.

There was also, during that campaign, another major first for the young Ulsterman: his initial entry into the winner's enclosure at the Cheltenham Festival after riding a brilliant finish on Dizzy in the County Handicap Hurdle. The winning distances were a mere neck and three-quarters of a length from two Irish challengers, Diplomatic and Steel Dawn, but both Tony and his mount's trainer, Peter Monteith, were over the moon with the hard-fought victory.

Some weeks later he rode Over The Deel to finish sixth over the National fences in the John Hughes Memorial Trophy 'Chase and two days after that lined up at the start for his introduction to the Martell Grand National. Partnering the John Howard Johnson-trained Ushers Island in the big race, they were just behind the leading bunch until a blunder at the first open ditch caused them to part company. A fortnight later, Ushers Island sprung a surprise when winning the Whitbread Gold Cup at Sandown, only this time the eight year old was ridden by Charlie Swan.

It was no doubt his victory with Dizzy at Cheltenham that brought Tony Dobbin the plum job of stable jockey to Gordon Richards at his powerful Greystoke stables in Penrith.

His first valuable triumph for his new employer was with the highly promising grey One Man in the Hennessy Cognac Gold Cup but some little time afterwards Tony was inexplicably 'jocked off' the horse in favour of Richard Dunwoody. Despite the disappointment, he continued to ride plenty of winners for the remainder of that period for Gordon Richards, as well as picking up some from other yards. The following term was equally rewarding, Tony amassing a total of 67 wins, which gave him the sixth slot among the top jockeys behind the champion Tony McCoy. Among his big race victories were the Premier Long Distance Hurdle at Haydock Park on his stable's Better Times Ahead and, from the same source, Addington Boy at Ayr, where he took the Edinburgh Woollen Mill's Future Champion Novices 'Chase.

Tony Dobbin's first taste of Aintree glory came early in the 1996–97 season, when riding a perfectly judged race to win the Crowther Homes Becher Steeplechase over three miles and three furlongs of the Grand National course on the Mary Reveley-prepared Into The Red. The smile of joy as he entered the winner's enclosure that November day showed perfectly just how much that success meant to him and one could but wonder how he would react if ever he entered that hallowed area after a National. Those wondering did not have long to wait to find out.

Among the many trainers Tony shared his services between, when not required for a Greystoke horse, was Steve Brookshaw, the nephew of the late, great jockey Tim Brookshaw. Among the horses in his care at Steve's Preston Farm stables at Uffington near Shrewsbury was a New Zealand-bred bay gelding named Lord Gyllene, who in his ten races in this country had won three and been unplaced just once. A winner three times over long distances at Uttoxeter during the early part of 1997, his latest attempt to make it a four-timer when running in the Marston's Pedigree Midland Grand National only just failed when he was caught close home and beaten into second place by

Seven Towers. Having struck up a perfect working relationship with Lord Gyllene, Tony was booked to partner him at Aintree in the Grand National and with the gelding's recent excellent form he figured prominently in all ante-post betting lists.

That Saturday at Aintree will always be remembered for the mass evacuation of the racecourse after a coded warning of a bomb being somewhere on the premises was received just minutes before the scheduled time of starting. Along with thousands of stranded racegoers, the local people assisted and comforted each other in their plight and all the National jockeys found themselves adrift in just their flimsy silks and breeches. With commendable energy and initiative, the management and staff of Aintree worked almost non-stop to restage the race the following Monday and in a most surreal atmosphere the 36 runners lined up for the event that not even cowardly terrorists could stop.

The Mick Fitzgerald-ridden Go Ballistic was the 7–1 favourite from Suny Bay at 8s, the Irish hope Wylde Hyde on 11–1 and Avro Anson and Smith's Band both heavily backed at 12–1. Antonin, Lo Stregone and Lord Gyllene each attracted plenty of money which made them 14–1 chances.

At one minute past four, as the tape rose to set them on their way, the roar from the greatly reduced attendance was far more muted than what one expects at the beginning of the great race but nonetheless the spirit of the occasion was the same as always and somehow this time there was a proud attitude of defiance.

Dextra Dove, Lord Gyllene and Smith's Band were the first to land over the initial obstacle and within strides, Tony Dobbin found his mount in the lead. Behind them the only faller was Full Of Oats and unusually there were no further upsets on the way to Becher's Brook. Very wisely, Tony allowed Lord Gyllene to dictate things up in front and, leaping really well over Becher's, his nearest rivals were the grey Suny Bay and Smith's Band. The next plain fence put Glemot and Back Bar out of the race and, striding out in front, Lord Gyllene cleared the Canal Turn ahead of Suny Bay, Smith's Band, Northern Hide, Wylde Hyde and Nahthen Lad. The field was well strung out by the time they crossed Melling Road to re-enter the racecourse proper and with the leader still setting a terrific pace many were already struggling to keep in touch. Don't Light Up and Straight Talk both fell before reaching the Chair but with a brilliant leap Lord Gyllene landed safely and was still in front over the biggest obstacle on the course. With Smith's Band almost level with the leader here, Suny Bay was still going easily on the inside of the course running to the Water Jump and it was at this point that Tony proved in the most convincing manner what a really fine horseman he is. Coming from somewhere further back as the leading trio reached the final obstacle on the first circuit, the riderless Glemot suddenly charged forward and, forcing his way in front of and across Lord Gyllene, appeared to be in the process of carrying Tony's mount to the left and off the course. The jockey's reflexes were spot-on, as he calmly checked his horse in mid-stride and brilliantly avoided a collision with the would-be intruder to clear the whole expanse of the water without losing his place at the head of the field. Hugging the inside rail, Lord Gyllene continued in front, jumping superbly in front of Suny Bay, Smith's Band, Northern Hide, Valiant Warrior, Avro Anson and Dextra Dove. Two fences before Becher's the Richard Dunwoody-ridden Smith's Band came to grief when he'd been looking threatening, and with Lord Gyllene still well in control with his impeccable jumping he never appeared likely to be headed. Becher's, the Canal Turn and Valentine's Brook were each met with perfect precision and making his way back towards the racecourse the only dangers to Lord Gyllene – apart from the remaining fences – were Suny Bay and Master Oats. The main threat, Suny Bay, ruined any chance he had at the final open ditch, the 27th, when he crashed straight through the fence and, although still on his feet, this error took a lot out of the grey. Coming to the final fence with such a commanding lead, only a fall could prevent Lord Gyllene from winning and, jumping it perfectly as he had done throughout the race, that danger was passed. Romping home to one of the easiest victories ever seen at Aintree, Tony Dobbin rode Lord Gyllene to a 25-length victory from Suny Bay, the 100–1 outsider Camelot Knight and Buckboard Bounce. Thirteen others completed the trip but for the winning connections this mattered little.

Soon after his victory in the Grand National, Tony Dobbin appeared on the BBC's *National Lottery* programme as their guest presenter and one could be forgiven for thinking it was far more trying and considerably less satisfying than riding a horse like Lord Gyllene in the toughest race on earth. By the end of that wonderful jumping season, Tony had ridden 73 winners, the most important of course being at Aintree that Monday in April.

Without a ride in the 1998 National, he did, however, win the John Hughes Memorial Trophy 'Chase at Aintree in 1999 and he finished 17th in that year's Grand National on Avro Anson. Upon the death of Gordon Richards, his son Nicky took over the licence at Greystoke, with Tony Dobbin still retained as first jockey. In November 1999 he rewarded the confidence placed in him by winning Aintree's Becher Steeplechase on the Nicky Richards-trained Feels Like Gold.

Less successful at Aintree in the Spring, when he donned Lord Gyllene colours this time to ride Listen Timmy, Tony pulled his mount up between the Water Jump and the 17th fence. In an otherwise perfect period of racing, he finished fifth among the top jockeys with 71 victories, of which the most notable were with Nordance Prince at Wetherby and Master Tern for Jonjo O'Neill at Kelso and at the Cheltenham Festival in the Vincent O'Brien County Handicap Hurdle. He also rode John Howard Johnson's Forrestal particularly well to snatch fourth place in the John Hughes Memorial Trophy at Aintree.

With his unquestionable talents still in great demand, Tony persists in totting up the winners and all who know racing agree that this is a jockey who, whatever the race and whatever horse he rides, is always trying to win.

Although he had to pull up Listen Timmy again at the Water Jump in that dreadful ground at Aintree in the 2001 Grand National, there can be no doubt that, with his unique talent, Tony Dobbin will feature for many a year to come among the greats of his profession. The man who seldom, if ever, is seen without a meaningful smile on his face deserves, as much as anyone, another National success. If that fine day comes, Tony Dobbin will be just the same down-to-earth, sincere person as he was that day he rode the race of his life aboard Lord Gyllene.

Paul Carberry

For well over three centuries, breeders of thoroughbred racehorses have placed great store in the importance of pedigrees and bloodlines in their desire to produce the perfect racing machine. Still considered by some to be little more than theory, there can however be no doubt that the study of genetics has played an enormously important part in the development of the British bloodstock industry.

In simple terms, the reasoning upon which thoroughbred breeding is based is the belief that by carefully studying the bloodlines of a mare and stallion before deciding to mate them it should be possible to reproduce the most favourable characteristics of the respective ancestors in a future offspring. This well may be the case, certainly in human genealogy it has frequently been seen that certain people very often inherit a particular trait, talent or ability from their forebears. In the world of sport this has never been better demonstrated than in the Grand National, which, through its long history, has seen many family names reappearing through numerous decades. The Beasleys, Anthonys, Piggotts and members of the Rees family all added tremendously to the rich tapestry which has made the Grand National the most romantic of all sporting events.

In the final year of the twentieth century, this phenomenon was yet again demonstrated in a manner befitting a family's dedication to this particular endeavour.

Paul Carberry was born on 9 February 1974 in Ireland and was barely 14 months old when his father Tommy rode L'Escargot to victory ahead of Red Rum in the 1975 Grand National. Paul's maternal grandfather was Dan Moore, a leading Irish racehorse trainer who did in fact prepare L'Escargot for four Nationals, including the one he won. A former jockey himself, Dan Moore came breathtakingly close to winning the 1938 Grand National when he was beaten with Royal Danieli, just a short-head in arrears of the tiny American stallion Battleship.

With a pedigree such as this, there could only possibly be one avenue of enterprise for young Paul and almost as soon as he could walk he found most joy when sitting astride a horse. From showjumping, hunting and point-to-pointing, the unique skills inherited from his ancestors were honed razor-sharp in the rapid development of one of the most stylish riders seen for a very long time.

With the unlimited facilities available at his father's training establishment at Ballybin in County Meath, young Paul took every opportunity to ride as many different horses as possible on the gallops, thus adding greatly to his experience. In April 1993, he took part in one of his earliest major events, the Jameson Irish Grand National at Fairyhouse. In a highly competitive field he gave the seven-year-old Joe White a delightful ride which gained them seventh place behind Charlie Swan on Ebony Jane.

Riding principally for the Navan trainer Noel Meade in his homeland, Paul Carberry partnered that stable's Shirley's Delight into third place in the Daily Express Triumph Hurdle at the 1994 Cheltenham Festival and a few weeks later he rode the same horse when finishing fourth in the Glenlivet Anniversary Four-year-old Hurdle at Aintree behind another Irish invader, Tropical Lake.

Two days later, Tommy Carberry gave his son Paul the leg-up on his Rust Never Sleeps before sending them off for their first encounter with the Grand National. On dreadfully heavy ground, the race developed into a very desperate slogging match with the casualty rate mounting all the way round, but young Paul was still in the hunt with Rust Never Sleeps jumping the Canal Turn for the final time. It was only at the last ditch that the 66–1 shot reached the end of his tether and, blundering over the obstacle, unseated Paul.

The obvious brilliance of the young Irishman had by this time attracted the attention of the immensely wealthy owner Robert Ogden, who engaged Paul as his jockey on a three-year retainer. The confidence displayed by Mr Ogden was amply rewarded.

Somehow managing to divide his services between England and his native land, Paul Carberry, with the energy and willingness of youth, kept up a regular pattern of riding on both sides of the Irish Sea, ever aware of the concern of his mother Pamela and father Tommy. Yorkshireman Graham Bradley played a very important part in this stage of the youngster's association with steeplechasing, steering Paul away from the pitfalls and temptations young men will always be faced with.

In January 1996 Paul came second on Ferdy Murphy's Frickley behind champion Tony McCoy's mount Warm Spell in the Bic Razor Lanzarote Hurdle at Kempton Park. Shortly afterwards he recorded a superb victory in the Tote Gold Trophy Hurdle at Newbury on Andy Turnell's Squire Silk. At Aintree in April, Paul Carberry went for the John Hughes Memorial Trophy 'Chase on an old friend from his native land, the 33–1 chance Joe White. Displaying a confidence and ability way beyond his years, Paul kept his mount well in hand the whole way and, delivering his challenge at exactly the right time, ran on to win by a head from Go Universal ridden by his friend and mentor, Graham Bradley. Just a neck away in third place was Mugoni Beach in one of the most exciting climaxes to a race ever seen at Liverpool.

Proving himself equally adept over the minor obstacles, 24 hours later Paul rode Pleasure Shared to a most convincing victory in the Belle Epoque Sefton Novices Hurdle and looked forward to a second attempt the next day at the Grand National. His mount this time was the Irish-trained Three Brownies and, in a fast-run race, Paul yet again provided his charge with the best possible assistance to finish sixth behind Mick Fitzgerald on Rough Quest. His final major appearance that year was on Son Of War for Peter McCreery in the Jameson Irish Grand National and after a hard tussle, they gained sixth place behind Franny Woods and Feathered Gale.

In the re-scheduled Monday Grand National of 1997 Paul's mount Buckboard Bounce was putting in his best work towards the finish of the race when gaining fourth place behind the runaway winner Lord Gyllene.

Continuing to make his mark on both sides of the Irish Sea, Paul Carberry's racecourse activities left little time for relaxation and when it did he played as hard as he worked. Again on heavy ground in the 1998 Grand National, Paul made the best of his way for a long time in the race on Martin Pipe's Decyborg, only to have to pull up his mount three from home.

It was a totally different story in the Jameson Irish Grand National at Fairyhouse shortly afterwards, when Paul rode his father's eight-year-old gelding Bobbyjo to a decisive victory – and in so doing, he created a record. It was the first time in the 123-year history of the race that a family pair of father and son had won the event.

A plan of campaign was arranged for the gelding's activities during the 1998–99 season, with Tommy Carberry's target being the Grand National at Aintree in April 1999. Strangely though, Paul only rode the horse once in the run-up to the big race. That was in the Leopardstown 'Chase early in the year when he came fifth behind Hollybank Buck. But in four other steeplechases

Bobbyjo was well below form and his only success prior to Aintree was in a two-mile hurdle at Down Royal when ridden by Paul's younger brother Philip.

During this period Paul maintained a regular flow of winners in Ireland, winning twice on Imperial Call at Naas and Punchestown and on Nomadic at Gowran Park. In the Royal Sun Alliance 'Chase at the Cheltenham Festival, he secured an all-the-way victory on the Noel Chance-trained outsider Looks Like Trouble and from there his principal objective was the National.

At the beginning of Grand National week Bobbyjo was freely available at 33–1 with the bookmakers and on that day Paul rode Cardinal Hill to a resounding success in the Jameson Gold Cup at Fairyhouse. By the time he took his place with Bobbyjo among 32 hopefuls at Aintree the following Saturday, however, the best price available on his National ride was 10–1.

The consistent Mick Fitzgerald-ridden Fiddling The Facts went off the 6–1 favourite for the National from Double Thriller and Call It A Day on 7s. Others attracting heavy support included Eudipe, Addington Boy and, of course, Bobbyjo. From a good start, they charged down to the first fence, where Double Thriller was the only faller. Baronet was the next to go three fences later and at the first Becher's Tamarindo fell together with Mudahim. At this stage Lorcan Wyer's mount Blue Charm held a fractional lead over General Wolfe, Brave Highlander and Nahthen Lad. Also well in attendance were Fiddling The Facts, Feels Like Gold and Call It A Day, while Bobbyjo was noticeably being kept to the inside and jumping brilliantly just to the rear. Setting a very good gallop, Blue Charm was still in front rejoining the racecourse proper, leading over the Chair from Feels Like Gold, General Wolfe, Eudipe and the rapidly improving Bobbyjo. Hard on the leaders' heels were the grey Suny Bay and Adrian Maguire on Addington Boy but Cavalero came down at the Chair. Other fallers on the way back to Becher's were Commercial Artist and Cyborgo. Paul had given his mount a copybook ride straight from 'the off' and, steering clear of Frazer Island, Eudipe, Fiddling The Facts, Choisty and Camelot Knight, who all came to grief at the Brook, Bobbyjo was still well in the race. Over the Canal Turn Blue Charm still headed the rest, followed by Brave Highlander, Nahthen Lad, Feels Like Gold and Bobbyjo and in this order they re-crossed the Melling Road for the final time. Running on strongly in the closing stages of the race, Merry People moved up dangerously, only to fall at the second last and from there on the result rested between just four. Blue Charm landed first on the flat, with every obstacle not just safely cleared but jumped perfectly, with Call It A Day, Bobbyjo and Addington Boy breathing down the leader's neck. Paul Carberry had been hard at work on his horse for some time before the penultimate fence, yet Bobbyjo kept responding and switched to the outside, rallied gamely to race clear and win by ten lengths from Blue Charm, Call It A Day and Addington Boy. Eighteen horses eventually completed the course, including the bravely remounted Merry People and, most importantly, not one horse or rider was injured.

The celebrations for the winner began within strides of passing the winning post when some family members of the winning connections rather foolishly invaded the area of the racecourse near the finishing line. Innocently but foolishly attempting to greet their heroes, each of the first three horses home shied at the intrusion to such an extent that Richard Dunwoody was unseated from the third placed Call It A Day.

When entering the winner's enclosure, Paul Carberry himself was caught up in the excitement of the moment, standing up in his irons to dismount by swinging from the rafters of the roof of the building. It was all very good stuff for the media boys and, though frowned on by some, it was really only youthful exuberance at the realisation that he had just ridden the first Irish-trained Grand National winner for 24 years. Somewhere in the back of his mind was also the fact that it was his dad, Tommy, who had brought about that victory too.

Paul attempted to follow a similar route to Aintree with Bobbyjo the following year but the horse was unable to gain a place in his five races before the 2000 Grand National. Paul though, still rode a more than reasonable number of winners during this period, including a successful association with the brilliant Florida Pearl in the James Nicholson Wine Merchant Champion 'Chase at Down Royal and Leopardstown's Hennessy Cognac Gold Cup. At Cheltenham in March, Paul again exerted his authority when winning the Capel Cure Sharp Supreme Novices Hurdle with Sausalito Bay for trainer Noel Chance, after which his attention was centred on Aintree 2000.

On the first day of the meeting, Paul rode Ross Moff to victory in the Barton and Guestier Handicap Hurdle, which for many was a portent of his prospects in the National.

Further encouragement came for Carberry supporters in the first race on Grand National day, when his brother Philip rode the Paddy Hughes-trained Sharpaten to a comfortable victory in the Cordon Bleu Handicap Hurdle. The National itself was something of an anti-climax for the Carberry family, with Bobbyjo far less foot-perfect than the previous year. A number of errors during the course of the race ruled out the gelding's chances long before the second Canal Turn and it can truly be said that it was only with the assistance of Paul Carberry that Bobbyjo survived the test to finish in 11th place behind another Irish challenger, Papillon.

Tragically, Bobbyjo met with an injury during his preparation for the 2001 Grand National and a recurrence of the ailment led to his death shortly before his Aintree appointment, leaving Paul unable to compete in that year's event.

With such an abundance of natural talent, it is inconceivable that Paul Carberry should not achieve the ultimate victory at Aintree again and when that time arrives it will be just reward for a life fully committed to steeplechasing and the attainment of success, particularly at Aintree.

Ruby Walsh

After waiting almost a quarter of a century for a Grand National victory to match their heady days of the 1950s, Irish trainers produced two big Aintree winners within the space of 12 months on 8 April 2000.

Even more remarkable was the fact that, as in 1999, it was another father and son partnership which took steeplechasing's greatest prize back across the Irish Sea. In truth, the similarities between the winning connections of both years were nothing less than uncanny but they proved, if proof were needed, that history really does have a habit of repeating itself when it comes to the Grand National.

Ted Walsh was born in Fermoy, County Cork, the son of Ruby Walsh senior, who besides having a public house ran a livery stable in the area. After moving to the United States in 1954, they returned within two years to their homeland. Renting a yard at Chapelizod, the Walsh family later moved again, this time to a farm at Kill in County Kildare and it was from here that Ted Walsh began to make a name for himself as a horseman of great distinction.

In a thrilling career as an amateur, Ted Walsh became leading rider among the unpaid ranks on no less than 11 occasions and made something of a habit of making successful forays on the Cheltenham Festival. A total of four winners at the Prestbury Park course came his way during his career in the saddle, the most notable being when riding Peter McCreery's Hilly Way to victory in the Two-Mile Champion 'Chase Challenge Trophy. When eventually turning his attention to training, Ted Walsh saddled Commanche Court to win the Elite Racing Club Triumph Hurdle at Cheltenham in 1997, a success he described at the time as the highlight of his career. His only ride in the Grand National was in 1975, the year Tommy Carberry set Irish eyes a-smiling by winning on L'Escargot. In that race Ted was aboard Peter McCreery's 33–1 chance Castleruddery but the horse refused at the fence before Becher's first time round.

While still turning out his fair share of winners from a small yard, Ted Walsh has demonstrated his versatility as a journalist and broadcaster with RTE and *Channel 4 Racing* and in this capacity his racing expertise and humorous nature are always well received on both sides of the Irish Sea.

Following in his father's footsteps, Ruby Walsh also became a highly talented amateur rider and in his first season as a professional in 1999 he partnered the winners of 96 races to become the Irish champion jump jockey. His most important victories were with such horses as Goldanzig, Alexander Banquet, Rince Ri and Imperial Call. In 1998, his last season as an amateur, Ruby rode his father's horse Papillon in the Jameson Irish Grand National at Fairyhouse and, after being badly hampered early in the race, recovered brilliantly to finish a very good second to Bobbyjo. Having finished fourth in the race the previous year behind Mudahim, it was felt by Ted Walsh that to be seen at his best Papillon needed a severe test of stamina. A long-term plan was decided upon: to aim the gelding at the 2000 Grand National. Although sustaining an injury in his third attempt at the Irish Grand National in 1999, hopes were high that he could be restored to fitness in time for the Aintree spectacular.

Mrs Betty Moran, the owner of Papillon, is an extremely wealthy American lady whose family fortune originates from their involvement with Smith Kline Beecham. Being brought up in a hunting and racing atmosphere in the United States, she became acquainted with Ted Walsh's father, Ruby, during the mid-1950s. Ted Walsh bought Papillon on behalf of Mrs Moran in 1995 for 5,300 guineas and at her request proceeded to train the horse for National Hunt racing on this side of the Atlantic. It took Ted Walsh some time to convince the owner that her horse should take part in the National, for she was fearful of Papillon receiving an injury in the race but with his persuasive assurances, Betty Moran relented and agreed to the Aintree venture.

Papillon was most disappointing during his races in the build-up to Aintree, appearing merely a shadow of his former self, and in six outings before the National he only displayed a glimmer of previous form in the last of these when finishing a good third under top-weight in a handicap hurdle at Leopardstown. Quite apart from these dismal performances, Ted had worries concerning his son Ruby. Having travelled to the Czech Republic in October 1999, Ruby had fractured his leg in a steeplechase fall there, which kept him out of the saddle for five months. It was only on 4 March, barely a month before the Grand National, that Ruby returned to action when riding his father's Make My Day into third place at Tramore. A week later at Navan, Ruby proved that, despite his recent injuries and lay-off, his nerve was unaffected when riding both Gabby Hayes and The Next Step to victory. The latter was a most appropriate winner, for 'the next step' for the whole Walsh family was an appointment at Aintree with Papillon.

Ted's last, and thus far only, representative in Aintree's showpiece was Roc De Prince when he sent out Mrs Thompson's gelding to finish in 17th place behind the winner Party Politics, which was trained by Nick Gaselee but also owned by Mrs Thompson.

With a full complement of 40 runners, the betting market was headed by

Martin Pipe's Dark Stranger at 9–1, with a late flood of money reducing the odds against Papillon from 33–1 the previous day to a significant 10–1 joint second-favourite with Star Traveller. Others attracting support in the betting were Bobbyjo at 12–1 and Young Kenny, Earthmover, Micko's Dream and The Last Fling all on the 14–1 mark.

From an even start they made the usual dramatic charge across the Melling Road to the first fence, at which Art Prince, Royal Predica, Micko's Dream, Senor El Betrutti and Trinitro all fell. Sparky Gayle unseated his rider Brian Storey at the next and the favourite, Dark Stranger, did likewise with Tony McCoy at the first open ditch. Another two, Choisty and Earthmover, came to grief and the survivors headed for Becher's Brook. Mick Fitzgerald led here on Esprit De Cotte from Star Traveller and Bobbyjo, with Brave Highlander, Lucky Town and Hollybank Buck immediately behind. The only casualty at the Brook was Red Marauder, misjudging the drop. Jumping the Canal Turn, Star Traveller had gained the ascendancy. Young Kenny went at the plain fence after Valentine's and at the next Star Traveller was accompanied by the riderless Trinitro as they cleared the open ditch some three lengths ahead of the rest. Ruby Walsh had settled Papillon perfectly in the early stages of the race and looked to be going comfortably in sixth place at this point but still the number dropping out continued to rise. Jockey Rupert Wakley parted company with Druid's Brook at the 12th and, back on the racecourse, Torduff Express and The Gopher went at the 13th, with Merry People dislodging his rider at the next. For once the Chair caused no problems, with Star Traveller still dictating the pace, closely followed by Esprit De Cotte, Hollybank Buck, The Last Fling, Lucky Town, Brave Highlander and Papillon. After a costly mistake at the seventh, Bobbyjo was also now well up with the leaders and back on the final circuit the race was still wide open. At the 20th fence Village King and Flaked Oats departed from the contest, soon followed by Esprit De Cotte and Stormy Passage at the second Becher's and at this point Star Traveller was still showing the way. Papillon was going very easily under a copybook ride from Ruby Walsh. Another starting to make a forward move from the rear was Mely Moss with Norman Williamson on top. Beginning to run out of steam after the Canal Turn, the long-time leader Star Traveller was pulled up at the fourth from home and at the next there were still plenty in with a chance. Papillon, Lucky Town and Mely Moss were just a couple of lengths ahead of a group including Niki Dee, Hollybank Buck, The Last Fling, Call It A Day, Addington Boy and Djeddah. Back on the racecourse with just two fences left, the result by now lay between Papillon and Mely Moss, with the remainder reaching the end of their tether, but the crowds in the stands were already in full voice, cheering what they realised was going to be a close finish. Half a length to the good landing over the final fence, Ruby Walsh recognised the threat posed by the too-close Mely Moss and, getting down to riding a finish, kept his mount in full-flight past the elbow. The brave Mely Moss battled on gamely but at the post it was Papillon by a length and a half from Mely Moss, with Niki Dee third in front of Brave Highlander, Addington Boy, Call It A Day and The Last Fling. Ten others also completed the course but hardly anybody noticed them as all eyes were focused on Papillon and his 20-year-old jockey Ruby Walsh.

At the post-race press conference, the beaming-faced trainer Ted Walsh made the following comment:

> It's great and that's an understatement. It was a wonderful feeling with Ruby on board and Betty Moran owning the horse. We have had him since he was a five year old. He jumped super all the way and Ruby gave him a lovely ride – the race is one in which you have to have so much luck in. We had all the luck today; everything just went our way and I am proud of the whole family. It is a great day to be alive. I have been a very lucky person in racing and this is one of the greatest days.

Hanging on every word during this post-mortem, the media people could not have wished for more from owner, trainer and jockey, who were beside themselves with joy.

Ruby Walsh was ebullient when describing his ride into the record books and part of Aintree's folklore, declaring that:

> The race went super for me. I was able to get a possie [position] straight from the start and, though he was a bit keen over the first two, he soon settled into a rhythm. I was tracking Paul Carberry on Bobbyjo when he made a mistake at the fence after Becher's and then I went and joined Richard Johnson on Star Traveller. My horse would not turn at the Canal Turn and I carried Richard halfway across the country, but after that I just decided to make the best of my way home. I can never say that I always thought I was going to win, as I thought about the Irish National halfway up the run-in and then we were beaten by Bobbyjo. I had looked round at the fourth last and all I could see was Jason Titley on Lucky Town and Norman Williamson on Mely Moss. They were both going very well and so I knew that I would not be able to take it easy as I would have liked to do. I just had to keep going at the gallop I was going. I could never get rid of Mely Moss, he was a real thorn in my side but my fellow has run on really well, all the way to the line. Most of this season has been a nightmare for me.

I broke my collarbone early on and I was only back a few days when I broke my leg in the Velka Pardubice. I came back in January and then had a fall when schooling, which opened the fracture again but this healed up quite quickly and I was able to have a couple of winners. I was a bit concerned when I first came back but having had the winners, I was able to get going again. I think I might do a little celebrating tonight.

A little over a fortnight later Ruby added another National to his seasonal tally, this time in his homeland at Fairyhouse in the Powers Gold Label Irish Grand National aboard another Ted Walsh-trained hero, Commanche Court. The same combination of horse, trainer and jockey repeated that victory less than a fortnight later when spread-eagling the field in the Punchestown Heineken Gold Cup.

With racing on both sides of the Irish Sea suffering throughout the next season as a result of the dreadful foot-and-mouth epidemic, it was only through a last-minute decision by the Irish Agriculture Minister that Irish horses were permitted to travel to Aintree for the 2001 Grand National.

Under the worst possible conditions, with the going extremely heavy because of constant rain over the preceding four days, it was a forlorn-looking assembly of 40 runners at Aintree on 7 April 2001. With co-favourites Inis Cara, Edmond and Moral Support at 10–1 receiving most attention, the major concern of all at Aintree on the day was whether in fact the race would actually take place in such horrendous conditions.

With only two fallers at the first (Spanish Main and Art Prince) a false sense of well-being may have been encouraged, but the pile-up caused by a loose horse at the Canal Turn reduced the race to a succession of disasters. After jumping the Water at the end of the first circuit, there remained realistically only five in the contest and when the leader Beau came to grief at the 19th, quickly followed by Blowing Wind and Papillon, the race was reduced to just two. It was the most complete annihilation of a Grand National field since that day in 1928 when only Tipperary Tim survived without falling. With little chance of catching those ahead of them, both Papillon and Blowing Wind were eventually remounted and courageously battled on to the bitter end behind the winner Red Marauder and Smarty. It was a brave but futile effort on the part of Ruby Walsh, whose mount was totally unsuited to the prevailing ground, but they finished in fourth place.

Ruby Walsh – and indeed his father Ted – have plenty of time left in their respective careers to repeat the bliss experienced that day when Papillon wrote his own unique chapter into racing's records. The sooner that wonderful performance so majestically displayed by Ted, Ruby and Papillon is re-enacted at Aintree the better for all – particularly steeplechasing itself, which benefits immeasurably from such outstanding displays of total commitment.

Richard Charles Guest

Richard Guest was born in Andover, Hampshire, on 10 July 1965, and with his uncle Joe already a successful steeplechase jockey, it is easy to see where his early attachment to horse racing began.

While little more than a schoolboy, Richard spent some time with the Newmarket flat trainer Jeremy Hindley before moving on to work for Michael Stoute. It was while riding work for the latter that Richard exercised a young racehorse called Shergar, the winner in 1981 of the Epsom Derby and tragically later the subject of a terrorist kidnapping which led to the colt's premature death.

In 1986, his first season as a conditional jockey with Weyhill trainer Toby Balding, Richard Guest won seven races under National Hunt rules and the following term increased his strike rate when riding 20 winners, including Neblin in the County Handicap Hurdle at the Cheltenham Festival. Another 18 victories the following season kept him in the public eye but it was during the 1988–89 campaign that Richard really hit the headlines.

At Fontwell in February 1989, Richard caused an upset when beating the odds-on favourite Vagador by 20 lengths aboard the Balding-trained Beech Road in the National Spirit Challenge Trophy Hurdle. Despite the ease with which he had won, Beech Road was allowed to start at 50–1 when turning out for the Waterford Crystal Champion Hurdle at Cheltenham just three weeks later. In an extremely competitive field of brilliant hurdlers, Richard and Beech Road won comfortably by two lengths from Celtic Chief and Celtic Shot.

On Grand National day at Aintree, the pair won again, this time at 10–1 in the valuable Sandeman Aintree Hurdle, providing Toby Balding with the first leg of a fantastic treble that day. The trainer's other two winners were Little Polveir in the National and Morley Street in the Mumm Prize Novices Hurdle, both partnered by Jimmy Frost.

After six years with Toby Balding, Richard accepted the position of stable jockey to Sue and Harvey Smith at their establishment near Bingley in West Yorkshire, a period he remembers with deep fondness. At Ascot in January 1992 he rode Kildimo for the Smiths in the First National 'Chase and with a well-judged challenge, won by seven lengths from Peter Scudamore on Solidasarock. Another victory for the Yorkshire team was achieved at Chepstow a few weeks later when he brought their ageing hurdler Rothko through late on to win the Philip Cornes Saddle Of Gold Hurdle Final.

Offered the ride on Romany King in the Grand National by his old boss Balding, Richard gladly agreed and on 4 April 1992 lined up at the start with his 39 rivals. Patiently ridden on the first circuit, Romany King made a forward move going back out for the last lap, jumping Becher's well in fifth place behind the leader Hotplate and with Carl Llewellyn on Party Politics just to his rear. Moving to the front after taking the Canal Turn, Romany King was going well and as the race entered its final phase appeared to have plenty still in hand. At the last open ditch before coming back onto the racecourse, Party Politics moved smoothly into the lead and set sail for home across the Melling Road followed by Romany King, Stay On Tracks, Docklands Express, Ghofar, Old Applejack, Twin Oaks, Laura's Beau and Cool Ground. Between the last two fences Romany King moved up again to pose a threat to the leader and even when Party Politics cleared the last in fine style Richard Guest put in a renewed challenge approaching the elbow. Edging closer to the horse in front with every stride, it was only in the final 200 yards that Party Politics at last stamped his authority on the proceedings, staying on to win by two and a half lengths from Romany King. In third place came Laura's Beau, followed by Docklands Express, Twin Oaks, Just So, Old Applejack and 15 others. That season ended with Richard Guest achieving a total of 43 winners, his best jumping period yet. He had grounds for great optimism for the future.

Such are the vagaries of the crazy world of sport, and steeplechasing in particular, however, that the highest of hopes are too often shattered and such was the case for Richard Guest over the next couple of years. His next appearance in the big Aintree event came in 1994, when reunited with Romany King, but they fell at the fourth fence and over the same country in November that year, Richard gave the tiny Into The Red a copybook ride to win the Becher Handicap Steeplechase. Aboard the same horse in the next two Nationals, Richard dead-heated for fifth place with Marcus Armytage on Romany King in 1995 and, 12 months later, again completed the course when 15th behind Rough Quest.

Through a period probably only describable as 'the doldrums', Richard Guest demonstrated his determination and self-belief by persevering when many had written him off. The offer of a position as assistant to the permit-holder Norman Mason at Crook in County Durham appealed to him greatly, mainly because of the genuine, down-to-earth personality of Mason. It was the beginning of a chapter in the Hampshire jockey's career which would provide many highs, as well as an almost fatal low.

Partnering the Richard Rowe-trained Yeoman Warrior in the 1998 Grand National, Richard pulled up his mount before the 19th fence and later that month fell foul of the stewards when accused of breaking Rule 151, otherwise known as the 'non-triers' rule. It was the third such incident involving the jockey, so the stewards at Perth suspended him, but in a moment of understandable frustration Richard handed them his licence and announced his retirement from the saddle.

Great play was made of the incident in the press and although many tried to persuade Richard to change his mind he was adamant in his belief that officialdom was being petty and heavy-handed.

Fortunately for the whole of steeplechasing, the abundance of talent emerging from Norman Mason's Brancepeth Manor Farm stables proved too much of a temptation for Richard and he returned to the saddle in time to ride Mason's Red Marauder to victory in the 1998 First National Bank Gold Cup.

In the 1999 Grand National he again took the commission from trainer Richard Rowe to ride – this time Frazer Island. Although jumping well throughout the first circuit, Becher's Brook at the second attempt proved just too much for them.

Back at the same venue the next year Richard rode Nosam for Norman Mason into 12th place in the John Hughes Trophy 'Chase, and aboard the same owner's Red Marauder in the National, came down at Becher's first time round. By way of consolation, they did gain much comfort when Richard piloted Red Ark to a superb success in Aintree's Perrier Jouet Novices Handicap 'Chase over the Mildmay Course.

The outbreak of foot-and-mouth disease in the north-east during the autumn of 2000 was sorely neglected and dreadfully mismanaged by the authorities, whose knowledge of the agricultural industry was scant and their attitude somewhat dismissive. Quite apart from the terrifying effect on those farmers and their families involved, the wider repercussions were dreadful and far-reaching.

Although in comparison of merely secondary importance, National Hunt racing was severely curtailed, a situation which was to remain for many months to come. In fact it eventually led to the abandonment of the 2001 Cheltenham National Hunt Festival. With the Irish Government seemingly attaching more concern to the problem than its British counterpart, a total ban was imposed on racing in Ireland and with it came an embargo on horses travelling to mainland Britain to compete.

The prospect of a Grand National meeting without the traditional attendance of any Irish competitors hung like a cloud over the rapidly approaching Aintree fixture and it was with tremendous relief that virtually at the eleventh hour the Irish Government eased their restrictions to allow horses over for Aintree on the condition that they stayed in this country for several weeks after racing.

Never in living memory had such inclement weather been witnessed at

Aintree on the approach to the principal event of the jumping year and with incessant rain turning the racecourse into little better than a quagmire, the Grand National was in doubt until the very day of the race.

The day before that fateful Saturday, a ray of hope was cast in the direction of Norman Mason and his jockey Richard Guest when they carried off the Heidsieck Diamante Bleu Novices Steeplechase with Red Striker in convincing fashion by 11 lengths from Hannigan's Lodger and Hunt Hill.

A late inspection by the clerk of the course on the morning of the National resulted in the go-ahead for the race and by the time the starter eventually sent the 40 runners on their way 3 horses shared favouritism at 10–1: Moral Support, Inis Cara and Edmond. The renowned mud-loving Beau was heavily supported at 12–1 and others finding favour among the betting fraternity included Papillon, Blowing Wind, Mely Moss, Smarty and Paddy's Return.

To the relief of everyone at Aintree and far beyond, the 2001 Grand National got underway against all probability and out into that murky area known as 'the country' the brave and hopeful raced – without any indication of just what lay ahead.

Art Prince and Spanish Main went at the first, quickly followed by Addington Boy, Tresor De Mai and Hanakham at the second fence. The early decimation continued at the first open ditch, where Hollybank Buck, Kaki Crazy and Paddy's Return also came to grief but as would be seen all too soon, Paddy's Return continued in the race without a jockey. Inis Cara and Earthmover fell at the fourth, The Last Fling at the next plain fence, and the first time at Becher's accounted for Northern Starlight, Strong Tel and Exit Swinger. But the worst was yet to come. With only a handful clearing the Canal Turn at the first time of asking, the riderless Paddy's Return cut straight across the bulk of the field to create a massive pile-up reminiscent of Foinavon's race in 1967. The result, sadly, was that barely ten remained in the race as they approached the Chair Jump in front of the stands. Here again, the dreadful ground and all they had already encountered brought more victims of a race which was in severe danger of becoming farcical. Back across the Melling Road, with a full circuit ahead of them, only five were realistically left in the contest, with Carl Llewellyn on Beau heading just four other forlorn-looking survivors. Somehow, at some point, Carl had lost control of his reins, which both finished up on the same side of his mount's neck, resulting in Beau racing without steering. Incredibly, however, they survived until the ditch at the 19th, when Beau unseated his rider. Red Marauder and Smarty got over the ditch safely but the two remaining survivors, Papillon and Blowing Wind, both hit the ground. With still so far to go it looked distinctly as if the bookies might make a clean sweep, with every horse in the race falling, but over the

Canal Turn and on the run back towards the racecourse the two sole survivors struggled bravely on. From Valentine's Brook Red Marauder held a fractional advantage over the Mark Pitman-trained Smarty and at this point it could be seen that both Blowing Wind and Papillon had been remounted but were a very long way behind. A mistake by Red Marauder four from home allowed Smarty to gain the lead and, racing back onto the racecourse proper, he held on to his advantage. Bringing Red Marauder with a determined challenge between the final two obstacles, Richard delivered his challenge at precisely the right moment and with his nearest rival by now completely exhausted, Red Marauder gamely plodded on to win by a distance from Smarty, with similar distances separating him from Blowing Wind and the only other to get round, Papillon.

The completely mud-splattered Richard Guest informed all at the post-race press conference:

> It was sheer hell out there – the going was absolutely desperate and Red Marauder must the be worst jumper ever to win the Grand National. Certainly second time round he was climbing over most of the fences but he stays forever and being the mudlark he is, I suppose he found everything to his liking today.

Whatever future historians may say, it is perhaps symbolic and correct that in the year when the whole of Britain was devastated by a cruel virus that respects nobody, a man and a horse could show the way to surviving the worst that the elements could throw at them.

The Grand National has, in my brief period of appreciating its spectacle, drama and incredible uncertainty, demonstrated just how far the human psyche and indomitable will can survive whatever fate may challenge it with. I personally have been enormously privileged to see all these unique men perform to their ultimate capabilities and, in so doing, add such immeasurable value to the records of human endeavour.

In a world often described as being without purpose or direction, one can gain reassurance that each spring at Aintree you will find a body of men completely and totally prepared to put their lives on the line for ten minutes of glory and – just maybe – a place in the record books. While such spirit exists within the soul of man, there remains hope for us all – and indeed for this troubled world.

ELEVEN

Jim Culloty

Born on 18 December 1973, less than nine months after Red Rum's first Grand National victory, Jim Culloty added his name to Aintree's Roll of Honour 25 years after that greatest of all National heroes' record-breaking third success in 1977.

The son of a Killarney accountant, Jim followed a similar path to that of so many of his countrymen whose absorption with all things horsey results in their seeking a career in the saddle. Gaining valuable experience during his school holidays by crossing the Irish Sea to work for trainer John Jenkins' stables in Royston, Hertfordshire, the youngster showed exactly where his future lay.

Settling in England on a more permanent basis in 1993, he rode initially for Cornwall-based point-to-point handler David Bloomfield as an amateur and during the 1994–95 season partnered a winner at Les Landes in Jersey. Moving on to the neighbouring county of Devon, Jim Culloty became associated with Mrs Jackie Retter's yard in Exeter and after joining Mrs Henrietta Knight's stables at Wantage, turned professional in late 1996.

Although his first appearance in the Grand National in 1997 was an all-too brief affair, with he and his mount Full Of Oats coming to grief at the first fence, it was nevertheless a most memorable occasion for it was the event which was interrupted minutes before 'The Off' by a malicious bomb threat. Postponed for 24 hours, the race has become renowned as the 'Monday National' and the citizens of Liverpool justifiably received overwhelming praise for their generous support of the many thousands of racegoers stranded due to the outrage.

It was to be another three years before Jim got another chance of Aintree glory and, although again failing to complete the course when falling with Village King at the 20th fence in that 2000 Grand National, the first year of the new century marked a major turning point in his career. A large proportion of Henrietta Knight's seasonal total of 58 winners were partnered by Jim Culloty, among them Lord Noelie who provided the Irishman with his first Cheltenham Festival success when taking the Royal & Sun Alliance Steeplechase. Another important landmark for the jockey came the following month when he made most of the running on the brilliant five-year-old hurdler Best Mate to convincingly win the Martell Mersey Novices' Hurdle at Aintree.

With the outbreak of foot-and-mouth disease in the autumn of that year, much of the subsequent National Hunt season was subjected to continuous abandonments, a situation which not only resulted in the loss of Cheltenham's National Hunt Festival, but also seriously threatened the forthcoming Grand National fixture. To the credit of racing's governing bodies, stringent precautions were implemented to avoid the spread of the disease through the transportation of horses and the attendance of spectators, to such effect that Aintree survived where so many other venues failed.

Once more aboard the Philip Hobbs-trained Village King in the 2001 Grand National, Culloty stood little chance of steering a clear course in the pile-up which ensued at the first Canal Turn on that rain-soaked day and became just one of eight victims eliminated as a result of the antics of the wayward, riderless Paddy's Return. The previous day, however, Jim rode Catfish Keith over one circuit of the National fences in the John Hughes Trophy Steeplechase and, though unplaced behind the winner Gower-Slave, was given an opportunity of witnessing a fine front-running performance by the fourth-placed gelding Bindaree. Little could he have imagined that day how their paths would cross again exactly 12 months later and how very different their contributions to racing history would be.

Through the early part of the new season the undoubted star of Henrietta Knight's stable was Best Mate, an Irish-bred gelding who'd made a startling transition from hurdling to competition over the major obstacles, and with Jim Culloty again aboard, they scored a highly impressive victory in the 2002 Cheltenham Gold Cup. One of the most delightful aspects of the post-race celebrations was the outstanding sportsmanship of the trainer's rivals, who with obvious joy congratulated Henrietta and her husband, the ever-popular former champion jockey Terry Biddlecombe. For Jim Culloty, winning the Gold Cup was a dream come true; a much hoped for but hardly expected realisation that the years of graft, dedication and total commitment had earned the acknowledgement of his peers.

With his Wantage stable without a Grand National contender, Jim gladly accepted the offer of trainer Mark Pitman to ride his Browjoshy in the big race but the gelding was some way out of the handicap and there existed considerable doubt about whether the horse would actually run. Yet again, however, fate intervened and as so many times in the long history of the Grand National, one man's misfortune presented a golden opportunity to another. Just days before the big race, jockey Jamie Goldstein broke his leg in a race fall, leaving trainer Nigel Twiston-Davies without a partner for the least experienced of his three representatives, Bindaree. The mount on the eight year old was offered to Jim Culloty and, with typical courtesy and consideration, Mark Pitman released the Irishman from their agreement concerning Browjoshy.

Unlike 12 months earlier, the elements blessed Aintree in that first week of April 2002 with glorious sunshine throughout the entire three-day fixture and yet a melancholy, mercifully rare at major sporting events, overshadowed the whole proceedings. The recent death of Her Majesty Queen Elizabeth The Queen Mother was deeply felt by many millions everywhere, though none more so than by devotees of National Hunt racing who fully and completely recognised the enormous contribution she had made to the winter sport. With commendable respect, reverence and humility, the many thousands attending Aintree's three-day festival of jumping complied wholeheartedly and affectionately with the racecourse management's tasteful tributes to a gracious lady whose association with the Grand National is sadly most remembered for the 'Devon Loch incident'. A minute's silence each day was fully observed with great dignity and the decision was made that all jockeys riding in the Grand National would wear black armbands.

Despite the absence of last year's winner Red Marauder, a full complement of 40 runners ensured another wide-open Grand National, but much play was made in the press about the fact that such proven staying 'chasers as Moor Lane, Amberleigh House and Browjoshy were relegated to mere reserves and ultimately forbidden to compete. At the top of the handicap such recognised splendid performers as Marlborough, Alexander Banquet, Kingsmark, What's Up Boys and Davids Lad added a distinct element of class to the race, while Blowing Wind, Ad Hoc and trainer Twiston-Davies' chief hope Beau headed the final pre-race betting.

Away to a good start, the 40 runners proceeded at a sensible pace across the Melling Road but, as on so many occasions in the past, the first fence exacted a costly toll. No less than eight of the competitors made their exit at the initial obstacle, among them such notables as Marlborough, Paris Pike, Red Ark and one of the six challengers from Ireland, Wicked Crack. With The Last Fling and Supreme Charm setting the pace, the survivors raced without further incident until the fourth fence, at which Logician, Niki Dee and Samuel Wilderspin fell. Two jumps later Becher's Brook put paid to the chances of Alexander Banquet, Frantic Tan, Ackzo and Iris Bleu, with Gun'n Roses II falling victim to the next fence, the smallest on the course. Closely pressed by Supreme Charm, The Last Fling maintained his advantage over and around the Canal Turn and, with the remainder well strung out behind, Smarty was the only other casualty before they approached the halfway stage in front of the stands. At the 14th Beau had moved into second place behind the leader but, landing awkwardly, unseated his rider and after the rest safely crossed the Chair and Water jumps, The Last Fling led them back out for the final circuit. Still well in touch with the front-runner, Supreme Charm was in second place ahead of Celibate, Davids Lad, Djeddah, Majed, Blowing Wind, Bindaree, Royal Predica and Mely Moss. With the race now entering the decisive stages, Murts Man went at the 17th, Super Franky at the next and Manx Magic together with Lyreen Wonder at the 20th, but by now Bindaree had moved smoothly into contention. Landing first over Becher's Brook, at which Majed departed, Bindaree was running well within himself, ably and considerately assisted by Jim Culloty, and striding out well they made their way towards the next with Davids Lad appearing the most dangerous rival. Preceded into the Canal Turn by his riderless stable-mate Beau and with another loose horse dangerously close on his inside, jockey Culloty demonstrated horsemanship at its finest by steering his mount clear while maintaining his lead, although the manoeuvre cost him precious lengths. Long-time leader The Last Fling fell here, together with Inis Cara and Spot The Difference, but Bindaree cleared Valentine's Brook confidently and with the precision he'd displayed throughout the race ahead of Davids Lad, Blowing Wind and two rapidly improving greys, What's Up Boys and Kingsmark. The French-trained Djeddah fell at the 27th, as also did Davids Lad, who brought down Ad Hoc in the process, and it was at this point that Richard Johnson on the blinkered What's Up Boys made his move. Closely tracking Bindaree all the way back across Melling Road for the final time, What's Up Boys came under pressure approaching the second last fence and, responding well, joined issue with the leader taking that obstacle. Landing within half a length of Bindaree, but appearing to be travelling the better, Johnson cleverly avoided interference from the riderless Beau who ran ahead and across him to the inside rail, and at the final fence it was Jim Culloty and his mount who were in most danger from the loose horse. Touching down safely and almost together, it was What's Up Boys who immediately struck the front, racing clear of Bindaree whose run to the inside rail was initially impeded by the pilotless Beau. Nearing the elbow, Culloty attempted to switch his horse to the outside, but at precisely the same moment Richard Johnson veered his mount away from the inside. With remarkable intuition, Jim Culloty instantly realised the inner passage was now clear. Riding understandably like a man possessed, the Irishman began the seemingly impossible task of reducing the gap between himself and the leader, gaining ground with every stride but with the distance to the winning post rapidly and cruelly reducing. Bindaree stayed on grimly, in tremendously courageous fashion, to gain the upper hand close to home and win readily by a length and three-quarters from the equally brave What's Up Boys, with the Tony McCoy-ridden favourite Blowing Wind 27 lengths further back in third place.

It was trainer Nigel Twiston-Davies' second National success in four years and a first victory in the race for owner Raymond Mould, whose wife Jenny owned Bindaree until her sad death from cancer in November 2000. In their moment of triumph both men were lavish in their praise of the tenacity of Bindaree and the skill of last-minute substitute jockey Jim Culloty who, in a somewhat breathless post-race interview, expressed his own delight with the following words:

> Bindaree is a brilliant jumper and he got out of jail at the last fence. Because I had trouble with a loose horse I could not kick on in front beforehand and after the last I was getting a bit caught for

speed. The second horse came by us after the last and for a split second I thought, Jesus we were beat. Then I got him up the rail on the run-in and he is as brave as they come. He stuck his head out and tried his hardest, it is just unbelievable. Thanks go to Mark Pitman who let me get off Browjoshy at very short notice to ride this horse. I really feel sorry for Jamie Goldstein, who was due to ride Bindaree but broke his leg earlier this week. Missing the National winner is every jockey's worse nightmare. I couldn't in my wildest dreams imagine winning the Grand National, it is just unbelievable now.

Jim became the first jockey to win both the Cheltenham Gold Cup and the Grand National in the same season since John Burke in 1976 and on that sunny Saturday afternoon at Aintree realised fully the joy of becoming a very worthy King For A Day.

AFTERWORD

The Uncrowned Kings

Since that day in 1839 when Jem Mason rode Lottery to victory in what we now know as the Grand National, countless riders have attempted to emulate his success and naturally the vast majority have failed. For whenever there is a winner, there has to be somebody who loses.

The horsemen featured in this book all tasted that rare moment of Aintree glory but there were others during that period of time who came repeatedly and agonisingly close to achieving their aim. It would be most remiss of me not to add a brief acknowledgement of their contributions to the prestige of the race.

Lord Anthony Mildmay, to whom we owe thanks for the existence of the Mildmay Course at Aintree, finished third and fourth on Cromwell in successive years at the end of the 1940s. George Slack came second on three occasions during the 1950s, twice with Tudor Line and again on Tiberetta.

Coming twice third in the race – aboard Royal Tan in 1956 and Mr What three years later – Tom Taaffe came close to the distinction of equalling both his father and brother in winning the race. That very popular champion Terry Biddlecombe was twice fourth, in 1966 and 1967, before finishing second with Gay Trip in 1972.

In more recent years, that most likeable of northern jockeys, Chris Grant, finished second three times: with Young Driver in 1986 and with Durham Edition two years later and again in 1990.

It is, however, when enthusiasts discuss the hard-luck stories which abound in the National that one man springs most readily to mind. Dick Francis, like many of his generation, lost some of the most valuable years of his career as a jockey serving in the Royal Air Force during the Second World War. He did, however, become one of the most talented jockeys in the immediate post-war period and when taking part in his first Grand National in 1949 he finished second on Roimond. Seven years later, riding the Queen Mother's gelding Devon Loch in the race, he had every fence safely behind him, they were within 50 yards of the winning post and well clear of any rivals. That fall on the flat so close to victory will remain a mystery forever, but the dignity and sportsmanship displayed that day by both Her Majesty the Queen Mother and Dick Francis set an example of which we can all be forever proud. They also upheld the finest traditions of the Grand National.